AF520010

NEW FRONTIERS OF KNOWLEDGE in INFORMATION SCIENCE

NEW FRONTIERS OF KNOWLEDGE in INFORMATION SCIENCE

Edited by

Dr.G.Devarajan Ph.D

Prof & Head

Department of Library & Information Science

University of Kerala, Thiruvananthapuram

Ess Ess Publications

4837/24, Ansari Road, Darya Ganj,

New Delhi-110002

✆ : 23260807

Fax : 23274173

E-mail: essess@del3.vsnl.net.in

First Published 2004

ISBN : 81-7000-377-6

Price : Rs. 800/-

Published by :

Ess Ess Publications

4837/24, Ansari Road, Darya Ganj,
New Delhi - 110 002
Phone : 23260807
Fax : 23274173
E-mail : essess@del3.vsnl.net.in

Laser Typesetting:

Mukesh Graphics

L-2/8, DDA Market,
Mangolepuri, New Delhi
Ph. : 27924405

Printed at :

Mehra Offset Press

Contents

PREFACE

Study and research are two paramount activities in a university. Duplication of research due to lack of current and consolidated list is a common phenomenon today among universities in India. A number of studies conducted in the universities, which usually remain unpublished, have great potentialities in the scientific, technological and socio-economic and cultural fields if they are properly disseminated in time. Infact the relative merit of research contributions can easily be assessed and research contributions utilized for societal development if the contents of these "frozen documents" could be published and made known to those who are interested. The publication of research studies in Library and Information Science has got contemporary significance in the present day information world.

This book is a humble attempt made by the editor as the culmination of fulfilling the objective of disseminating the contents of the research studies conducted in the various Library and Information Science schools in the Indian Universities in the field of Library and Information Science. This is the Second book under the series "Research in Library and Information Science". Nine selected research studies conducted at various levels namely M.Phil and Ph.D are included in this compendium. The topics selected by the authors for their study are current, significant and unique. The subjects such as Fiscal Allocation in University Libraries ,Design and Development of Ayurveda Information System. National Library of Bangladesh, Industrial and Technological Information Centres for Small Scale Sector, Information Needs of Veterinarians, Bibliometric Study of Reference books in Malayalam, Information Needs of College Teachers, Role of Libraries in Societal Development among Rural Women and Information Needs of Pure Scientists etc included in this book. A Book Index is incorporated as auxiliary for the effective use of the book. It is hoped that this book will be well received by students, teachers and researchers in the field of Library and Information Science.

The editor records his profound thanks to the authors of the theses/dissertations for contributing the relevant portions of the studies for inclusion in this book. The editor also records his great appreciation and sincere thanks to Mr. Sumit Sethi, M/s Ess Ess Publications, New Delhi for Bringing out this book in good format within record time.

Thiruvanathapuram **Prof. (Dr.) G. Devarajan**

25/10/2003

1

FISCAL ALLOCATION IN THE UNIVERSITY LIBRARIES

Prof.(Dr.) G. Devarajan

INTRODUCTION

The library is an important instrument of education. In the changing educational environment in India, the role of libraries in education, especially in higher education is very significant. The role of university library is well recognised as a tool and an integral part of higher education to achieve quality education. But today the University libraries in India are confronted with a number of problems which hinder the achievement of the objective of higher education at the desired level. Inadequate fiscal investment and unscientific fiscal management are the most serious of these problems.

LIBRARIES IN EDUCATION

Education is an all-pervasive means of personal development, which leads to societal change. The purpose of education is given in the Education Commission Report as: "In a democracy, the individual is an end in himself and the primary purpose of education is to provide him with the widest opportunity to develop his potentialities to the full"(1). Library plays an important role in this by providing him with wide opportunities to learn, think and develop his capabilities on his own lines. It is a social institution which plays a crucial role in the socio-economic and cultural spheres too.

India is faced with a number of challenges, external as well as internal. The importance of education to meet these challenges is stressed in the policy document on education of the Government of India as: "Education is the most effective instrument to meet these challenges. Only education can imbue people with the knowledge, the sense of purpose and the confidence essential for building a dynamic, vibrant and cohesive nation capable of providing its people with the wherewithal for creating, fuller and more purposeful life" (2).

To enable the education system to play its role effectively in the process of national development along democratic lines, it is essential to ensure universalisation of education through formal channels alone will not be sufficient to achieve this objective.

Education through informal channels viz. distance education is one of the effective ways by which this can be achieved. That is why the New Education Policy, 1986 has laid great stress on distance education. For an effective distance education programme a well-established library system is an essential pre-requisite. Its role in formal education also is not less important.

PROBLEMS OF HIGHER EDUCATION

The most important indicator of a country's future may be the state of its higher education. Higher education enables people to reflect on the critical, social, economic, cultural, moral and spiritual issues facing humanity. It contributes to national development through dissemination of specialized knowledge and skills.

There are a number of problems in the field of higher education in India. The major problems listed in the document 'New Education Policy' are the following:

(i) Problems associated with developing countries like scarcity of resources, dependence on and high competition from developed countries in the areas of high and specialized technologies etc and urgent need for faster development and progress put many constraints on teaching and research in higher education.

(ii) Pressure of a large number of students aspiring for higher education for personal, social and economic betterment.

(iii) Expansion of knowledge in its content and diversity and emergency of many new areas like computers, microelectronics, space science, energy, biotechnology, communication etc;

(iv) Emergence and adoption of communication and microelectronics based technologies are transforming the industrial, social and cultural life of this country and the world;

(v) Non-homogenous student body can't be properly educated and trained by the existing educational system which was evolved on the principles of centralization and uniformity;

(vi) Grading and certification function of the universities for admission to higher courses of study and for selection to various employment opportunities has brought in outside, as well as inside pressures on teachers and educational institutions vitiating the entire teaching and learning process;

(vii) Dominant culture in the educational institutions is authoritarian and hierarchical;

(viii) Lack of motivation in the system has resulted in the limited success or often failure in many reforms based on sound principles and started with well-planned programmes and preparation;

(ix) Less importance often bordering on neglect given to the university system in Research and Development work has eliminated challenge from the system, and resulted in falling standards;

(x) Accountability is entirely absent in the system and good, bad and indifferent institutions, all get the same grant and support; and

(xi) Financial resources provided to higher education are not enough to carry out its responsibilities. Often the grant-in-aid and its controlling operation by the funding agency, usually a Government agency, is so restrictive and bound in long procedures and delay that it disheartens and dissuades those working for educational reforms and changes(3).

The problems in the higher education mentioned above are indeed the problems faced by the universities in India. In the midst of all these problems the universities , the centres of our national development are forced to function for achieving the objectives of higher education.

FUNCTIONS OF A UNIVERSITY

The university is an important agency for imparting higher education. The University has important responsibilities to the society as well as to the educational system. The traditional functions of a university are mainly acquisition, preservation, dissemination and extension of the frontiers of knowledge, the balanced education of individuals and the training of personnel for all walks of life. The Education Commission (1964-65) was of opinion that universities are undergoing profound changes in their scope, functions and organisation and are in a process of rapid evolution. In broad terms, the functions of the universities in the modern world as stated by the Education Commission are:

- to seek and cultivate new knowledge, to encourage vigorously and fearlessly in the pursuit of truth, and to interpret old knowledge and beliefs in the light of new needs and discoveries;

- to provide the right kind of leadership in all walks of life, to identify gifted youth and help them develop their potential to the full by cultivating physical fitness, developing the powers of the mind and cultivating right interest, attitudes and moral and intellectual values;
- to provide society with competent men and women trained in agriculture, art, medicine, science, and technology and various other professions;
- to strive to promote equality and social justice and to reduce social and cultural differences through diffusion of education; and
- to foster in the teachers and students, and through them in society generally, the attitudes and values needed for developing in the 'good life' in individuals and society(4).

Apart from the aforesaid basic functions, a modern university especially in a country like India has to undertake several other functions as well. These functions are given in the document entitled 'Development of higher education in India' prepared by the University Grants Commission. They are:

- inculcate and promote basic human values and the capacity to choose between alternate value system;
- Preserve and foster our great cultural traditions and blend them with essential elements from other cultures and people;
- Promote a rational outlook and scientific temper;
- Enrich the Indian language and promote their use as important means of communication, national development and unity;
- Promote the development of the total personality of the students and inculcate in them a commitment to the society through involvement in national service programmes;
- Act as an objective critic of society and assist in the formulation of national objectives and programmes for their realisation;
- Promote the development of science and technology and of

an indigenous capability to apply it effectively with special emphasis on national problems; and

- Contribute to the improvement of the entire educational system so as to observe the community(5).

OBJECTIVES AND FUNCTIONS OF A UNIVERSITY LIBRARY

A University Library is established with the intention of aiding in the successful accomplishment of the objectives of its university such as teaching, research, publication programmes etc. Considering the multifarious objectives of a modern university, the university library has to shoulder onerous responsibilities. The role of the University library in higher education is important and it is emphasised in different reports brought out by various library and education commissions in India and abroad at different times.

The role of a library in a University system is stressed by the University Grants Committee (United Kingdom) in its report (1921) thus: The character and efficiency of a university may be gauged by its treatment of its central organ the library. We regard the fullest provision for library maintenance as the primary and most vital need in the equipment of a university(6).

In India, the University Education Commission (1948- 49) headed by Dr. S. Radhakrishnan describes the importance of the University Library in higher education thus: "Teaching is a co-operative enterprise. Teachers must have the necessary tools for teaching purposes in the shape of libraries and laboratories and also the right type of students. The library is the heart of all the University's work, directly so, as regards its research work, and indirectly as regards its educational work, which derives its life from research work. Scientific research needs a library as well as its laboratories, while for humanistic research the library is both the library and laboratory in one. Training in higher branches of learning and research is mainly a question of learning how to use the tools, and if the library tools are not there, how can the students learn to use them. "President Truman's Commission on Higher Education says: "The library is second only to the instructional staff in its importance for high quality instruction and research. Both for humanistic and scientific studies, a first class library is essential in a university"(7).

To quote S.R. Dongerkey, "a well stocked and uptodate library is a *sine qua non* for every modern University"(8).

The importance given by the Kothari Commission Report (1964-66) on education to the role of libraries in higher education is reflected in these words: "No new university, college or department should be set up without taking into account its library needs in terms of staff, books, journals, space etc. Nothing could be more damaging to a growing department than to neglect its library should be an important centre of attraction on the college or university campus"(9).

The role of University library in higher education is emphasised in the Atkinson Commission Report (1976) in the following words: "The library is the core of a university. As a resource it occupies the central and primary place, because it serves all the functions of a university, teaching and research, the creation of new knowledge and the transmission to posterity of the learning and culture of the present and the past" (10).

The Parry Committee Report (1967) reiterated the University Grants Committee Report of United Kingdom (1921) by adding a statement that "this is as true today after forty five years as it was when it was written"(11).

According to Gelfand, the fundamental role of the library is educational. It should not be operated as a mere store house of books attached to a reading-room, but as a dynamic instrument of education. It should feed the intellect of the student, encourage the researches of the faculty, and invite all who enter its house to partake fully of its intellectual and cultural fare" (12). To quote M.B. Line, "the foundation of the university library is to bring together information or knowledge on the one hand and human beings on the other"(13).

The report of the Library Committee of the University Grants Commission (1957) headed by Dr. S.R. Ranganathan has dealt with in detail the role of the University Library in academic development especially in the field of higher education(14).

Paul Buck's famous observations about the University Library referred to as his 'Credo' are worth mentioning here. His observations are:

(i) The library is the heart of education.

(ii) Methods and fashion in education change from generation to generation, but each generation uses the library as a means of realising its items; hence the library remains the great conservator of learning;

(iii) A quality education is impossible without a quality library;

(iv) You can't have quality faculty without a quality library;

(v) A library is vital to proper exploitation of our intellectual resources;

(vi) The library is essential to maintenance of free access to ideas, and to the functioning of the untrammeled mind(15).

FACTORS AND PROBLEMS IN UNIVERSITY LIBRARY DEVELOPMENT

There are a number of factors affecting the normal development of a university library. In the opinion of Wilson and Tauber the essentials that are basic to successful operation of the University library and the co-ordination of its programmes with the teaching and research programmes of the University are:

(i) resources for instruction, research and extension;

(ii) a competent library staff;

(iii) organisation of materials for use;

(iv) adequate space and equipment;

(v) integration of the library with administrative and educational policies;

(vi) integration of the library with community, state, regional, national and international library resources;

(vii) adequate financial support; and

(viii) a workable policy of library government(16).

In order to make the university library the heart of the parent institution it is essential that the authorities, the faculty and the librarian should realise their obligations to the objectives of higher education. Their obligations may be stated as follows:

(a) The authorities i.e the University, the University Grants Commission and the Government, State as well as Central Government, should provide adequate funds for library service with the conviction that, in its turn, it (library service) would help to develop scholarship and increase the productive capacity of the nation;

(b) The faculty should give up the age old textbook centered, examination oriented and mass talk method of teaching, and should encourage library centered individual and group guidance method through tutorials, discussions and seminars etc to make education really effective and worthwhile; and

(c) The librarian should collaborate with the faculty and provide necessary literature, supplementary and parallel reading, keeping in view that library service does not merely aim at satisfying the immediate requirements of reader, but also aims to assist the reader in strengthening his creativeness and satisfying his intellectual curiosity(17).

University libraries in India and other third world countries are confronted with several problems as obstacles in their course of development. M.A. Gelfand has pointed out a number of obstacles faced by the university libraries in developing countries. They are:

(i) Lack of clearly defined university and library objectives, of co-operation and understanding from University authorities and faculties, of trained library personal and adequate clerical staff, of library resources in the university and in the country at large;

(ii) Serve import and currency restrictions;

(iii) Inadequate financial support;

(iv) Inadequate physical facilities;

(v) Failure to appoint a competent university librarian, to give him authority commensurate with his important responsibilities, and to recognise the educational and professional qualifications of librarians;

(vi) Unduly complex purchasing and other administrative regulations; and

(vii) The inhibiting enforcement of strict personal accountability for book losses. In addition to the specific 'obstacles' which are listed above, a number of factors may affect the development of university libraries. These may need to be considered in planning library development in the interests of the nation as well as of the university. These include:

a. number and type of specialised research institution.

b. The state of library services in the nation;

c. Conditions in particular universities; and

d. The status of librarianship(18).

The obstacles and factors for University Library development listed above are both external and internal. Of these, the most crucial one in the Indian situation is inadequate fiscal support.

IMPORTANCE OF FINANCE

Finance holds the key to all human activity. It is the guide for regulating decisions and expenditure. According to D.P.Misra "Finances are the *sine qua non* of every organised human endeavour, and success in all planned public projects is often proportionate as much to the amount of finances made available as to the wise manner in which they are put to use. Education, of all public projects, is one which vitally, although indirectly, affects the growth and continuity of community life. No study of such an important public activity as education can be complete and fruitful unless it also covers its financial aspect" (19).

The finance plays a significant role in the organisation and administration of a library. A library should be assured of adequate finances, otherwise it cannot discharge its obligations and guarantee the continuity of proper service to the users. The quantum of funds made available towards library resources and personnel determines to a large extent the quality of a library and the services provided by it. The educational system of any country will be reflected negatively if the fiscal allocations are inadequate. Today librarians and information managers are faced with a number of problems like quantitative growth of documents, increase in the number of library users, diversified nature of user's requirements, escalating cost of documents, unrealistic budget provision, etc. Inflation has adversely affected the university libraries in the third world countries. But the university authorities seldom take the above factors into account while considering the university library budget. In this connection the role of the parent body is important. Here the observation made by C.G, Viswanathan is worth quoting. He has stated that 'All institutions need stable and adequate financial support and guarantee from the authorities creating them. In fact, it is the full responsibility of the parent body to maintain all its institutions, in such a way, as to expect satisfactory services from them to the community served" (20).

Regarding the nature of finance in the university libraries in the developing countries, Carl M White has observed: "No great university library comes to mind which can't point to stable financial support as a corner-stone of its success. The reason is quite simple. High standards in work of this kind can't possibly be achieved, when funds for maintaining a competent staff, occupied by a steady flow of work, are provided by jerky fits and starts. If the library is to rid itself of a formidable menace to normal development, the University will be obliged to join with the University Grants Commission in establishing library financing on a footing which increases dependence on regular maintenance funds and reduces dependence on non-recurring grants" (21).

James D Hart has emphasised the necessity of adequate finance for various university programmes. "Adequate financial support is basic to the maintenance of any programmes of library development and service that is to be significantly effective. To supply the necessary funds for the staff to administor the resources, and for building to house the materials is a responsibility of the university administration which is cognisant of the role played by the library in the academic programme"(22).

UNIVERSITY LIBRARY FINANCES IN INDIA

It is sad fact that, generally speaking, university libraries in India are not provided with adequate finances. The Education Commission as early as 1948-49 had suggested that "there is no doubt that in most of our universities the annual grants for libraries are very inadequate" (23). The Kothari Commission Report (1964-66) on Education has recommended that, "there is no formula for estimating with precision how much money a university should invest in its libraries. It has been found that the expenditure on library in relation to total educational expenditure of the university, has gone up from 1.88% in 1951-52 to 4.04% in 1960-61, by which time the grants provided by the UGC had begun to make an impact. The University Education Commission has suggested about 6.5% of educational budget as reasonable expenditure on libraries. But this could vary say from 6.5% to 10% depending on the stage of development of each university library. It may also be suggested that, as a norm, a university should spend each year about Rs.25 for each student registered and Rs.300 per teacher" (24).

UNIVERSITY LIBRARY FINANCES IN KERALA

The state of finances of the university libraries in Kerala is not different from the national average. The position of university library finances in Kerala, a state with the highest literacy rate in the Indian Union, warrants a detailed investigation since the university libraries play a vital role in the advancement of higher education and research.

As a planned economy the lion's share of the university finances comes from plan allocations. As such it comes as a part of the planning of higher education. Eventhough large amounts are seen invested in education in every five year plan it is felt that the major portion goes to staffing, building, laboratories etc. The university libraries which ought to get an equitable fiscal share do not get it. Because of this, university libraries in Kerala do not function at the desired level of adequacy and efficiency to fulfil the objectives of higher education. The studies conducted on university libraries especially on fiscal aspects are few in numbers in India. In Kerala, this study is the pioneer attempt in the field. Considering all the aforesaid factors an attempt is made by the investigator to investigate the financing of the Kerala, Calicut and Cochin University libraries during the plan periods.

OBJECTIVES OF THE STUDY

The main objective of the study is to examine the state of financing in the Kerala, Calicut and Cochin university libraries in Kerala during the Five-year plan periods. More specifically the study is aimed at the following:

(i) What are the sources of finance; their magnitude and trend?

(ii) To examine the rate, trend and pattern of expenditure on salary, books and periodicals, contingencies, binding, equipments and furniture in relation to total university library expenditure;

(iii) To estimate the library expenditure in relation to student enrolment and total university budget; and

(iv) To ascertain the impact of finance on library resources and services based on user's point of view.

HYPOTHESIS

The study starts with the following hypotheses:

(a) The finances of the university libraries in Kerala are inadequate and far below the minimum as per the standards recommended by the library and education commissions.

(b) The libraries fail to perform their functions at the desired level and organise satisfactory responsive services.

METHODOLOGY

The study is basically an analytical one. For this purpose both primary and secondary data were collected. The following research methods were adopted in the study.

(i) Literature Survey

(ii) Questionnaire

(iii) Observation

(iv) Interview

LITERATURE SURVEY

An exhaustive literature search in the field of study was conducted. A number of published and unpublished sources were consulted. The official published sources included university budget papers, university annual reports, UGC reports, State and Central Government budget papers, five year plan proposals, Annual plans, progress report of annual plans etc published in various years. Other published literature, both primary and secondary, in the field of study was also used extensively. Besides, a number of unpublished records viz. Allocation registers, circulation registers, payment registers, overdue registers, cash book, acquittance registers and other related office files were consulted. The data collected from all these sources were used to analyse and compare the sources of finance, fiscal allocation and utilisation of the same in the university libraries in Kerala.

QUESTIONNAIRE METHOD

A Questionnaire was prepared and distributed among the users (Appendix I). Since the population under study is large in number, sampling technique was used. To avoid sampling errors, stratified sample was taken from different strata of users via. Researchers, teachers, students and graduate members.660 questionnaires were distributed among the users in three university libraries. Out of these, 494 were received duly filled up. Of the total questionnaire, 204 (out of 283) were received from the Kerala University library, 147(out of 192) from the Calicut university library and 143(out of 185) from the Cochin University library.

Questionnaire method was used with the intention of collecting data pertaining to the reader's opinions to ascertain the level of adequacy of the collection and services provided by the libraries under the study and also to elicit user's opinion in respect of anticipated sophisticated library services. Based on this data the actual requirements is identified and the financial implications were ascertained. In order to verify the findings arrived at from the questionnaire, observation and interview methods were also applied.

OBSERVATION METHOD

Observation method was used for primary data collection in the different sections of the libraries under study to identify the various programmes/activities and to ascertain the adequacy of collection, equipments, services and manpower in order to fulfil the user's requirements.

Interview method

Interview was conducted among librarians in charge of various sections and university librarians. This was conducted by using interview schedules given in appendices II and III.

SCOPE OF THE STUDY

In Kerala there are seven universities Viz. University of Kerala, Cochin University of Science and Technology, University of Calicut, Kerala Agricultural University, Mahatma Gandhi University, Sanskrit University and Kannoor University. Of these, Kerala Agricultural University does not have a university library. It has only departmental/ college libraries. Mahatma Gandhi University is a newly established one which has only just started building up its library. Hence the study is limited to three universities having university libraries viz. Kerala, Calicut and Cochin. The study is also limited to the first seven Five-Year Plan Periods.

ORGANISATION OF THE STUDY

The study is organised in nine chapters as;

i) Introduction
ii) Survey of Related literature
iii) University Libraries and Fiscal Allocations : International and National Trends
iv) Universities and University Libraries in Kerala : Genesis and development
v) Revenue : Sources and Magnitude and Trends
vi) Expenditure : Analysis, Pattern and Trends
vii) Fiscal estimate Based on method of Proportion and Per Capita Method
viii) Evaluation of Responsive services
ix) Findings and Recommendations

FINDINGS AND RECOMMENDATIONS

The analysis of the data collected has revealed a number of crevices in the financing of the three university libraries investigated.

The issues are many and vary from inadequate revenue to unscientific fiscal allocation and expenditure. The major findings that have evolved from the discussion in the previous chapters are summed up here under the major heads 'Magnitude and trends of revenue', 'Trends and pattern of expenditure', 'Estimate of Library expenditure' and 'Finance vs. responsive library services'. Magnitude and trends of revenue

UNIVERSITY REVENUE

The sources of University revenue in Kerala are both external and internal. Of these, external sources contribute the major portion of University revenue. Grants from the State Government constitute the major portion of income of the Universities. The income from internal sources is nevertheless on the increase from year to year.

The study revealed that the total revenue of the universities viz. University of Kerala, University of Calicut and Cochin University of Science and Technology has increased significantly from one plan to another. The growth rate is the highest in the Cochin University of Science and Technology and the lowest in the University of Calicut.

The annual growth rate of income in the University of Kerala, University of Calicut and Cochin University of Science and Technology is 51.57%, 42% and 178.22% respectively.

The higher percentage of growth rate of Cochin University of Science and Technology reflects the policy of the State Government and UGC in providing stronger financial support to special universities like Science and Technology universities than to general universities. This uneven growth rate of income among the Universities has resulted in an imbalanced development of universities in Kerala.

UNIVERSITY LIBRARY REVENUE

The funds allocated from the university budget and grants

received from the UGC constitute the major sources of income of the University libraries in Kerala.

ALLOCATION FROM UNIVERSITY BUDGET

The funds allocated to libraries out of university budget include both recurring and non-recurring grants. A total amount of Rs.7, 11,98,758 had been received by the University Libraries under the recurring head during the Plan periods. The recurring grants to libraries from their universities have been increasing steadily from plan to plan. In the Kerala University Library the allocation in the 7th Plan was 279 times more than the 1st Plan allocation. The 7th plan allocation of the Calicut University Library was 7 times that of the allocation for the 5th Plan whereas the allocation for the Cochin University Library during the 7th Plan was 4 times that of the 6th plan. (As already shown in table 23 recurring grant out of University budget was available to Calicut and Cochin University libraries only from the 5th and 6th Plans respectively.)

A total amount of Rs.12,99,801 had been received by the University Libraries from the University budget under the non-recurring head during the Plan periods. Out of this, the maximum amount had been received by the Kerala University budget under the non-recurring head during the Plan periods. Out of this, the maximum amount had been received by the Kerala University Library. This is due to the fact that Kerala University Library is the oldest university library in Kerala which received grants during all the Five year Plan periods.

GRANTS FROM THE UGC

Grants from the UGC constitute another significant source of revenue of the university libraries. The grant received from UGC by the Kerala University Library under the 7th Plan has been 95 times that of the grant under the first Plan, but only 2 times that of the 4th Plan. The ratio of the 4th Plan allocation to the 7th Plan allocation in the Calicut and Cochin Universities was 1:2 and 1:3 respectively.

A total amount of Rs. 1,30,67,257 had been received as recurring grants by the University libraries from UGC till the 7th Plan. Of this, the share of the Cochin, Kerala and Calicut University Libraries was 46.91%, 28.46% respectively. The above figures show that Cochin University Library has received the maximum as recurring grants from UGC, even more than the grant received by the Kerala University Library, the oldest University Library in Kerala. The recurring grants to the university libraries by the UGC have not been uniform during the plan periods. This is one of the reasons for the imbalanced growth of libraries in Kerala.

As regards non-recurring grants, these have not been received by the university libraries from UGC during every plan. A total amount of Rs.29,45,322 had been received from the UGC by the Libraries till the 7th plan. Out of this, Kerala University Library had received the maximum amount (Rs.20,54,739).

GIFTS AND OTHER SOURCES OF INCOME

In Kerala, no endowment has been instituted by philanthropists for the development of university libraries. However gifts in the form of books have been received by the university libraries. These included gifts from individuals and institutions.

The amount collected by way of overdue charges, cost recovered from members for damaged or lost books, Xerox copying charges, amount collected through sales of waste paper etc are not available to university libraries for utilization but is credited to the university account. Of the three university libraries under study, Kerala University Library had collected the maximum amount under this head.

A total amount of Rs.7,4511138 had been received from various sources by the university libraries till the 7th Plan. Of this, the maximum i.e. Rs.40986387 had been received by the Kerala University Library. The Cochin University Library received Rs.1,9121877 and Calicut University Library received Rs.1,4402874.

There was a wide variation noticed in respect of revenue of the university libraries during the plan periods. The variation from Plan to Plan was very high in the Kerala University Library. A year-wise comparison of University allocation and UGC grants to libraries in Kerala shows that the university allocation to libraries had shown a steady increase over the plan periods whereas the UGC grants had been of a varying nature.

The link relatives of Universities allocation and UGC grants have shown that allocation to libraries from University budget ranged from 139.7% to 535.66% and 160.18% to 232.79% during the Plan period in the Kerala University Library and Calicut University Library respectively. But in the case of UGC grants the percentage varies from 1.44 and 52862.22 in the Kerala University Library whereas this varies from 4.03 to 1088.54 and 34.14 to 743.38 respectively in the Calicut and Cochin University libraries.

The proportion of library revenue in relation to university revenue varied from 0.29 to 4.65. The lowest proportion had been recorded by the Kerala University Library and the highest by the Cochin University Library.

The study revealed that there is a high degree of positive correlation between the total university revenue and total library revenue in the University libraries in Kerala during the Plan periods. The correlation coefficient is +0.997 in the Calicut University Library; and +0.994 in the Cochin University Library.

UNIVERSITY EXPENDITURE

The expenditure in the universities in Kerala is only natural, shows an upward trend from one plan to another. A total amount of Rs.25146.89 lakhs had been spent by the Universities till the 7th Plan. Out of this, the maximum (Rs.13049.21 lakhs) had been spent by the University of Kerala which was in existence during all the 7 Plan periods. The University of Calicut and Cochin University of Science and Technology which were established much later during the 4th plan period had spent only Rs.7467.94 lakhs and Rs.4629.74 lakhs respectively. The growth rate of expenditure during the Plan periods in the University of Kerala is 28 times from 1st to 7th Plan and 8 times from 4th Plan to 7th Plan. The growth rate is 9 times and 40 times in the University of Calicut and Cochin University of Science and Technology respectively from 4th Plan to 7th Plan. There is a substantially higher growth rate of expenditure in the Cochin University of Science and Technology as compared to the other two universities. A Plan-wise expenditure pattern shows that the rate of increase is not uniform from Plan to Plan in the Universities.

UNIVERSITY LIBRARY EXPENDITURE

A total amount of Rs.7,45,11138 had been spent by the university libraries in Kerala till 7th Plan. Out of this, the maximum (55%) had been spent by the Kerala University Library. The Calicut University Library and Cochin University Library of Science and Technology had spent 19.32% and 25.66% respectively. The rate of increase on expenditure is 263 times in the Kerala University Library from 1st Plan to 7th Plan. In the case of Calicut University Library and Cochin University Library the growth rate is 11 times and 41 times between the 4th Plan and 7th Plan respectively. But the growth rate in the Kerala University Library is only 7 times from 4th Plan to 7th Plan, much lower than that of the other two universities.

RECURRING EXPENDITURE

The recurring expenditure (Rs.7, 0320012) constitutes the lion's share of the total library expenditure in the university libraries. The Calicut University Library stands first with 98% of its total expenditure for recurring items during the Plan periods. The Cochin University Library and Kerala University Library had spent 94.66% and 92. 97 % respectively under recurring items. This trend in the expenditure on recurring items confirm the fact that the expenditure in a library is primarily recurring. The growth rate of recurring expenditure from Plan to Plan is more or less uniform. The growth rate from the 1st Plan to 7th Plan in the Kerala University Library is 246 times while it is 6 times from the 4th to 7th Plan. The growth rate is 13 times and 39 times respectively in the Calicut University Library and Cochin University Library from 4th Plan to 7th Plan.

NON-RECURRING EXPENDITURE

A total amount of Rs.4, 191126 had been spent by the university libraries on non-recurring items of expenditure. Out of this, the maximum (Rs.28, 84376) had been spent by the Kerala University Library. The second position (Rs.10, 19547) goes to Cochin University Library and the third position (Rs.2, 87203) to Calicut University Library. The general trend in the non-recurring expenditure in the libraries is irregular and haphazard.

As regards the expenditure of each university on various items the following pattern and trends are observed.

In the case of expenditure on salary the maximum percentage (65.95) had been incurred by the Calicut University Library and the percentage had been the least (31.96%) in the Cochin University Library of the total university library expenditure. In Kerala University Library it was 61.10%. The average percentage of expenditure on salary is 54.56% of the total University Library expenditure in the University Libraries as a whole. The expenditure on salary in the Kerala University Library and Calicut University Library is above the existing norms in India and it is below the norms in the case of Cochin University Library.

As regards the expenditure on books and periodicals, the Cochin University Library had spent the maximum (60.94%) percentage out of its total expenditure. A lower percentage (29.15%) of expenditure on books and periodicals was incurred by the Kerala University Library. In Calicut University Library it was 30.82%. The average expenditure on books and periodicals in the University libraries in Kerala as a whole is 37.63%. The expenditure on books and periodicals in the Kerala University Library and Calicut

University Library is below the prescribed standards and it is above the standard in the Cochin University Library.

In the case of contingent expenditure, the Kerala University Library spent 2.94% of its total expenditure. The lowest percentage on this item was of the Calicut University Library(1.23%). The State average of expenditure on contingent items in the university libraries is 2.31%.

All the three university libraries under study had spent only a negligible percentage on binding. The average expenditure under this head is only 0.76%. As compared to the norms prescribed by experts, the expenditure under this head is found to be far below the minimum standard suggested by experts.

The Kerala University Library had spent 5.31% on equipments. Cochin University Library and Calicut University Library had spent only 2.95% and 0.26% respectively on equipments. The average expenditure on equipments in the University Libraries is 3.72%.

Under the head purchase and repair of furniture the Cochin University Library had spent a slightly higher percentage as compared to the other two university libraries. The average expenditure under this head in the university libraries in Kerala is only 1%. On the whole the expenditure on contingencies, binding, equipments and repair and purchase of furniture do not conform to the set standards/ norms prevailing in India.

The ratio of expenditure on salary, books and periodicals and other items varies from library to library. It is 5:2:1 in the Kerala University library, 19:9:1 in the Calicut University Library and 1:2:2 in the Cochin University Library.

A comparison of expenditure on salary, books and periodicals and other items in the university libraries in Kerala with that of the prescribed national and international library standards shows that the ratio of expenditure in Kerala is different from the approved standard/norm. The expenditure on salaries in the Calicut and Kerala University Libraries is much higher than national and even international standards while Cochin University Library has recorded a higher percentage of expenditure on books and periodicals and lower percentage of expenditure on salary.

The percentage of university library expenditure in relation to university expenditure in Kerala varies from 0.35% to 5.66% during the Plan periods. The highest percentage of library expenditure in relation to university expenditure was incurred by the Cochin University Library during the 7th Plan and the lowest had been incurred by the Kerala University Library during the 1st Plan period.

The study revealed that the coefficient of correlation between the total library expenditure in the University libraries during the plan periods is a highly positive one. It is +0.998, +0.994 respectively in the Kerala, Calicut and Cochin University Libraries respectively.

ESTIMATE OF LIBRARY EXPENDITURE

The study revealed that the year-wise estimate of university library expenditure in relation to University expenditure varied from 0.28% to 7.41%. The lowest proportion had been shown by the Kerala University Library during 1954-55 to 1956-57 and the highest proportion had been by the Cochin University Library during 1973-74. The average proportion of library expenditure in relation to university expenditure in the Kerala University Library is 3.14%. The rate of proportion had increased from year to year with slight fluctuation in certain years.

In the Calicut University Library the proportion had increased from year to year with slight variations in certain years. The growth rate of proportion was not uniform and significant. The average percentage of library expenditure in relation to total university expenditure in the Calicut University Library is only 1.93%.

The proportion of library expenditure in relation to university expenditure during various years is not uniform in the Cochin University Library. The average proportion of library expenditure to total university expenditure in the Cochin University Library is

4.13%. The Cochin University Library had shown the highest proportion of average expenditure on libraries. The Kerala University Library occupies the next position and the Calicut University Library the last position. Comparing the proportion of library expenditure with accepted standards in India it can be seen that the fiscal investment in the university libraries in Kerala is not satisfactory. The deviation from the existing standard is the highest in the case of Calicut University Library and the least in the Cochin University Library. The Kerala University Library, Calicut University Library and Cochin University Library ought to have got additional grants of Rs. 405.lakhs, Rs.322.72 lakhs and 98.16 lakhs respectively during the plan periods to be on a level with the standard prescribed by the Radhakrishnan Commission Report. An additional fiscal investment of Rs.2199.98 lakhs, Rs.1349.56 lakhs and Rs. 734.75 lakhs was necessary for the Kerala University Library, Calicut University Library and Cochin University Library respectively to conform to the norm suggested by Dr.K.N. Raj Commission.

The average per capita expenditure in the Kerala, Calicut and Cochin University libraries is Rs.11.38, Rs.8.61 and 91.05 respectively. The state average of per capita expenditure in the University libraries is only Rs.13.58. By applying the norm suggested by Dr.S.R.Ranganathan (Rs.100 per student) the Kerala, Calicut and Cochin University Libraries fall short by Rs.319.1 lakhs, Rs.1528.98 and Rs.18.8 lakhs respectively.

FINANCE VS. RESPONSIVE LIBRARY SERVICES

For a need-based library service adequate space for reading for users, adequate resources, equipments and manpower are prerequisites. The study revealed the following on the above aspects.

The space for reading for users in the various sections of the Kerala University Library is inadequate in the periodicals section and partially adequate in the reference section and Kerala Studies section whereas the space for reading for users is adequate in the Calicut University Library and Cochin University Library. This is not because the space is less in the Kerala University Library than in the other libraries but because the number of readers is more.

The physical facilities and equipments are not available at the desired level in the Kerala University Library and Calicut University Library.Reading materials like current periodicals, back volumes of periodicals, books and monographs and reference books are partially adequate for the users in the Kerala University Library and Calicut University Library. But materials like technical reports, conference proceedings, patents and standards, dissertations, indexing and abstracting periodicals, bibliographies and non-book materials are totally inadequate for the user's requirements. As regards the users of the Cochin University Library non-book materials are fully adequate and books and monographs are partially adequate for their requirements. But current periodicals, back volumes of periodicals and bibliographies are inadequate. In short, the different types of reading materials, which are very essential to users for study, teaching and research programmes are not available in adequate number. This has stood in the way of the University libraries in Kerala in fulfilling the requirements of users and effectively supporting the objectives of the universities.

The manpower of the university libraries in Kerala is competent and adequate in number to provide services to the user community. But the services provided by the university libraries are not upto the mark. This is due to a number of interrelated factors like inadequacy of materials, equipments, lack of proper manpower planning and deployment and above all lack of motivation among library staff. So a detailed investigation is needed in this regard.

The user community in the university libraries in Kerala is not adequately aware of the existing services provided by the libraries. Also the existing services are not suitably organised for fulfilling the actual requirements of users. This is due to lack of proper user education and user studies.

As regards the services presently provided by the university libraries, the users have different opinions. The majority of users (60.84%) in the Cochin University Library have opined that the existing services provided by this library are inadequate for their requirements whereas the percentage of inadequacy is 56.86% in the Kerala University Library. But the majority of users in the Calicut University Library are satisfied with the existing services. The higher rate of inadequacy of services in the Cochin University Library is explained by the fact that the users are more service conscious as the nature of their academic and research work needs intensive library support.

The users have suggested a number of new services to be started in order to fulfill their requirements. Majority of the users in the Kerala University Library, Calicut University Library and Cochin University Library have indicated SDI service as their first choice. The second preference is shared by News paper clipping service and user education among users in Kerala University Library whereas News paper clipping service and Referral services are the second and third preferences among users in the Calicut University Library. The user community of the Cochin University Library prefer to have Library bulletin service and News paper clipping services as their 2nd and 3rd preferences respectively.

The above findings are indices of the deficiency of resources and services in the university libraries in Kerala. Adequate resources and services necessitate adequate fiscal support. A detailed investigation and evaluation of the existing service and prospective services required by the user community and the steps required to be taken for this purpose is necessary.

The user community in the university libraries in Kerala is in favour of a switch over from the present manual system to computer-based library operations and services so as to fulfil their requirements speedily, effectively and with precision. The above findings and discussions are fruitful in substantiating the objectives of the study. The study proved that the financing of the university libraries in Kerala is inadequate and far below the minimum as per the standards recommended by Library and Education Commissions. It has also proved that the university libraries fail to perform the functions at the desired level of adequacy and efficiency and organise satisfactory responsive services. Thus the findings have tested and substantiated the validity of the hypotheses made in the study.

RECOMMENDATIONS

The findings of the study have brought out many facts which are of interest and significance to educationists, university authorities, funding agencies,university librarians and users as well. The university library plays a crucial role in higher education and national development especially in the third world countries like India needs no reiteration. There are at present various deficiencies, which obstruct university library development. It is essential that they are removed and libraries are enabled to perform their role effectively. Even though the study is confined to university libraries in Kerala, it can be deemed as typical of the fiscal allocation in the university libraries in India and the developing countries in general. A few recommendations are given here which, if implemented would be helpful in mitigating fiscal problems confronted by the university libraries.

(i) The university Grants Commission should evolve a policy based on rational norms for funding university libraries which would ensure their balanced and even growth and enable them to lend effective support to the academic and research programmes of the universities.

(ii) In deciding the norms for funding university libraries the recommendations of the various Education/Library Commissions and Committees should be taken into consideration. It is better to link library revenue and expenditure to the total university revenue and expenditure than to work it out on the basis of per capita expenditure of students and teachers. This is because the total university revenue/ expenditure is bound to go up from year to year due to various factors such as new courses started, increased enrolment of students, diversification of research programmes, general inflationary trends etc and if the library expenditure is worked out as percentage of the total university revenue/ expenditure the funds available to each library would substantially go up from year to year. The disadvantage of calculating library expenditure on the per capita basis is that the rate of expenditure fixed will have a tendency to remain static with practically no enhancement of library revenue/ expenditure.

(iii) The Kothari Commission's recommendation of 6.5% to 10% of the total institutional budget for the library depending on the stage of development of the library merits consideration for acceptance by the universities.

(iv) The distribution of the library budget among various heads of expenditure should be more rational than at present conform to national and international norms.

(v) The percentage of expenditure on salaries has been found to be too high and much above the prevailing standards, in the case of the University of Kerala and the University of Calicut. This is because of the present irrational funding of University Libraries. While the funds made available in one year may lead to workload necessitating additional staff recruitment, in the succeeding year there may be a sharp fall in the fund leading to reduced workload as revealed by the study. The staff once recruited will continue to stay in office and while the expenditure on this account due to increments, salary revisions etc goes up, the allocation for other items especially books and periodicals does not keep pace with this and sometimes even goes down. The imbalance in the expenditure ratio of salaries and other items is a concomitant of this lack of rational funding policy. All efforts should be made to remove this imbalance by increasing the allocation for each items every year as warranted by the conditions in each University.

(vi) The binding of books and periodicals, although very important, is practically neglected in the University libraries as evidenced by the very low percentage of expenditure incurred on this. The expenditure should be around 3% of the total library budget or 5% of the book budget as recommended by experts.

(vii) The expenditure on other contingent items should also be substantially enhanced in order to conform to prescribed norm. i.e. 6%- 10% of the library budget as suggested by experts.

(viii) The book resources in the libraries especially primary sources like journals, reports, standards, patents, theses and dissertations etc essentially needed for research should be strengthened in order to meet the requirements of the users adequately.

(ix) In view of the lack of satisfaction among the library users with the services now offered by the libraries in response to expressed needs, the services should be diversified and made more efficient. Selective Dissemination of Information Service (SDI), Current Awareness Service(CAS), News paper clipping service etc for which a demand has been expressed by users should be organised to the extent needed and permitted by available sources.

(x) User Education programmes aimed at imparting the requisite skills to library users to enable them to exploit library resources fully should be organised by each University Library.

(xi) Services should be oriented to user needs and for this purpose surveys of user needs should be conducted periodically by the libraries.

(xii) The general dissatisfaction regarding the delay and lack of precision in the services can be removed by introducing automation in the library operations and services as favoured by the majority of users covered in this study. The libraries should plan automation in a phased manner.

Automation is also necessary to enable each library to participate in the Information Library Network (INFLIBNET) project contemplated by the UGC in the 8th Plan.

In conclusion it must be emphasised again that only through the universities adopting and implementing a sound and rational fiscal policy in respect of their libraries can the book resources be strengthened, their organisation streamlined and services made more effective so that adequate library support can be ensured for the fulfilment of the objectives of the Universities.

APPENDIX I

(Note : Please put tick mark where box is available and write wherever necessary)

A. GENERAL

1. Name
2. Designation

Student	Research Scholar	Teacher	Others
☐	☐	☐	☐

3. Foreign languages known other than English

Russian	German	French	Others
☐	☐	☐	☐

4. Area of your subject interest.

B. PHYSICAL FACILITIES

1. Do you use the University Library regularly?

Yes	No
☐	☐

2. How do you find the general layout of the library?

Easy to follow	Difficult	Inconvenient
☐	☐	☐

3. When you wish to use the library, do you find a place in the following sections.

	Always	Usually	Sometimes	Never
a) Physical Section	☐	☐	☐	☐
b) Reference Section	☐	☐	☐	☐
c) Stack room Section	☐	☐	☐	☐
d) General Reading Section	☐	☐	☐	☐
e) Any other Section (Please specify)	☐	☐	☐	☐

4. What is your opinion regarding the physical facilities (Chairs, tables, fan and light arrangements) available in the library.

Adequate	PartiallyAdequate	Inadequate
☐	☐	☐

C. COLLECTION

1. To what extent are your requirements such as learning, teaching and research met by the following collections in the University Library?

	Adequate	Partially Adequate	Inadequate
i) Current Periodicals	☐	☐	☐
ii) Back volumes of periodicals	☐	☐	☐
iii) Books, monographs, Text Books	☐	☐	☐

iv) Reference Books	☐	☐	☐
v) Technical Reports	☐	☐	☐
vi) Proceedings of Conferences and seminars	☐	☐	☐
vii) Patents and Standards	☐	☐	☐
viii) Dissertations & Thesis	☐	☐	☐
ix) Indexing, Abstracting and Reviewing Periodicals	☐	☐	☐
x) Bibliographies	☐	☐	☐

2. Do you get your reading materials in due time?

Always	Sometimes	Never
☐	☐	☐

3. Do you feel that useful periodicals subscribed earlier in the University Library are discontinued?

Yes	No
☐	☐

If your answer is 'YES', please mention such periodicals which must be essentially subscribed by the library in the order of your preference.

i)

ii)

iii)

iv)

v)

4. Are there any particular periodicals (not indicated in 3 above) you would like to read but are not available in the University Library?

Yes ☐ No ☐

If your answer is 'YES', please list the name of periodicals

i)

ii)

iii)

5. Do you use non-book materials like microfilm, microfiche etc in the University Library?

Yes ☐ No ☐

6. Do you visit other libraries in case your requirements are not fully met by the University Library?

Yes ☐ No ☐

If the answer is YES,please name the libraries

i)

ii)

iii)

iv)

D. STAFF

1. Have you ever asked for assistance from library staff for the following purposes

	Yes	No
a) To locate books	☐	☐
b) To locate current and back issues of periodicals	☐	☐
c) To understand the various reference books	☐	☐
d) To compile a bibliography	☐	☐
e) To locate a specific piece of information	☐	☐
f) For other purposes (Please specify)	☐	☐

2. What is your opinion about the library staff in the University Library about the following:

	Yes	No
a) Always ready to help	☐	☐
b) Too busy to help	☐	☐
c) Not adequate in number	☐	☐
d) Incompetent to help	☐	☐

3. Have you ever felt that you are not getting the required staff assistance due to inadequacy of library staff

Yes	No
☐	☐

SERVICES

1. The following are some of the services rendered to the users by the University Library. Do you utilize such services?

	Yes	No
i) Reference service	☐	☐
ii) Latest addition list of books	☐	☐
iii) Reprographic services	☐	☐
iv) Interlibrary loan services	☐	☐
v) Reservation of books	☐	☐
vi) Current content services	☐	☐
vii) Any other service (Specify)	☐	☐

2. Do you think that the aforesaid services are adequate for your learning, teaching and research work?

Yes	No
☐	☐

If your answer is 'No', do you think any of the following additional services are necessary? (Indicate your preference by 1,2,3, etc).

a) News paper clipping service (a service based on important information taken from news papers) ☐

b) Selective Dissemination of Information (SDI) (An intensified personalised service given to the user by routing latest information in his/her field of specialization) ☐

c) Referral Service(directional service given to the user regarding availability of information in another institution). ☐

d) Translation service ☐

e) Library Bulletin (Publication which contains Research in progress, research already completed and other relevant information) ☐

f) Bibliographical services (compilation of bibliographies on demand from users) ☐

g) User education (Instruction given to the users to help them make the best use of library materials) ☐

h) Data service ☐

i) Any other service (Specify) ☐

3. Do you think that the present system of manual library operations and services in the University is time consuming and not very effective?

Yes ☐ No ☐

If your answer is YES, do you think that the use of computers in the University Library can improve the situation?

Yes ☐ No ☐

F. SUGGESTION

Please give your suggestions for eliminating the existing problems especially financial problems and improving library services in the University Library.

APPENDIX II

INTERVIEW SCHEDULE FOR SECTION HEADS IN THE UNIVERSITY LIBRARIES

1. Name of the Section
2. What are the important objectives and functions of the section

   i)

   ii)

   iii)

   iv)

   v)
3. Working hours of the section
4. What is your opinion about the working space in your section

   a) Working space for staff Adequate/Inadequate

   b) Working space for users

   (If it is a service section like Reference Section, Periodical Section, etc)

   If your answer is 'INADEQUATE' suggest approximate area (in sq.ft.) required to work the section effectively..........
5. Do you feel that adequate library equipments are available in the section to meet the objectives of the section

   If your answer is 'NO' please suggest the essential library equipments (including conventional and modern) to be purchased and their approximate cost.

Name of equipments	Cost
i)	
ii)	
iii)	
iv)	
v)	

6. Do you feel that reading materials/ services available in the section are adequate to meet the requirements of the users

   Adequate ☐ Inadequate ☐

   If your answer is 'INADEQUATE' do you think that this is mainly due to inadequate finance.

   Yes ☐ No ☐

7. Strength of personnel working in the section (Give numbers)

   Professional ☐ Semi-Professional ☐ Non-Professional ☐

8. What is your opinion about the present manpower position in the section?

   Excess ☐ Adequate ☐ Inadequate ☐

9. What are the programmes/activities/ services and the number of personnel engaged to execute each programme.

Name of the Programme	*No. of Professional Staff*	*No. of Semi Professional Staff*	*No. of Non-Professional Staff*
i)			
ii)			
iii)			
iv)			
v)			

10. Have you left out any programme/s or service/s at any time in the section due to lack/inadequacy of staff

    Yes ☐ No ☐

11. Do you have any new programme/s or service/s other than existing ones to be started to achieve the ultimate objectives of the section

Yes	No
☐	☐

If your answer is 'YES' list the programme/s and number of additional staff required to execute the programme/s or service/s.

Name of the Programme/s	*No. of Professional Staff*	*No. of Semi Professional Staff*	*No. of Non-Professional Staff*
i)			
ii)			
iii)			
iv)			
v)			

12. What is your opinion about the application of computer in your section as a means of enabling it to function more speedily, effectively and economically.

13. Please give your suggestions to overcome the problems especially fiscal problems in your section.

APPENDIX III

INTERVIEW SCHEDULE FOR UNIVERSITY LIBRARIANS/ DEPUTY LIBRARIANS

1. Name of the University Library
2. What are the major objectives of the university library?

   i)

   ii)

   iii)
3. What is your opinion about the provision of space in the University Library

	Adequate	Inadequate
a) Working space for Staff	☐	☐
b) Working space for users	☐	☐

   If your answer is 'INADEQUATE' suggest approximate area (in sq.ft.) required to work the library effectively…………
4. Do you think the library equipments presently availble in the library are adequate to fulfil the objectives of the library.

Yes	No
☐	☐

   If your answer is 'NO' please suggest the essential library equipments to be purchased and their approximate cost.

Name of equipment/s	Cost
i)	
ii)	
iii)	
iv)	
v)	

5. What is your opinion about the adequacy of the following for fulfilling the requirements of the users.

	Adequate	Inadequate
a) Reading materials	☐	☐
b) Staff	☐	☐
c) Services	☐	☐

6. How do you feel about the present manpower position in the library.

Excess	Adequate	Inadequate
☐	☐	☐

7. Have you left out any programme/service during the last 10 years due to lack of staff and finance.

Yes	No
☐	☐

8. What type of budgeting technique/method followed in the library for the budget preparation.

   a) Line Budgeting

   b) Programme Budgeting

   c) Performance Budgeting

   d) By comparison with past expenditures

   e) By using arbitrary standards and norms

   f) Any other (specify)

9. Do you think that the present method of budget allocation is adequate to fulfill the objectives of the library.

Yes	No
☐	☐

If your answer is 'NO' indicate the approximate adhoc amount required for the following.

Item	Approximate cost
a) Purchase of books and periodicals	
b) Equipments	
c) Extension of the library building	
d) Staff salary (For appointing additional staff)	
e) For starting additional service	
f) Stationary	
g) Contingencies	

10. Please give your suggestions inorder to overcome the problems especially fiscal problems in the University Library.

REFERENCES

1. India, Education Commission (1964-66) (Chairman :D.S.Kothari) Report: Educational and National development. Delhi, MOP,1966. P.4.
2. India, Education (Mini.of-). Challenge of education: A policy perspective. New Delhi, The Ministry, 1985, p.1.
3. Association of Indian Universities (New Delhi). New Education Policy. New Delhi, Association of Indian Universities 1985. p.5-7.
4. India, Education Commission (1964-66) (Chairman :D.S.Kothari) *op.cit*. p.274-75.
5. University Grants Commission (New Delhi). Development of higher education in India : A policy frame. New Delhi, UGC,1978.
6. University Grants Committee (United Kingdom). Report.London.HMSO.1921.
7. India, University Education Commission (1948-49) (Chairman :S.Radhakrishnan) Report. Vol.1. Delhi, MOP.1951. p.111-112.
8. Dongerkery, SR Libraries in university education. *In*

comparative librarianship ed. By NN Gidwani. Delhi. Vikass,1973,p.15.

9. India, Education Commission (1964-66) (Chairman :D.S.Kothari) *op.cit*. p.287.

10. University Grants Committee (United Kingdom)(Chairman : R. Atkinson). Capital provision for university libraries: Report of a working party. London, UGC,1976.

11. University Grants Committee (United Kingdom) (1963) (Chairman : Thomas Parry). Report. London, HMSO,1967. p.9.

12. Gelfand, M.A. University libraries for developing countries. Paris,Unesco,1968,p.24-25.

13. Line,M.B. The functions of the university library. ***In*** University and research library studies, ed by W.L. Saunders. Oxford,Pergamon Press,1968.p.148.

14. University Grants Commission (New Delhi) (1957) (Chairman : S. R.Ranganthan). University and College libraries. New Delhi, UGC,1965.p.17

15. Buck,Paul.Libraries and Universities. Harvard,Harvard University Press,1964.p.9.

16. Wilson,L.R. and Tauber, M.E. The University library. Ed2.New york, Columbia university press,1956.p.19.

17. Shrinath Sahai Development of university libraries in India since independence. ***ILA Bulletin.*** 12(1) 1976.p.37.

18. Gelfand, MA *op cit*. p.14,20.

19. Misra, DP Forward to 'Educational finances in India' by Atmanand Misra. Bombay, Asia, 1962.p.vii.

20. Viswanathan,CG. University libraries in India : Principles and policy. Delhi, The author, 1972.p.20.

21. White, Carl M.A. Survey of the university of Delhi library. Delhi, University of Delhi,1965.p.85.

22. Hart, James D.Interim report of the library committee. ***University Bulletin***, University of California 2,1954.p.133-134.

23. India, University Education Commission (1948-49) (Chairman : S.Radhakrishnan) *op cit.*p.111.

24. India, Education Commission (1964-66) (Chairman:D.S. Kothari) *op cit.*p.288.

2

DESIGN AND DEVELOPMENT OF INDIAN NATIONAL INFORMATION SYSTEM FOR AYURVEDA

Dr. Joshy George P.

INTRODUCTION

All known cultures of the past Egyptian, Babylonian, Jewish, Greek, Indus-valley etc. have their own equally glorious and useful systems of health care. In India, development and growth of such a body of knowledge known as Ayurveda, meaning science of life, was coeval with the growth and evolution of Indian civilization and culture. Vedas, which are considered to be the repositories of recorded Indian culture, have mention of this knowledge both in the theoretical and practical form. There is discussion of theories about the composition of living and non-living matters, the physical, biochemical, biological, psychological and spiritual components of man and the vital motive forces working both inside and outside the body. In other ancient works such as *Charaka Samhita, Sushruta Samhita* etc. there are mention of such current medical subjects like anatomy, physiology, aetiology, pathology, treatment and environmental factors. This medical knowledge has been the work of ages. It is the outcome of the great power of observation, generalization and analysis combined with patient labour of hundreds of investigators spread over thousands of years. This knowledge has played so important part in the development of Indian culture that it has been documented in an integrated form in the Vedas, which are considered to have been originated from Gods[1]. The ancient Ayurveda was closely related to astrology.[2]Judy Pugh of the university of British Columbia detects three separate arts in Indian astrology: the art of dialogue, the art of prediction and the art of remedy. [3]The basis of the ancient Ayurveda can be found in some of the astrological texts like Maharishi Parasara's *Brihat Parasara Hora Sastra*. Most of this mythological and medico-religious genesis of Ayurveda is even today shrouded in the mist of antiquity.

Around 1500 B.C. Ayurveda's fundamentals and applied principles got organised and enunciated. *Atharvaveda*, one of the four most ancient books of Indian knowledge, wisdom and culture, contains 114 hymns or formulations for the treatment of diseases. In this sense Ayurveda is considered to have divine origin representing one of the oldest organized system of medicine for positive health and cure of human sickness. Making use of systematic careful observation and documenting detailed experiences over the past several thousands of years, it has grown into a very comprehensive health care system with two major school and eight specializations, it has a School of Physicians and a School of Surgeons referred in literature as '*Atreya Sampradaya*' and '*Dhanvanthari Sampradaya*' respectively[4].

The most important and massive ancient compilation of the Schools of medicine is known as *Charaka Samhita*. It contains several chapters dealing at length with therapeutic or internal medicine. About 600 drugs of plant, animal and mineral origin are described in it. Besides, this compendium also deals with other branches of Ayurveda like anatomy, physiology, aetiology, prognosis, pathology, treatment and medicine etc[5].

An equally exhaustive ancient compilation, *Sushruta Samhita* exists relating to school of surgery. It deals primarily with various fundamental principles and theory of surgery, more than 100 kinds of surgical instruments including scalpels, scissors, forceps, specula etc. are described along with their use in this valuable document. Descriptions of how to go about doing incision, excision, extraction, and bandaging etc. are detailed in this compendium. In addition, this document also mentions of such other topics as anatomy, embryology, toxicology and therapeutics. It has a mention of about 650 drugs[6].

In course of time Ayurveda, which started as a magico-religious practice, matured into a fully developed medical science with eight branches which have parallels in the modern western system of medicine. The growth of these eight specialities gave Ayurveda another name as *Astanga* Ayurveda. The medical knowledge was divided into the following eight branches:

1. *Kayachikitsa* - Internal medicine
2. *Kaumarabhritya* - Paediatrics
3. *Grahachikitsa* - Psychiatry
4. *Salakyatantra* - Opthalmology
5. *Salyatantra* - Surgery
6. *Visatantra* - Toxicology
7. *Rasayanatantra* - Geriatrics
8. *Vajikaranatantra* - Knowledge of Virilfics[7]

Ayurveda deals elaborately with measures of healthful living during the entire span of life and its various phases. Besides dealing with principles for maintenance of health, it has also developed a wide range of therapeutic measures to combat illness. These principles of positive health and therapeutic measures related to physical, mental, social, and spiritual welfare of human beings. Thus Ayurveda become one of the oldest system of medicine dealing with both the preventive and curative aspects of life in a most comprehensive way.

RELEVANCE OF THE STUDY

Development of a National Information system is essential for the further development of Ayurveda in India. When compared to other major systems of medicine like Allopathy, Homeopathy etc., at present the Ayurveda is not getting the due recognition as a system of medicine. The Acupuncture, a part of Chinese indigenous medicine could acquire a worldwide recognition. But still the Ayurveda, one of the major medical systems with thousands of years of history and the one, which has proven as a harmless and effective medical system, has not yet got the worldwide recognition and it is still practiced only in India and some other Asian countries. Even in India the Ayurveda is loosening its prominence. Among the various factors for this situation, a major reason is lack of sufficient research and proper communication among the experts in this field. Even the study and research activities taking place in the various parts of the country are not properly coordinated. They are carried out in isolation. There is no effective scientific communication in this field. Not much bibliographic activities are carried out in this field. Development of a National Information System has a major role to solve these problems. In Ayurveda many valuable documents are kept as closed documents by a number of persons, families and organisations. Many of the ancient documents are kept unused in the various manuscript libraries and in personal and family collections, especially in the traditional "Vaidya families" of Kerala and other parts of India. For the overall development of Ayurveda these ancient compilations should be identified, properly documented and made available to all the practitioners and researchers in this field. A National Information Agency with sufficient government backing can unearth many of these valuable treasures.

Now a days western countries are showing interest in herbal

and indigenous medicine, the multinational companies are involved in patenting these information collected from third world countries. From India a lot of information are flowing out in this way. An effective National Information system can play an important role to check this loss.

There are many claims for the Ayurvedic remedies for the dreaded diseases like AIDS, cancer etc. But most of these claims are ignored or not properly attended in our country. A National Information System can help to put forward such claims effectively and to communicate the study results properly. Thus in many ways a National Information System can play a key role in the development of Ayurveda. So any effort to design and develop such a system is most relevant now.

TITLE OF THE STUDY

The title of the study is "Design and development of Indian National Information System for Ayurveda".

Definition of the key terms

Most of the terms in the title are self-explanatory. The terms which are not self-explanatory and those in which the context in which the term is used is to be specified are defined below.

National Information System: An information system is defined as 'an organised procedure for collecting, processing, storing, and retrieving information to satisfy a variety of needs'[8]. When the activities of an information system is restricted to the jurisdiction of a nation it becomes a national information system. Here in this study all the above said activities of the information system is designed in the context of the nation India.

Ayurveda: The word 'Ayurveda' is composed of two Sanskrit terms viz. '*ayus*' meaning 'life' and '*Veda*' meaning the 'knowledge' and taken together it means the 'science of life'. It deals with the method of keeping the human body and mind in a state of perfect health. Charaka has defined Ayurveda as the 'science through the help of which one can obtain knowledge about the useful and harmful types of life, happy and miserable types of life, things which are useful or harmful for such types of life as well as the very nature of life'[9]. Thus more than a medical system Ayurveda is considered as a 'way of life'. But here in this study the term Ayurveda refers to the ancient system of medicine which is still practiced in India.

OBJECTIVE OF THE STUDY

The objectives of the study are:

i. To study the infrastructure available in libraries and information centres attached to the various Ayurveda institutions in India.

ii. To study the information needs of the various categories of users in Ayurveda such as qualified and conventional practitioners, scientists, teachers and students;

iii. Makes an assessment of whether the present information infrastructure available in Ayurveda is adequate to satisfy the needs of the users or not; and

iv. Based on the assessment made on the above objectives designing a National Information System for Ayurveda, which will satisfy the needs of the information users in Ayurveda.

METHODOLOGY

The following methodologies were used in the study for data collection.

LITERATURE SURVEY

The history and basic principles of the Ayurveda and other Indian systems of medicine were studied mainly through literature survey.

The present status of Ayurveda and other Indian systems of medicine in India, data relating to the number of medical personnel, research centres, hospitals, educational institutions etc. were studied mainly using secondary data collected from the publications of the planning and evaluation cell under the ministry of health and family welfare, Government of India. The background studies regarding the various information systems and library and information networks were also made through literature survey.

QUESTIONNAIRE METHOD

The library and other information infrastructure available in various Ayurveda institutions were studied mainly through questionnaire method. Data collected from CCRAS and its various subsidiary research institutions including 2 Indian Institutes of Ayurveda, 3 Central Research Institutes, 17 regional centres and 47 research units. Data from 10 representative samples of other state level and private research centres were also collected. Apart from these data were collected from National Institute of Ayurveda, Pharmacopoeia laboratory, Gujarat Ayurveda University, Department of Medical Sciences of Banarus Hindu University and 72 Ayurveda colleges.

The information needs of the various categories of the Ayurveda users were also collected mainly through questionnaires. Representative samples from different regions of the country were selected and questionnaires were distributed to 83 scientists, 97 teachers, 91 doctors, 96 conventional practitioners and 89 students. Sixty seven (80.72%) scientists, 74 (76.28%) teachers, 71 (78.82%) doctors, 61 (63.54%) conventional practitioners and 76 (85.39%) students were returned the filled up questionnaires.

INTERVIEW METHOD

The data collected though questionnaires were corroborated by the information collected through interview method. 145 persons responded through questionnaire were also interviewed to get more information as well as clarifications. These constitute 20 librarians, 23 doctors, 28 conventional practitioners, 27 scientists, 30 teachers and 17 students. Interviews were of unstructured in nature. In interviews with the librarians the problems faced by them in information collection, storage and dissemination in libraries were discussed. In interviews with the users the problems faced by them in getting information in right time, their opinion about the services provided by the Ayurveda libraries and the new services expected from libraries and the problems faced by the Ayurveda medical system in general were discussed. The opinions of the librarians and users regarding the structure and functions of the National Information System in Ayurveda were also discussed in detail. Since the dissemination of information in Ayurveda through publications are lesser in number and scattered in various languages, the information collected through this method were very useful.

The data collected though various methods were analysed to study the strong and weaker points of the present set-up. The information needs of the various categories of users were studied. Based on these inferences a new National Information System for Ayurveda which satisfies the needs of the various categories of Ayurveda users and one which helps the all-round development of the Ayurvedic medical system is designed.

HYPOTHESES

The hypotheses leading to the present study are:

1. The present information infrastructure available in Ayurveda in India is not satisfactory and inadequate to meet the information needs of the users.
2. The present institutional and information infrastructure are not coordinated and organized which calls for the design of a national information system for an effective and efficient information services in Ayurveda in India.

SCOPE OF THE STUDY

The study involves the designing of the National information system for Ayurveda. The various levels of organisations of the system, its infrastructure, manpower and the functions to be carried out are to be defined. For this the existing infrastructure available in India, the information needs of the various Ayurvedic personnel including scientists, teachers, students and practitioners, the present mode of communication and transfer of information among themselves etc. are to be studied. Lot of information relating to Ayurveda is still remains unpublished and undocumented, a major share is in the form of manuscripts so all these aspects are to be considered while designing a National Information System for Ayurveda. As the study is of all India coverage it involves extensive surveys to study the existing infrastructure available in the country, information needs of the personnel involved in this field, various sources in which Ayurveda literature is scattered etc. Based on these survey results the Information System is to be designed.

LIMITATIONS OF THE STUDY

Even if the study focuses all India; it is not desirable to cover all the institutions and all information users in Ayurveda. So representative samples were taken and studied. In case of research centres all the major research centres in India are covered, but in case of Ayurveda colleges only about 50% of the institutions were covered. In case of information users in Ayurveda also data were collected from representative samples.

The publications in Ayurveda are comparatively lesser, multilingual and scattered. So in many cases interviews with the experts were also undertaken to reach into conclusion.

The study proposes only the design of an Indian National Information System for Ayurveda. The various levels of organizations in the system and the functions of each of these subsystems were defined but the financial implications in the development of each subsystem were not worked out.

ORGANIZATION OF THE THESIS

The thesis is organized under 9 chapters. They are:

Chapter 1: Introduction

The title, objective, scope, relevance, methodology, limitations etc of the study are mainly discussed in this chapter.

Chapter 2: Review of related literature

Similar studies already conducted in the related fields are reviewed here.

Chapter 3: Ayurveda and other Indian systems of medicine: Genesis and development

The genesis, development and the basic principles of Ayurveda are discussed in detail in this chapter. The history and basic principles of other Indian systems of medicine are also explained briefly in this chapter.

Chapter 4: Institutional infrastructure of Ayurveda and other Indian systems of medicine

This chapter gives a statistical account of various Ayurvedic institutions engaged in research, education, treatment etc. A detailed description of the nature of Ayurveda research is also given. A brief statistical data relating to other Indian systems of medicine is also provided in this chapter.

Chapter 5: Related National and International Information systems and Library networks

In this chapter various library and information systems and networks related to Ayurveda such as medical and biological subjects at the national and international level are discussed. Various information systems, library networks and other communication infrastructure available in India are explained in detail.

Chapter 6: Present information infrastructure available for Ayurveda in India

The data collected through questionnaires and interviews about the present library and other information system infrastructure available in our country are analysed and interpreted here. An evaluation of the present information infrastructure is made and the drawbacks of the present system are listed.

Chapter 7: Information needs and information seeking behaviour of Ayurvedic information users

The data collected on the information needs and information use pattern of the various categories of information users such as researchers, teachers, students and practitioners in the field of Ayurveda are analysed and interpreted here. A comparative study of the information needs and information seeking behaviour of different types of users is also made in this chapter.

Chapter 8: Indian National Information System for Ayurveda (INISA): Design, Structure and Functions.

Here the information collected, analysed and interpreted are used for the design and development of an Indian National Information System for Ayurveda (INISA) which would satisfy the Information needs of the information users in the field of Ayurveda. The various levels of organisation of the proposed information system, structure and functions of each of these levels or subsystems etc. are provided here.

Chapter 9: Findings and conclusion

In this chapter the findings of the entire study are summed up and conclusions are drawn.

Appendix I

Questionnaire used for the collection of data from libraries attached to various types of Ayurveda institutions.

Appendix II

Questionnaire used for the collection of data from

1. researchers and teachers
2. qualified practitioners
3. conventional practitioners
4. students.

FINDINGS AND CONCLUSION

The major findings of the study are given below. The main objective of the study is to design a National Information System for Ayurveda which will satisfy the needs of the information users in Ayurveda. In order to carry out the designing of the information system the infrastructure available in various libraries and information centres attached to the various Ayurveda institutions in India and the information needs of the various categories of users in Ayurveda were studied in detail. To conduct these surveys the questionnaire and interview methods were used. In order to collect the background information such as genesis and development of Ayurveda and other Indian systems of medicine, institutional infrastructure of these medical systems, related national and international information systems and library networks etc. literature survey method was mainly used. Based on the findings and inferences of these surveys National Information System for Ayurveda is designed. A brief summary of the survey results and the structure and functions of the information system designed are presented below.

Genesis, development and basic principles of Ayurveda and other Indian systems of medicine. The exact origin of Ayurveda is lost in the mist of antiquity. Hindu mythology attributes a divine origin for Ayurveda. The Vedas, especially the *Atharvaveda* contains hymns on formulations for the Ayurveda treatment. Ayurveda is even treated as the *upaveda,* or accessory Veda to the *Atharvaveda* by many scholars. In the remains of Harappan civilization also found some substances such as deer antler and bitumen, which are used in classical Ayurveda. We can consider the Ayurveda as a medical system evolved out of the great power of observation, generalization and analysis combined with patient labour of hundreds of investigators spread over thousands of years.

The '*Athreya Samhita*' compiled in around 9th century BC is considered as the oldest known Ayurveda medical text now existed. The '*Charaka Samhita*' compiled by Charaka at the turn of the first millennium BC, is still the most important of all Ayurvedic texts appeared so far. Ayurveda's most famous text on surgical treatment is '*Sushruta Samhita*' compiled by Sushruta. Some of the famous Ayurveda texts of ancient period include *Ashtanga Samgraha, Ashtanga Hridaya, Madhava Nidhana, Sharangadhara Samhita* and *Bhavaprakasha*.

The basic principles of Ayurveda are *Panchabhootha Siddantam, Thridosha Siddantam* and *Saptha dhatu Siddantam*. Some commonly used therapies in Ayurveda are *Snehana* (unctuous therapy), *Svedana* (Sweat therapy) and *Panchakarma*. The ingredients of ayurvedic medicine falls mainly in three categories. First and most important one is those coming from vegetable kingdom. Eighty percent of the total medicinal ingredients belong to this category. Other two categories are those from animal kingdom and from mineral kingdom.

The indigenous medical systems practiced other than Ayurveda in India are Unani, Siddha, Yoga, Naturopathy and Amchi. Unani system was originated in Greece and flourished in India during Mughal period. The siddha system is known as the medical system of dravidian culture and was originated and practiced in south India, especially in Tamil Nadu. Naturopathy is known as drugless medical system. The fundamental principles of it were derived from the philosophical system of ancient India. Yoga is not basically a medical system, it is a means for controlling the body and mind and thereby achieving the spiritual heights and eternal joy. The different physical postures and breathing exercises in Yoga can be used judiciously for therapeutic purpose. Amchi is basically the Tibetan medical system which is practiced in the Himalayan regions in India. It has its roots in Ayurveda.

INSTITUTIONAL INFRASTRUCTURE OF AYURVEDA

The major institutional infrastructure of Ayurveda includes institutions for research, education and treatment. For the government level administration, at the centre there is a department of Indian systems of medicine and homeopathy under the Ministry of Health and Family Welfare. At the state level there are directorates and / or departments of Indian systems of medicine generally under the control of the Minister of Health and Family Welfare in each State.

Systematic research in Ayurveda under the patronage of Government of India started in 1969 with the establishment of Central Council for Research in Indian Medicine and Homeopathy (CCRIMH). In the year 1978 CCRIMH was split into four separate councils. One among them, the Central Council for Research in Ayurveda and Siddha (CCRAS) is engaged now in developing independent and multi-dimensional research in the various fundamental and applied aspects of Ayurveda. Under CCRAS there are research organisations at different levels like Indian Institutes of Research, Central Research Institutes, Regional Research Institutes, Regional Research Centres, Research Projects, Research Schemes and Research Units. There are research institutes under the patronage of state government and private sector also.

The education and training facilities in Ayurveda are presently being monitored by the Central Council of Indian Medicine (CCIM). There is a National Institute of Ayurveda at Jaipur, Rajasthan and an Ayurveda University at Jamnagar, Gujarat. There are at present 154 recognized under-graduate colleges of Ayurveda in India and 33 post-graduate colleges/institutions imparting post graduate education in Ayurveda.

As on 1-4-1998 there are 2189 hospitals and 14252 dispensaries for Ayurveda in India. The total hospital bed strength is 33145. As on 1-1-1999 total number of Ayurveda practitioners in India are 366812. Out of which 270349 are institutionally qualified and the rest are the conventional practitioners.

RELATED NATIONAL AND INTERNATIONAL INFORMATION SYSTEMS

Systems and Library Networks

At present there is no information system exists in Ayurveda. But there are information systems in the related fields like modern medicine and biomedical field. Two most important information systems in these fields are MEDLARS and EMBASE. Both these systems are providing information services at international level through different media like print, CD-ROM and On-line databases.

In India there are various national information systems like National Information System for Science and Technology (NISSAT), Biotechnology Information System (BTIS), Environmental Information System (ENVIS) etc. The information and library networks in India include NICNET, INFLIBNET, INDONET, SIRNET, ERNET, DELNET, CALIBNET, BONET, and MALIBNET etc. All these information systems and networks in India are at different stages of development.

PRESENT INFORMATION INFRASTRUCTURE AVAILABLE FOR AYURVEDA IN INDIA

Data were collected from libraries attached to CCRAS and various research institutes, National institute of Ayurveda, Pharmacopoeia laboratory, Gujarat Ayurveda university, Institute of Medical Science department of Banarus Hindu University and representative samples of Ayurveda colleges. The major findings of the study are given below

Among the libraries of the research institute the only library maintaining reasonably good standard is the CCRAS library. The libraries attached to the subsidiary centres of CCRAS are in really pathetic condition. There is no library staff in these libraries. Only a small collection is maintained in these centres under the charge of a scientist. The collection is not classified or catalogued. The library attached to the Pharmacopoeia laboratory is also not in a good condition. Here the librarian's post is being kept vacant for a long period. There are only less than 2000 volumes of books and are not classified. National Institute of Ayurveda library has collection of more than 20,000 volumes. The collection is classified and catalogued. Gujarat Ayurveda University library is the largest in collection. It has a collection of 27635 books 11000 bound volumes of periodicals and 2400 dissertations. The library is using its own scheme to classify the books. But there is no catalogue in this library. The library attached to the Institute of Medical Sciences department of Banaras Hindu University is common for Ayurveda and modern medicine. It has a collection of about 60,000 books out of which 20,000 are on Ayurveda and other Indian systems of medicine. The collection is classified and catalogued. Barring few exceptions the Ayurveda college libraries are not maintaining the standard of good library. The collection of books in these libraries varies from 7000 to 20,000. Periodical subscription is generally very poor. In most cases it is in between 10 and 15. Out of the 72 libraries studied 23 libraries have not classified their collection. Among the different types of library services, the only effective service provided by most of these libraries is the issue of books and periodicals. Many libraries are also providing reference service at its minimum level. Most of the libraries spend less than 25000 rupees for books and less than 5000 for periodicals annually.

The survey shows that the Ayurveda libraries in India are generally not maintaining the standard of good modern day libraries in other subject fields. The collections are generally poor both quantitatively and qualitatively.

The information on manuscripts is important in Ayurveda and 38 libraries were found to have a collection of rare books/ manuscripts. But there are no organized efforts to preserve and publish the information in these rare documents.

Many libraries have not yet classified and catalogued their collection. Among the libraries classified their collection the commonly used classification systems are CC, DDC or the schemes specially devised by the individual libraries. The commonly used cataloguing codes are CCC and AACR. The classification schedules and lists of subject headings available now are inadequate for technical processing of Ayurveda documents. That is the main reason for using specialized schemes and codes for classification and cataloguing in many of the Ayurveda libraries. Because of this practice there is no uniformity in the technical processing of documents in Ayurveda libraries.

The Ayurveda libraries have generally failed to provide modern library and information services to their users. Majority of libraries still focus on traditional service, issue and return of books and periodicals. Other services offered by few libraries include reference service, reprography service and current awareness service. Only one library provides CD-ROM and On-line database search facility. No library is providing services like SDI, translation etc.

Only two libraries were found to be using the computers. Here also all the sections are not computerized. According to the librarians the main reasons for not computerizing the Ayurveda libraries in India are negative attitude of the management, non-availability of the sufficient qualified staff with knowledge in computerization and inadequacy of the library fund.

Except CCRAS library no other library have regular publications like bulletins, newsletters, new additions list etc. The main reason for not publishing even the new additions list by these libraries is lack of computerization.

Except one library no library have interlibrary loan arrangement with other libraries. There is no union catalogue of Ayurveda libraries. There is no network of these libraries as well. Each library is functioning as independent units and there is no uniformity in the practice of technical processing of documents and providing information services in these libraries.

All the libraries under survey are faced with financial

constraints. Inadequate budget allocation hinders the libraries from maintaining a good collection and providing modern information services to the users. Another problem faced by these libraries is lack of sufficient number of qualified staff members. This is a major reason for the poor services offered by Ayurveda libraries in India.

INFORMATION NEEDS AND INFORMATION SEEKING BEHAVIOUR OF AYURVEDA INFORMATION USERS

In order to conduct the survey among the users of Ayurveda regarding their information needs they were divided into various categories like scientists, teachers, qualified practitioners, traditional practitioners and students. As their information needs are different and their accessibility to the libraries and other information centres are different, separate questionnaires were framed for each category of users. The study gives following results.

The information sources generally used by the Ayurveda users are books, periodicals, seminar volumes, theses and manuscripts. Practitioners of Ayurveda commonly use books and current periodicals. Members of all categories found to use non-book materials. Scientists (61.19%) and conventional practitioners (60.65%) are the two categories of users which use the non book materials, especially the manuscripts, heavily.

While researchers, teachers and students make use of the libraries attached to their parent institutions, majority of the practitioners are not using libraries regularly, they depend mainly on personal collection of books and periodicals. Those who using the libraries are not generally satisfied with the present library collection and the services offered by the libraries. While 43.28% of the scientists, 22.97% of the teachers and 36.84% of the students think that the present library services are inadequate, 49.25% of the scientists, 56.75% of the teachers and 32.89% of the students thinks that these services are partially adequate. Additional services expected by them are information search, literature search, bibliography compilation, computerized catalogues and CD-ROM and On-line database search facilities.

All the scientists, 93.24% of the teachers, 81.69% of the doctors, 45.9% of the conventional practitioners and 60.52% of the students are facing the difficulty of not getting the right information in right time.

Majority of the users viz. the scientists, teachers, qualified practitioners and students are regular readers of journals. While a major share of scientists (64.17%) shows interest in reading the literature from other Indian systems of medicine, only a small group from other categories shows interest in literature on other Indian systems of medicine. There are regular readers of allopathic journals from different categories of users.

Seminars are important media for information transfer among the users in Ayurveda. Seminars are well attended by all the categories of users. Members from all the categories of users are consulting other qualified and traditional practitioners for practical information. This shows that the presence of informal communication is prevalent among the Ayurveda users. This tendency is most prevalent among the traditional practitioners. 75.4% of the traditional practitioners are consulting each other for practical information. A major share of the scientists, teachers and practitioners are members of some common forum for sharing practical information. At the same time members from different categories of Ayurveda users complained that there is reluctance from the part of Ayurveda practitioners in revealing rare formulas of treatment, especially the practice of "*ottamoolies*".

Practice of specific treatment measures (*ottamoolies* etc.) not commonly practiced by every practitioners are prevalent in Ayurveda. 72.13 % of the traditional practitioners, 40.29% of the scientists, 28.37% of the teachers, 25,35% of the qualified practitioners and 23.68% of the students were shown interest in these specific treatments.

A small group each from different categories of users except students were claimed to have developed new drug formulations for treating their patients. But in most cases they are not manufacturing it on commercial basis.

Members from all categories, especially the traditional practitioners possess rare documents in their personal collection. Many of them are willing to share it with the colleagues and to provide a copy of them to a national information system, if organised.

All the scientists, teachers, doctors, students and 96.72% of the traditional practitioners think that a National Information System for Ayurveda is essential in India.

DESIGN, STRUCTURE AND FUNCTIONS OF INDIAN NATIONAL INFORMATION SYSTEM FOR AYURVEDA

In the light of the studies conducted on the information infrastructure available in Ayurveda and information needs and use pattern of users of Ayurveda an Indian National Information System for Ayurveda (INISA) is designed. The functions of the INISA are mainly derived from the opinion of users expressed in questionnaires and interviews.

While designing the INISA the important features of Ayurveda information scene such as lack of good libraries and information centres with modern facilities, lack of bibliographic control, lack of tools for technical processing, reluctance in publishing the information, multilingual nature of information, inadequate finance etc. were considered.

Design and structure of INISA

The INISA will have the following levels of organizations in the order of hierarchy

* National Information Centre
* Regional Information Centres
* State Information Centres

* Local Information Centres
* User nodal points

National Information Centre (NIC) will be the apex body. It will be located in CCRAS, New Delhi. The NIC will be the administrative headquarters of the INISA. The main database will be maintained in the master computer kept at NIC.

There will be four Regional Information Centres (RICs) one each for the north, south, east and west which will be located at the CCRAS' Central Research Institute at New Delhi, Regional Research Centre at Bangalore Regional Research Institute at Kolkatha and Central Research Institute at Mumbai respectively. The RICs will evaluate the information received from the subsidiary centres and the useful information will be technically processed and send to NIC. The RICs will also maintain a regional database.

Each state will have a State Information Centre (SIC). It will be located in any of the CCRAS Research centre in the state, if exists, or some other Ayurveda institutions like state level research institutes or Ayurveda college can be identified as SIC. The SIC will coordinate the activities of Local Information Centres in the state. It will evaluate the information collected from the State and will send to the concerned RIC. The SIC will also maintain a state level database.

Under the State Information Centre there will be a number of LICs. LIC will be developed one each for a district or for two or more districts depending upon the prevalence of Ayurveda in that area. Depending upon the availability CCRAS research centres, state level research centres, Ayurveda colleges, Ayurveda hospitals, dispensaries etc. can be spotted as the location for LIC. The LICs will conduct surveys to collect rare information possessed by individuals and traditional *Vaidya* families in its area. It will also conduct surveys to identify and record the medicinal flora and fauna in its area. All the information collected will be transferred to the concerned SIC. The LIC will also maintain a local databank on various aspects of Ayurveda treatment facilities available in its purview. Other functions of LIC include maintenance of a good library, herbarium, museum of medicinally important animals and a medicinal garden.

The ultimate users of the online version of the INISA database are at the nodal points. Any Ayurveda institution or user can be the clientele of INISA database. The infrastructure for taking the INISA online connection such as the computer, modem, telephone connection etc. is to be established by the clientele.

All the INISA information centres and nodal points are linked each other through computer/telecommunication networks and the INISA database is accessible to all the approved users.

Various products and functions of INISA

The most important function of INISA is the creation and maintenance of INISA database which collects all the relevant information in the field of Ayurveda. On this database on-line search facility can be provided to the users. Its print and CD-ROM versions are also should be published.

In order to collect information on Ayurveda and related subject fields the INISA should conduct extensive surveys. The important among them are those to find out rare medical information, survey of medicinal flora and fauna and survey on Ayurvedic educational and treatment facilities.

The INISA should strengthen the existing Ayurveda library system. It should establish a National Ayurveda Library at its NIC, Regional Ayurveda Libraries at RICs, State Ayurveda Libraries at SICs and Local Ayurveda Libraries at its LICs. The INISA should also try for the promotion of resource sharing among Ayurveda libraries.

Using the database and resources of the libraries attached to the INISA, it should provide information services like Current Awareness Service, Selective Dissemination of Information, Indexing and Abstracting Services, Literature Survey, Reference Service, Document Delivery Service, Translation Service, Reprography Service etc. to the Ayurveda users.

Other important services to be provided by INISA are

- Patent information service
- Consultation service to library and information centres, cultivators of medicinal plants, to the Ayurvedic information users and to the patients.
- Preparation of technical processing tools for Ayurveda documents.
- Training programmes for library staff and users.
- Programmes for the propaganda of Ayurveda.
- Creation of web site in Internet.

Future development prospects of INISA

The main future development prospects for INISA are

i) development of INISA as an International Information System

ii) expansion of INISA as a National Information System for all Indian systems of Medicine.

CONCLUSION

The study gives an idea about the genesis, development, history, basic principles etc. of Ayurveda and other Indian Systems of Medicine. There is also a detailed description of the institutional infrastructure available for research, education and treatment in these subject fields.

The objectives of the study were:

i. To study the infrastructure available in libraries and information centres attached to the various Ayurveda institutions in India;

ii. To study the information needs of the various categories of users in Ayurveda such as qualified and conventional practitioners, scientists, teachers and students.

iii. Makes an assessment of whether the present information infrastructure available in Ayurveda is adequate to satisfy the needs of the users or not; and

iv. Based on the assessment made on the above objectives designing a National Information System for Ayurveda which will satisfy the needs of the information users in Ayurveda.

The survey results given in the chapter titled "Present information infrastructure available in Ayurveda" substantiate the first objective. The second objective of the study is substantiated though the survey results given in the chapter titled "Information needs and information seeking behaviour of Ayurvedic information users". These two analysis chapters together substantiate the third objective. The results of analysis clearly states that the present information infrastructure is inadequate to satisfy the needs of the Ayurveda users. The chapter titled "Indian National Information System for Ayurveda (INISA): Design, Structure and Functions" meets the fourth objective.

The two hypotheses, which led to the present study, were

* the present information infrastructure available in Ayurveda in India is not satisfactory and inadequate to meet the information needs of the users
* the present institutional and information infrastructure are not coordinated and organized, which calls for the design of a national information system for an effective and efficient information services in Ayurveda in India.

The results of the surveys mentioned above clearly substantiate the validity of the hypotheses formulated in the study and led to designing of a National Information System for Ayurveda which will satisfy the needs of the information users in Ayurveda.

Here the study was carried out on all India basis. So the peculiar features of the information infrastructure and user needs at the minute level, which is valid for individual states and localities were not studied in detail. Further research is possible in this subject as prevalence of the Ayurveda and specific needs of the local users of Ayurveda in individual states, and localities can be studied in detail and based on which the special functions needed to be carried out, if any of the SICs and LICs of the INISA in the concerned localities can be defined. Research is also possible on the economic aspects involved in the implementation of the INISA project. The future development prospects for INISA are to develop it as an International Information System and to expand it as a National Information System for all Indian Systems of Medicine. Here also further research is needed to implement these development plans.

Here in this study the design, structure and functions of a National Information System for Ayurveda is proposed. If implemented it will be a right step for the future development of Ayurveda, an age-old medical system that has proven the test of the time. More over it is part of our cultural heritage and it is the duty of the Indians to make sure it will exist and flourish in the future.

REFERENCES

1. India, Ministry of Health and Family Welfare, Department of ISM and Homeopathy. Indian Systems of Medicine and Homeopathy in India 1992. Delhi: Controller of publications, 1996. p.1.
2. Svoboda, Robert E. Ayurveda: Life, health and longevity. New Delhi: Penguin books, 1993. p.175.
3. Tarabilda, Edward F. Ayurveda Revolutionized. Delhi: Motilal Banarsidass publishers, 1998. p. 60.
4. India, Ministry of Health and Family Welfare, Department of ISM and Homeopathy. Indian Systems of Medicine and Homeopathy in India. op.cit., pp.1-2.
5. Ibid, p.2.
6. Ibid.
7. Ibid.

8. Harrod, L M. Harrod's librarians glossary: 9000 terms used in information management, library science, publishing, the book trades and archive management. 8th ed. comp. By Ray Prytherch. Hants: Gower, 1995.

9. Bhagwan Dash. Fundamentals of Ayurvedic medicine. Delhi: Bansal & Co. 1980. p2.

3

NATIONAL LIBRARY OF BANGLADESH: RETROSPECT AND PROSPECT

Dr. Narun Nahar

INTRODUCTION

The Third International Congress of Libraries and Documentation Centres held in Brussels in 1955, emphasised the need for each country developing and maintaining a central library, generally a national library, as an institution capable of preserving for the future the whole of the country's literary output and of ensuring that bibliographical work proceeds on uniform lines(1). The Regional Seminar on the Development of National Libraries in Asia and the Pacific Area, held in Manila, Philippines, in 1964, under the sponsorship of UNESCO also stressed the need for the establishment of a national library in each member state where one did not exist, at the earliest possible time(2).

There has been an unprecedented proliferation of literature in each branch of knowledge in almost all countries of the world since the second World War and this posed the serious problem of their control and accessibility. The UNESCO, in co- operation with the International Federation for Documentation (FID), the International Federation of Library Associations (IFLA), and the International Council on Archives (ICA) initiated steps to ensure the universal availability of World literature through projects like Universal Bibliographic Control(UBC), National Information Systems (NATIS) and Universal Availability of Publications (UAP). The establishment of a national library in each country which can exercise effective bibliographic control of indigenous literature and provide access to literature held by the libraries in the country with the help of a National Union Catalogue was considered a necessary step for the realisation of these objectives. Bangladesh, like other countries, has been influenced by these recommendations and guidelines.

Independent of these international developments, the need for a National Library found patronage within the country in no less a forceful manner. Bangladesh existed as East Pakistan (a part of Pakistan) between August 15, 1947, the date of independence of the sub-continent and December 15, 1971, the date of creation of Bangladesh. During this period and later, professional and public opinion expressed itself on several occasions through the mass media and professional forums like Seminars, Conferences etc. for the establishment of national library.

Prior to December 15, 1971, when Bangladesh did not have its independent identity, there was a move for the establishment of a national library in West Pakistan and of a Central Library in East Pakistan as a subordinate unit.

At the fourth Annual Conference of the Pakistan Library Association held at Lahore from December 26-29, 1961, Dr. Mamud Husain, Vice Chancellor of the Dhaka University and President of Pakistan Library Association in his Presidential address observed:

"It is indeed regrettable that we have yet not been able to

possess a national library and the National Bibliography. In the Peshwar Conference of this Association held in the year 1959, the then Education Minister referred to a scheme of a national library in Pakistan, but to this date nothing worth noting seems to have been done at the government level to materialize this"(3).

The same concern was expressed by Dr. Mahamud Husain at the Fifth Annual Conference of PLA held at Dhaka from January 5-8, 1963 in the following words:

> "On the national level, the plans for the national library do not appear to have advanced much further since I last addressed the Lahore Conference of the Pakistan Library Association in 1961. If an auxiliary national library is not created for East Pakistan other measures must be adopted"(4).

This situation of stalemate seems to have continued and Dr. Mahamud Husain as President of PLA, again referred to this in a tone of despair in his presidential address at the Eighth Annual Conference of PLA held at Karachi from January 22-24, 1971, which was the last conference to be held in United Pakistan. To quote him again:

> "The national library which should have been the fountain of the library system of the country is still in the stage of extremely slow development. In fact we do not have a national library as of today since the Liaquat National Library (now Liaquat Memorial Library at Karachi) is no longer a national library and two national libraries at Islamabad and Dhaka are yet to be built up"(5).

PROFESSIONAL JOURNALS AND NEWS PAPERS

The need for a national library also found advocacy in the form of articles in the professional journals and editorials in the daily news papers.

EDUCATION COMMISSION

The Government of Bangladesh, soon after the birth of

Bangladesh in 1971, appointed an Education Commission to make recommendations for the development of education in the country on sound lines. The Report of this commission published in 1974 contains observations and recommendations relating to the establishment of a national library. The English version of these observations and recommendations contained in Chapter 30 of the report is given below.

National Library

The National library should be the greatest research centre of the country and a cultural bridge between this country and the world outside. It must be invested with the right to receive free copies of the publications under the Copyright Act. It must be charged with compilation and publication of the National Bibliography and with the duty of publication of bibliographies in different branches of knowledge. It will therefore require legislation and will have to be built up as an autonomous body. Incidentally we also recommend that the three Government Public Libraries at Divisional Head Quarters will also have to be given copyright privilege. The present Central Public Library may be converted into the proposed National Library. The National Library branch of the present Directorate of Archives and Libraries should merge in the National Library.

The first step towards the establishment of the National Library should be the creation of the post of the Chief Librarian thereof, filling the post and entrusting him with organisation work"(6).

Seminar on libraries in National Development

Following the founding of Bangladesh the East Pakistan Library Association was renamed as Library Association of Bangladesh. A seminar on "Libraries in National Development" was held under the auspices of the Library Association from July 22-5,1976. Two papers Viz. (1) National Library : Its role in national development by Ahmad Husain and (2) National Library for

Bangladesh, by Dr. A.M. Abdul Huq were presented at the seminar. The seminar supporting the views expressed in the Report of The Education Commission, 1975, adopted the following resolution:

" Highest priority should be accorded, as recommended by the Commission, to the conversion of the Bangladesh Central Public Library (loosely termed in some instances as Bangladesh Central Library) into the National Library of Bangladesh which will minimise much cost, both capital and establishment, and eliminate wastage of time. Bangladesh has suffered tremendously due to the absence of a national library in-so-far as, for instance, no comprehensive collection on the nation's history specially its struggle for independence is available at one place, nor has a representative collection on a world basis available to the public has grown.

Immediate creation of the following posts of the National library with the status indicated against them and filling the posts is necessary so that incumbents may begin work including planning of expansion, legislation etc.

Post	Number	Rank, Status
Director General	One	Additional Secretary to the Government Director (in charge of four Four Deputy Secretary to the Basic division) Government"(7).

BIRTH OF THE NATIONAL LIBRARY

Thanks to the overwhelming opinion in favour of a national library prevailing at the time of the birth of the Peoples' Republic of Bangladesh as a Sovereign Independent State in December 1971, there was an atmosphere that was conducive to the Government taking steps for the establishment of a national library. This, it did, as per declaration vide Gazette Notifications No. LB/IL-13/75/386 dated 29-8-1975, LB/KL-13/75/387 dated 29-8-1975 and LB/IL-13/75/546 dated 8-11-1975 (8),establishing the national library and empowering the Directorate of Archives and Libraries to serve the dual purposes of (I) the National Library and (ii) the National Archives. Both were installed on rented premises.

The functions of the National Library at present are (i) the collection and preservation of the literature published in the country and deposited under the copyright and Depository Laws (1974); (ii) compilation and publication of (a) an Annual National Bibliography entitled Bangladesh National Bibliography and (b) a yearly index of the Articles in the daily newspapers of Bangladesh both in English and Bengali.

The Bangladesh National Library is beset with many problems hindering its development. Inadequate funds, space and staff are its major constraints. The foundation stone was laid as early as in 1978 at Sher-E-Bangla Nagar, a few miles away from central Dhaka and the construction work is in progress, but there is still not knowing when the building will be completed and the national library will be housed in its own building performing all its functions and rendering all the services expected of it.

PRESENT STUDY

It is in this context that the present study has been undertaken with the following objectives:

(i) to review the economic, academic, research, intellectual and cultural environment of Bangladesh;

(ii) to assess the existing state of other library resources and services in the country;

(iii) to study and investigate the concept and functions of national libraries in the world as revealed by the current literature available;

(iv) to trace the origin and development of national libraries of the developed and developing countries;

(v) to investigate the present set up of Bangladesh National Library under the Directorate of Archives and Libraries;

(vi) to prepare a model plan for the organisational structure and functions of the current concept of the National Library and its services taking into account the views expressed by library professionals and scholars both at home and abroad and by the general public as ascertained through questionnaires and personal interviews;

(vii) to determine priorities for the implementation of the different functions of the National Library;

(viii) to prepare an action plan for implementation of Bangladesh National Library Project.

PROCEDURE

The author elicited the views of different sections of people like educationists, research workers, Heads of National libraries and other library professionals on the desirable organisational pattern and the functions of the national library and their priority, through personal interviews and questionnaires circulated both at home and abroad. The personal interviews were naturally confined to Bangladesh and a few cities in India including Calcutta, where the National Library of India is located. The responses were satisfactory and helpful.

To study the historical background of the National Library and the library resources and services in Bangladesh the author perused all the available literature, data books, government documents and official files and met the officials of the Ministry of Education, Cultural Division and Director, Directorate of Archives and Libraries, Government of Bangladesh.

On the basis of the opinions collected on the functions of the national library and their priority the author has attempted to suggest a model plan of organisational and functional structure for the Bangladesh National Library taking into account the modern trends of information storage and retrieval.

METHODOLOGY

Historical method

Although this is not essentially a historical study, the historical method was used in part to trace the earlier library movement and the efforts for the establishment of a national library during the British and Pakistani rule.

A comprehensive bibliography listing books and articles on the national libraries of different developed and developing countries was prepared with the help of secondary sources like "Library Literature" and "Library and Information Science Abstracts" and items to which access could be gained were perused. The bibliography is given at the end of the thesis.

The citation of references is generally in accordance with the rules laid down by the Indian Standards Institution.

The general concepts, functions and bibliographical and documentation services of national libraries are neither the same nor detailed enough to serve as guidelines for the establishment of a new functional national library. Literature such as Encyclopaedia of librarianship, Encyclopaedia of Library and Information Science, Ranganathan's Library Development Plan, Librarians Glossary, available Government documents and files etc. gave some relevant ideas. The investigator also examined relevant literature in the National Library of India, Calcutta, DRTC Library and other institutional libraries in Banglore, University Library of Mysore and the Kerala University Library, Trivandrum.

PERSONAL CONTACTS AND INTERVIEWS

The investigator interviewed several library professionals and others, associated with libraries and potential users of the National Library in Bangladesh and ascertained their views regarding the desirable organisational structure, functions and services of the National Library of Bangladesh. Among those contacted in this connection were the Librarian, Deputy Librarians and other senior officers of the National Library of India, Calcutta and other senior professionals in India.

Questionnaire Method

Three questionnaires were prepared, one for eliciting the views of the Heads of National Libraries, University Librarians, Heads of Library Schools etc. in India and abroad.(Appendix AI).

Another questionnaire to elicit the views of professionals, planners, educationists etc. of Bangladesh was also prepared regarding the functions of National Library (See Appendix AII).

A third questionnaire regarding the priorities to be observed in the National Library taking up the functions was also prepared (Appendix AIII). The details as per this questionnaire were collected through personal interviews.

EXAMINATION OF FILES AND RECORDS

The investigator collected information from the files and records relevant to this study available in the officers of the Ministry of Education and Culture, Directorate of Archives and Libraries, Directorate of Public Instruction, Higher Secondary Education Board, Library Association and the major libraries of Dhaka.

The author has also drawn on her own experience of working in the National Library of Bangladesh.

MODEL PLAN FOR THE ORGANISATIONAL STRUCTURE OF THE NATIONAL LIBRARY

An attempt is made in this chapter to suggest Model plan for the organisational structure of the National Library of Bangladesh. C.V. Penna in his book 'The planning of library and documentation services' has outlined the planning techniques for the development of library services which include the following:

a) a review of acquired experience;

b) diagnosis;

c) determination of requirements and financial implications;

d) programming;

e) publicity;

f) execution and evaluation(9).

Using Penna's planning stages as a checklist, this study for the establishment of a National library in Bangladesh has followed the following procedure.

1. reviewed the experiences of various planners as mentioned in the literature on the subject. Among other sources this experience has been collected from;

   a) the final report on the Meeting of Experts on the National Planning for Library services:

      In Latin America: Quito, Equador, 1966(10).

      In Asia : Colombo, Sri Lanka, 1967(11).

      In Africa : Kampala, Uganda, 1970(12).

      In Arab Countries : Cairo, Egypt, 1974(13).

   b) Questionnaires on the proposed organizational structure of the National Library, completed and returned by librarians/directors of foreign National libraries including India and other professionals as well as by Bangladesh library professionals and potential national library users.

   c) the National Library acts of selected countries.

2. Made an assessment of (diagnosed) the current state of library and information services in Bangladesh and also summarised the present position and condition of Bangladesh National Library functioning under the Directorate of Archives and Libraries.

3. Studied the goals, objectives and functions of different national libraries and with them as guidelines, arrived at the goals, objectives and functions of the proposed national library.

4. Indicated the financial implications of the proposed national library. The financial implications are as worked out by the Planning Commission and Shown in the Appendix D.

OBJECTIVES

The National Library should be the premier library of the nation playing the key role of leadership in the overall library and information system of Bangladesh. It must be the medium for all co-operative and co-ordinating efforts in the library and information science field. It must be vested with the power to initiate and execute programmes that will be able to meet national needs to serve larger national interests. It should be the apex of the entire library and information system and should be organised with due regard to the distinct geographical, economic, cultural, and administrative conditions prevailing in the country as a whole. In short, the National Library of Bangladesh, as any other national library, should be the channel for the nation to discharge its library obligations and responsibilities, both to the citizens of the country and to the international community. The weaknesses and deficiencies in the library scene should be sought to be removed by the establishment of a strong library system for which the National Library should be adequately equipped to give the necessary leadership. The Library services required by the people of the country without any distinction of sex, caste, age, economic or social status, and all other considerations should be made available to all. Academic libraries, right from school level upwards, research libraries, and other special libraries meant for different groups of people and the public library system should be strengthened. The National Library should function as the umbrella under which all these different types of libraries will flourish and serve as instruments for national progress.

ORGANISATIONAL STRUCTURE

The policy of the present Bangladesh Government is to amalgamate different units of similar nature into one unit to minimise overhead costs. According to this policy, the National Library of Bangladesh should be based on a unitary system. There should be a National Commission for Library and Information Services or Bangladesh National Library Authority at the top of the organizational structure. It will be responsible for the development of library services and should set up through legislation. The National library will function under the overall supervision of this commission. As already stated, it will be an agency which is "essential for the coordinated and efficient development of all types of libraries in a country"(14). The National Library will be headed by an officer designated as director.

There will be an Advisory body constituted of scholarships, librarians, government officers, and others to advise the National Library on matters, relating to policies and functions. The chairman of the National Commission will be the chairman of the Advisory body and the Director will be its member secretary. All administrative and financial affairs will be directly supervised by the National Librarian or the Director. The National Library will be having the following major divisions which are indicative of its functions.

1. National Bibliographic Division consisting of four sections.
2. Collection Development Division (or Acquisition Division) consisting of six sections.
3. Processing Division with two sections.
4. Services Division with six sections.
5. Research and Planning Division with four sections.
6. Administrative Division.

Each of the first five divisions will be headed by a Deputy Director and under him there will be an Assistant Director in charge of each of the sections falling under it as indicated in the chart. The Administrative Division will be headed by an Administrative Officer who will be on a par with a Deputy Director in pay scale and status.

ANALYSIS OF THE QUESTIONNAIRE

Three questionnaires were framed, one for eliciting opinions from heads of different national libraries of the world regarding the objectives and organizational structure of the Bangladesh National Library, one for ascertaining the views of the nationals of Bangladesh including library professionals regarding the functions to be undertaken by the National Library, and the third for obtaining the views of people in Bangladesh to determine the priorities of the functions. The answers to the first two questionnaires were obtained by post and the answers to the third were mostly collected by the investigator after interviewing the persons concerned. In choosing the persons for answering the second and third questionnaires representative samples from different sections were taken. The statement of objectives and organizational structure and functions have been so framed in the questionnaire that they largely reflect these aspects as they obtain in different national libraries. Therefore the statements regarding the objectives and functions and also the suggested organizational structure are in the nature of hypotheses to be tested by the opinions collected from professionals and others. The investigation has largely proved the validity of the hypotheses.

QUESTIONNAIRE – I ORGANISATIONAL STRUCTURE

As already mentioned, this questionnaire was designed to collect opinions from the heads of different national libraries of the world, university libraries and the national librarian and heads of important libraries in India. Out of sixty persons to whom the questionnaires were sent 45 (75%) responded.

Question 1 (a) and (b)

1. (a) Kindly peruse the objectives stated in the model plan for the National Library of Bangladesh

   If they are adequate Yes. If they are inadequate No

Responses are shown in Table 1.

TABLE I

Answer	*Number of Persons*	*Percentage*
Yes	40	88.1%
No	5	11.1%

1(b) Expressed clearly

Yes No

The answers to this question were also the same as to question 1(a).

Therefore the objectives of the National library as stated in the questionnaire can be regarded as adequate and also expressed clearly.

Question No. 2

Kindly peruse the statement under the Heading "Structure" and state if you are in Agreement with it. If not kindly suggest modification that you consider appropriate.

It was found that 95% of the replies were in agreement with the suggested structure.

Question No.3

Kindly peruse the brief description of the proposed organizational structure of the national library with its activities and services.

i) Do you agree with the suggested organizational structure?

ii) If not please give your suggestions for the organizational structure

iii) Give your views regarding the activities and services suggested.

iv) If additional activities and services are required kindly indicate them. About 98% respondents expressed themselves in agreement with the given organisational structure and activities and services. 3% of the respondents suggested that the Conservation Division may be separated and 1% suggested provision for a Children's Division.

Question No.4

Any other points relating to the proposed National Library not covered by the questions above that you consider worth mentioning.95% of the respondents had no additional suggestions to offer. 5% made a few suggestions such as the establishment of an External Services Division and a Data base Bibliographic Division. A few wanted the remaining of the Research and Planning Division as Research and Development Division.

QUESTIONNAIRE II : FUNCTIONS

The questionnaire to elicit opinions about the functions to be undertaken by the National Library (Appendix AII) was sent to 40 Bangladesh library professionals, educationists, researchers, journalists, etc. Number of responses was 38 or 95%. The responses to the different functions indicated in the questionnaire are analysed in Table 2.

It can be seen from the table that functions A and I received the highest score, cent per cent of the respondents having supported them. This is indicative of the concern of the people regarding the need for preserving at one place the entire national bibliographic production and its proper control through a national bibliography. Two other functions which received the support of 37 of the respondents i.e. 97.3 per cent are F and H viz. the provision of reprographic services and the maintenance of a National Union Catalogue. The other functions listed in the table, except D, also received high scores. As regards D only 18 respondents thought that the provision of hostel and other amenities was essential. This may be because it was difficult for the respondents to visualise

TABLE 2

RESPONSES TO QUESTIONNAIRE RELATING TO FUNCTIONS

Total number of responses: 38

Functions	*No. of responses in agreement*	*Percentage*	*No. of responses not in Agreement*	*Percentage*
A. Collect all the documents published in Bangladesh	38	100%	Nil	-
B. Collect all the documents published elsewhere but has relevance to Bangladesh	36	4.7%	2	5.3%
C. Preserve all documents connected with the culture and life of Bangladesh	36	94.7%	2	5.3%
D. Provide hostel and other amenities for scholars – Bangladesh and foreign to stay in Dhaka over a period of time	18	47.3%	20	52.7%
E. Provide comfortable reading room facilities to users within the library	35	92.1%	3	7.9%
F. Provide document reproduction (Reprography) service nominal cost	37	97.3%	1	2.7%

Functions	*No. of responses in agreement*	*Percentage*	*No. of responses not in Agreement*	*Percentage*
G. Provide for mailing non-rare documents under safety to users (through other libraries)	37	97.3%	1	2.7%
H. Maintain a National Union catalogue of books, reports, periodicals and other kindred documents	37	97.3%	1	2.7%
I. Publish a National Bibliography of documents as a monthly basis.	38	100%	Nil	-

functions of this kind as essential in the context of the non-existence of even the more essential functions listed.

The support given to function E by as many as 35 respondents or 92.1 per cent that the National Library should provide comfortable reading room facilities to all types of readers is evidence of the anxiety of the respondents to have access to a comprehensive collection of documents which a National Library is able to build up and organize. The second part of the questionnaire reads as follows:

The National Library of Bangladesh should be adequately funded

a) through national legislation or

b) through a government order for a regular grant.

Responses to this question are shown in table 3.

The responses are in strong support of the funding of the National Library through legislation so that the National Library is well- fortified from the possible ill-effects of policy changes when change of government takes place and it is assured of a regular income for its healthy growth and development.

In order to test the urgency felt by the citizens of Bangladesh for the establishment of a National Library a question was included to ascertain the year for the inauguration of the National Library preferred by the respondents. 4 years between 1985-2000 were given and the respondents asked to indicate their preferences.

The responses are shown in table 4.

Responses to the question No.3

Total number of responses : 38

TABLE 3. Total Number of responses: 38

Proposal	*Number of responses in agreement*	*Percentage of responses*	*Number of responses not in agreement*	*Percentage*
Through national legislation	34	89.5%	4	10.5%
Through a government order for regular grant	4	10.5%	34	89.5%

TABLE 4

Year of Inauguration	*Number of responses*	*Percentage*
a. 1985 A.D.	18	47.40%
b. 1990 A. D.	11	28.90%
c. 1995 A. D.	6	15.80%
d. 2000 A.D.	3	7.90%

The answers provide evidence of the desire of the people to have the National Library inaugurated as early as possible.

Question No. 4 is : There should be a National Library policy formulated by to guide the function and other libraries. This policy should be formulated by:

a. the parliament

b. the Government

c. the autonomous Bangladesh National Library Authority (BNLA)

The responses are shown in table 5.

Responses to question No.4

Total number of responses : 38

TABLE 5

Agency	*Number of responses in agreement*	*Percentage*
The Parliament	13	34.20%
The Government	8	21.10%
An autonomous Bangladesh National Library Authority (BNLA)	17	44.70%

The responses show that the establishment of a Bangladesh National Library Authority for the development of library services in the country including the establishment of the National Library and the formulation of a National Library Policy by this authority is more favoured than the formulation of the policy by the parliament or the Government. This may be because an authority exclusively created for this purpose will be more fully involved in the cause than the Parliament or the Government with their multifarious responsibilities could. Ofcourse, this does not mean that Parliament or the Government will not be concerned with the matter. It only means that the primary work relating to the development of library services would be the responsibility of an exclusive autonomous authority and the Government and the Parliament would then take up the matter for further legal and administrative follow up.

In question No. 5 opinions regarding other functions (other than those listed in the questionnaire) were invited and some of the respondents suggested that the National Library of Bangladesh should fall in line with the major National libraries of the world in its functions and services.

QUESTIONNAIRE – III : PRIORITIES

Questionnaire III was meant to ascertain opinions regarding priorities. The Investigator after analysing the replies categorised the functions as first priority functions, second priority functions and third priority functions as shown below.

a) first priority functions :

i) acting as the central collection of Bangladesh literature

ii) acting as a Legal Deposit Library

iii) acting as the National Bibliographic Centre

iv) Producing the National Bibliography

v) Collecting foreign literature

  a) about Bangladesh

  b) by Bangladesh authors living abroad

  c) on particular subjects according to the needs of the country.

vi) compilation of select bibliographies

vii) maintaining the National Union Catalogue

viii) planning and co-ordinating interlibrary lending

ix) providing leadership to the country's libraries

x) participating in the planning of library sciences in the country, and

xi) collecting, preserving and organizing Bangladeshi manuscripts

b) Second priority functions:

i) providing access to the National Library's catalogue for other libraries and information agencies

ii) providing indexing services to articles in Bangladeshi periodicals and newspapers

iii) providing services to the government

iv) for acting as a centre for exchange of publications, within the nation and internationally,

v) formulating standards for information handling,

vi) providing reprographic services and

vii) providing translation services.

c) Third priority functions:

i) conducting research on library techniques,

ii) providing professional training

iii) providing books for the blind and persons otherwise handicapped. One of the functions not listed but important in the opinion of the investigator is the maintenance of a Bibliographic Database relevant to the country. The National Library is the institution which enjoys the benefits of the Legal Deposit Law, produces the National Bibliography, and National Union Catalogue. Maintaining a bibliographic database is clearly a byproduct of this and therefore can be included in the group of first priority functions.

The functions of a National Library do not remain static. They would changes according to changes in the educational and cultural environment of the country. Similarly the priorities of the functions of the National Libraries can also be different for different countries according to the social, economic, and political conditions.

The distinction between a developed country and a developing country is not a criterion for determining and implementing the national library functions because it is seen that the National Libraries of some of the developing countries perform more functions than those of some developed countries. Examples of the former are the National Libraries of Botswana, Philippines and Singapore and as examples of the latter Belgium, Greece, Ireland and the Netherlands can be cited.

NATIONAL LIBRARY AND NATIONAL DEVELOPMENT PLAN

An important step towards the establishment of a National Library in Bangladesh is the inclusion of the National Library Planning and Services in the National Development Plan. This is a clear indication of the official recognition of the importance of the National Library and helps to create a concept of libraries as an important element in the overall national development.

COST ESTIMATE

The financial provision available and necessary for the proposed National Library needs to be examined. Appendix D gives the financial schedule of work and the yearwise sanction of grant given by Bangladesh Government. The meeting of the Experts on National Planning for Documentation Services in Africa suggested the cost norms of National Libraries as $ 5,000 per 1,000 volumes. The same meeting identified a National Library's recurring cost for 1980 as $ 8,500 million for a low target and $ 12,500 million for a moderate target and $ 17,000 million for a high target(15). Planning a National Library for Ceylon, a Meeting of Asian Experts estimated the expenditure on a National Library to be 0.03 per cent of the recurring expenditure on education in 1977, with 0.8 per cent of the educational expenditure collected for all types of libraries including the National Library(16) As an example of an actual National Library Budget, the National Library of Singapore's budget was $5,266,300 or 1.3 per cent of the Ministry of Education's budget and 0.16 per cent of the National Budget for the fiscal year 1979(17). The African experts estimated the recurring cost required for the development of library services in 1980 to be 2.9 per cent of the total educational cost for a low target, 4.9 per cent for a moderate target, and 7.3 per cent for a high target (18). In the case of Bangladesh the total cost of the project for the establishment of the National Library was estimated to be taka 465.18 lakhs i.e. $ 3,101,200 approximately(19) and this was subsequently revised as taka 621.4 lakhs including the foreign exchange component of taka 45.60 lakhs(20).

MANPOWER

A basic requirement to be looked into in planning the establishment of a National Library is the provision of the required manpower. The National Library has to be Manned by well-qualified staff in adequate strength. The number of persons required depends on the functions and duties of the National Library.

The Meeting of Experts on the National Planning for Library Services in Latin America suggested in 1996 that the minimum staff required by the National Library should consist 50 persons: one director, one technical assistant director, twelve posts for office and maintenance staff(21).

In the Bangladesh National Library there are now only 22 posts. It is estimated that 110 posts in addition to 15 posts for maintenance and special services for staff are required for the efficient discharge of the functions and services envisaged by the library. The details are given below.

Director	:	1
Deputy Directors	:	6
Assistant Directors	:	22
Bibliographers	:	4
Acquisition Librarians	:	3
Technical Assistants (senior)	:	8
Technical Assistants (Junior)	:	8
Supervisors (Conservation)	:	2
Technical Assistants (Conservation)	:	4
Technicians	:	12
Assistants (Services)	:	20
Translators	:	4
Typists	:	6
Secretarial Staff	:	10
Maintenance and Special services	:	15

STAFF IMPLEMENTATION

Now that the functions of the National Library have been identified and their Priorities determined the progressive implementation of these functions may be examined.

PRESENT ACTIVITIES

At present the activities of the National Library are confined to the following. Under the Copyright Deposit Law the National Library is to get one copy of each publication published in the country. But the act is not vigorously enforced as evidenced by the failure of many publishers to deposit their publications. The result is that there are many gaps in the collection of the national literature held by the library.

It is not only that the collection is incomplete, the available collection is subjected to many constraints like inadequacy of space and staff. Also there are no book funds for acquiring other books published in foreign countries.

Since 1972 the Bangladesh National Bibliography based on the Publications received under the Copyright Deposit Act is compiled and published. So far four annual volumes covering the period upto 1977 have been published. Another bibliographical activity is the compilation of the Annual Index of Articles in the Daily Newspapers. Both these publications are not uptodate, primarily because of the dependence of the National Library on the Government Printing Press for this purpose.

ACTION PLAN

The building of the National Library Agrgoon, Sher-e-Bangla Nagar is under construction and the first task is to complete the first phase of the building so that the most important activities and functions of the National Library can be started. The construction has lagged far behind schedule and all efforts should be made to expedite the construction.

In discussing the action plan the investigator wishes to divide the planning process into three terms viz. 1. Short term 2. Medium term 3. Long term. Short term (1985-87)

It is likely to take, even with the best of efforts, 2-3 years for the building to be completed for the first phase of activities to be initiated and organized.

a) Planning the best use of the available space in consonance with the present organizational set up and objectives of the National Library and the recruitment of the staff in vacant positions.

b) Vigorous enforcement of the Copyright Deposit Act to ensure that the library receives one copy of every indigenous publication.

c) Provision of reading facilities and recurring services.

The following steps need special attention

a) Provision of adequate funds and foreign exchange for acquiring foreign books on Bangladesh and books written by Bangladeshies abroad and other publications required for scholarly pursuits.

b) As regards the indigenous publications two copies should be acquired, one for current use and one for preservation for posterity.

c) Filling up the present gaps in the indigenous collection of publications by soliciting gifts, acquiring several copies, etc.

d) The setting up of a printing press and bindery to ensure the timely publication of the national and other bibliographies and indexes.

e) Setting up a strong reprographic section, particularly keeping in view the needs of scholars.

The National Library does not now have its separate identity being a part of the Directorate of Archives and Libraries. Time is ripe now for giving it a separate and distinct identity by being bifurcated from the Directorate. In this connection the question has to be examined whether the library should be under Government control or should have an autonomous status. Dr. Abdul Huq is of the opinion that "by an ordinance the National Library be created as a semi-autonomous institution with the authority vested in it to be the principal library of the nation and the principal organ of the Government on all library and related matters. It must have the powers to effectively co-ordinate all library and bibliographical activities within and without Government"(22). Such autonomous status is enjoyed by almost all National Libraries of the world.

Side by side with the above steps immediate attention is to be paid to the implementation of the following recommendations by J.S.Parcker,(23) an Unesco expert whose services were made available in 1979 for the development of libraries in Bangladesh with special emphasis on public libraries.

RECOMMENDATION NO. 1:

The National Library be encouraged to develop a national programme for the preservation and conservation of rare, valuable and little-used library materials.

RECOMMENDATION NO. 2:

Provision to be made under the Second Five Year Plan for the establishment for a National Library co-ordinating Committeee, representing all types of libraries and responsible for ensuring the co-ordinated development.

RECOMMENDATION NO. 3:

Provision be made under the Second Five Year Plan for the enactment of library Legislation which will facilitate the implementation of the recommendations of this report.

RECOMMENDATION NO. 4:

Efforts be made to achieve improved co-ordination of bibliographical activity and particular to publish the National Bibliography more frequently and more promptly.

MEDIUM TERM (1987-1990)

At the next stage the following activities may be taken up:

a) Provision of reference and bibliographical services
b) Standardisation of classification and cataloguing
c) Compilation of the National Union Catalogue
d) Preparing a plan for the introduction of new technology in libraries

e) Providing services to the Government

f) Planning and Co-ordinating inter-library lending

g) Promoting translation services.

LONG TERM (1990 – 1996)

During this period the Library should expand its activities to cover:

i) Conducting research on library techniques

ii) Providing professional training, and

iii) Providing books for the blind and persons otherwise handicapped.

By the end of this period the library should gain the recognition of being in a position of leadership in the library and information science field in the country and act as the centre for a single, unified, and highly developed National Information System.

SUMMARY AND CONCLUSIONS

Summary

This investigation presented in ten chapters has attempted the following:

i) Established the need for a full-fledged National Library for Bangladesh. In this connection the efforts during the pre-independence, post independence, and the post-liberation periods for the development of library services in general and the National Library in particular have been traced. The international efforts in this regard in the context of the development of concepts like Universal Availability of Publications (UAP) and Universal Bibliographic Control(UBC) have also been discussed.

ii) The geographic, administrative, educational, and cultural milieu of Bangladesh which have a bearing on the development of library services with the National Library at the apex have been described.

iii) The literary scene in Bangladesh comprising all types of libraries, information and documentation centres has been critically evaluated.

iv) The published literature which is fairly extensive, as the bibliography included in this thesis would testify, was perused and the concept, definitions and functions of National Libraries, as far as could be ascertained from the literature, have been described.

v) A comparison of a few selected National Libraries with regard to the types and functions has been made in order to serve as guide lines for arriving at the organizational structure and functions of the National Library of Bangladesh.

v) The historical background, present structure, and problems and prospects of Bangladesh National Library have been described in Chapter 6,7 and 8.

vi) On the basis of the ideas formed by the investigator through her own consultation of the relevant literature and experience of working in the National Library so far, and on the basis of the replies received to questionnaires regarding the organizational structure, functions and priorities from heads of National Libraries, other library professionals and others, suggestions have been made in respect of the following:

a) model organizational structure of the National Library

b) functions to be undertaken by the National Library

c) priorities for the implementation of functions

CONCLUSIONS AND RECOMMENDATIONS

i) The National Library which now functions without a separate identity as part of the Directorate of Archives and Libraries should be bifurcated and put under an autonomous agency which may be designated Bangladesh National Authority (BNLA).

ii) The building currently under construction for the National Library should be completed as early as possible and the National Library shifted there.

iii) The organizational structure of the National Library should be as given in chart given in Appendix A questionnaire I with such minor variations as may be found necessary.

vi) Copyright Deposit Law should be vigorously enforced to ensure the receipt by the National Library of a copy each of all indigenous publications. While the collection of publications so built up should be preserved for posterity, the library should acquire an additional copy for current use by scholars.

iv) The publication of the Bangladesh National Bibliography and the Index to Articles in newspapers should be brought up-to-date.

v) The other functions of the National Library enumerated in the study should be implemented in three phases with 1996 set as the target year for the Library to become a full-fledged one performing all its functions and playing an effective leadership role in the library and information science field in the country.

vi) The manpower necessary for the effective working of the National Library should be provided according to a phased programme corresponding to the implementation of the functions.

REFERENCES

1. UNESCO. National libraries : their problems and prospects.1960.Unesco.Paris.p.6.
2. Regional Seminar on the Development of National Libraries in Asia and Pacific Area. *In* Unesco Bulletin for Libraries. July- August 1964.p.158.
3. Proceedings of the 4th Annual Conference of Pakistan Library

Association, Lahore, December 26-29, 1960. PLA, Karachi,1962.p.17.

4. Proceedings of the 5th Annual Conference of Pakistan Library Association, Dhaka, January 5-18 , 1963. PLA, Dhaka, 1964. p.12.

5. Proceedings of the 8th Annual Conference of Pakistan Library Association, Karachi, January 22-24, 1971. PLA, Karachi, 1972.p.1.

6. HUSAIN (Ahmad). English rendering of the "Chapter 30-Granthagar" (Library) of the Report of the Bangladesh Education Commission dated May,1974. *In* The Eastern Librarian. 10. 19756.p.185-86.

7. Observation of the Council of the Library Association of the Bangladesh Education Commission, 1975. *In* The Eastern Librarian . 10. 1976. p.194.

8. Development Scheme of the National library of Bangladesh : Second Five Year Plan (1980 – 85). 1979. Government of Bangladesh, Ministry of Sports and Culture; Dhaka. P.3 (For restricted use only).

9. PENNA (C V) . The planning of library and documentation services. rev. and enl. By P.H. Sewell and H. Liebaers. 1970. 2nd ed. Unesco. Paris.p.49.

10. Meeting of Experts on the National Planning of Library Services in Latin America. Qyito. 7-14. February,1966. Report. *In* Unesco Bulletin for libraries. 20. Nov – Dec, 1966.p.278-295.

11. Meeting of Experts on the National Planning of Library Services in Asia. Colombo, Ceylon,11-19. December,1967. Final Report. 1968.Unesco. Paris.

12. Expert Meeting on National Planning on Documentation and Library Services in Africa, Kampala, Uganda, 7-15 December, 1970. Final Report.1971.Unesco.Paris.

13. National Planning of Documentation and Library Services in Arab countries. *In* Unesco Bulletin for Libraries. 28, July-August 1974,p.182-187.

14. Meeting of Experts ... Asia. op.cit. p.9.

15. Experts Meeting on National Planning ... Africa. op.cit. p.16.

16. Meeting of Experts ... Asia. op.cit. p.17.

17. National Library : Report for the period April, 1979 – March 1980. 1980. National Library of Singapore. Singapore. p.28.

18. Experts Meeting ... Africa. op.cit. p.16.

19. Development Scheme of National Library of Bangladesh : 2nd Five Year Plan (1980-85). Government of Bangladesh, Ministry of Sports and Culture, Dhaka. P.1 (Restricted use only).

20. Ibid.

21. Meeting of Experts ... Latin America. op.cit. p.288

22. ABDUL HUQ (A M). National Library for Bangladesh. *In* The Eastern Librarian. 10. 1976. p.46.

23. PARKER (J S). Bangladesh Public Library Survey : Vol 1, 2, 3 submitted to the Ministry of Sports and Cultural Affairs, Government of Bangladesh.1979.

APPENDIX A

QUESTIONNAIRE I

Model plan for the organisational structure showing major functions for the proposed National Library of Bangladesh

Objectives:

The National library should be the apex of the entire library system and information centres. In other words, the National Library should play the role of leadership in the overall library system and information networks in Bangladesh.

Structure:

The National Library of Bangladesh should be based on a Unitary system in consonance with the present Government Policy of amalgamating different units of similar nature in one unit to minimise overhead cost, provision being kept for co- ordinating the library resources of the whole country through Union Catalogue and inter library loan facilities.

Organisational Structure:

A National Commission for Library and Information Science to be responsible for the development of library services will be set up through legislation. The National Library will be set up through legisaltion. The National Library will function under the over all supervision of this commission.

The National Library will be headed by an Officer designated as National Librarian or Director.

There will be an Advisory Body constituted of scholars, librarians, Govt. Officers and others to advise the National Library on matters related to policies and functions. The Chairman of the National Commission will be the Chairman of the Advisory Body and the National Librarian (Director) will be its member Secretary.

The National Library will have the following divisions which are indicative of its functions:

1. Bibliographic Division
2. Collection Development Division or Acquisition Division
3. Processing Division
4. Service Division
5. Research and Planning Division
6. Administrative Division

Each of the first five Divisions will be headed by a Deputy Librarian with an Assistant Librarian in charge of each of the sections falling under a Division. The Administrative Division will be headed by an Administrative Officer who will be on a par with a Deputy Librarian in pay scale and status.

QUESTIONNARE AND INTERVIEW

1. Kindly peruse the objective stated in the model plan for the National Library of Bangladesh.

   a) Is it adequate Yes No

   b) Is it expressed clearly Yes No

2. Kindly peruse the statement under the heading 'Structure' and state if you are in agreement with it. If not kindly suggest modifications that you consider appropriate.

3. Any other points relating to the proposed National Library not covered by the questions above that you consider worth mentioning.

QUESTIONNAIRE II

Your opinion for developing the National Library of Bangladesh

I. PERSONALIA

a) Name

b) Occupation

c) Address with designation

1. The National Library should do the following Please put (Tick mark) in the appropriate blocks

   a) Collect all the documents published in Bangladesh

   b) Collect all the documents published elsewhere but has relevance to Bangladesh

   c) Preserve all the older documents connected with culture and life of Bangladesh

   d) Provide hostel and other amenities for the scholars of Bangladesh and foreign countries to consult and read literature

   e) Provide comfortable reading room facilities to users within the library

   f) Provide document reproduction (Reprography) at a nominal cost

   g) Provide for mailing of non-rare documents under safety to users (through other libraries)

   h) Maintain a National Union Catalogue of books, reports, periodicals and other kindred documents

   i) Publish a National Bibliography of documents on a monthly basis

2. The National Library of Bangladesh should adequately be funded

   a) through a national legislation

   b) through a Government Order for regular grant

3. The National Library of Bangladesh should be developed into a large institution like Dhaka University in finance as well as working latest by

   a) 1985 A.D.

   b) 1995 A.D.

c) 2000 A.D.

4. There should be a National Library Policy formulated to guide the functioning of the National library and other libraries Policy is to be formulated by

   a) The Parliament

   b) The Government

   c) An autonomous Bangladesh National Library Authority (BNLA)

5. Any other opinion (in brief 1000 words)

QUESTIONNAIRE – III

(For the personnel interview)

FUNCTIONS OF THE NATIONAL LIBRARY

Kindly put the No. 1,2,3 etc. according to the priority:

	Functions	**Rank**
1.	Acting as the legal deposit library	
2.	Acting as the central collection of Bangladesh literature	
3.	Collecting foreign literature · about Bangladesh · By Bangladeshi authors living abroad · On special particular subject according to the needs of the Country	
4.	Acting as a National Bibliographic Centre	
5.	Producing the National Bibliography	
6.	Producing National Union Catalogue	
7.	Participating in the planning of library services in the country	
8.	Providing leadership to the country's libraries	
9.	Providing services for the select Bibliography	
10.	Acting as a centre for exchange of publications, nationwide and internationally	

11. Planning and co-ordinating interlibrary lending
12. Providing services to the Government
    * Providing professional training
13. Providing indexing services to the articles in the nation's periodicals and newspapers
14. Formulating international standards for information handling
15. Conducting research on library technique
16. Providing books for the blind and persons otherwise handicapped
17. Collecting, preserving and organising the country's manuscripts
18. Provide translation services
19. Provide reprograph and memograph services
20. Providing access to the National Library's catalogue for other libraries and information agencies

4

INDUSTRIAL AND TECHNOLOGICAL INFORMATION CENTERS FOR SMALL SCALE SECTOR

Dr. V. Sivaraman

INTRODUCTION

The knowledge of Information and information explosion had started gaining importance even in the early 60's and giving warning signals to Information Scientists to device proper control and channelisation for easy flow of information to the users. The great Indian Library and Information Scientist Dr.S.R. Ranganathan had aptly formulated his five laws of Library and Information Science, which are applicable forever. Taking into consideration of his two laws viz "Every reader his/her information" (Every reader his/her book) and every information it's user (Every book his/her reader), the author of this study has been motivated to work for a system to cater to the needs of the entrepreneurs of small scale sector in the state of Kerala.

In this study, the significance of Information, Information

Technology, Industrial Information system, the scenario of National and International Information system are mentioned briefly. The information needs of entrepreneurs/users from SSI sector and organizations disseminating information in Kerala are highlighted. The need for the research study is stated clearly for the state of Kerala. The total coverage of the study is highlighted in each chapter to have a bird's eye-view of the content.

THE SIGNIFICANCE OF INFORMATION AND INFORMATION TECHNOLOGY IN INDIA

Information is an essential ingredient for the socio-economic fabric of any country. If there is a distinct socio-economic structure, there will also be a distinct information structure to govern. The development of documentation and Information services in a country is very much in consonance with her national development activities. In fact, the tempo of these services is a factor to intensify of the country's research and development endeavour. A natural consequence of the tremendous national research efforts and activities in different disciplines of knowledge was the demand for active library, documentation and Information services at different levels.

As a result of the revolution in information and communication technologies caused by the convergence and integration of emerging communication technologies and computers, the communication information environment has been transformed in such a way that social scientists speak of the dawn of a new era – "the information age". With decreasing cost of microcomputers and increasing availability of suitable software, this technology is used increasingly for Information Storage and Retrieval Purposes – ISRP.

However, there appears no visible impact of modern information technology on information services management in the country. Inhibiting factors include lack of suitable software, lack of trained manpower in system management and moreover lack of financial resources. In spite of all these gaps, the infrastructure framework of Library and Information services exists in India and it only requires to be strengthened and coordinated.

* Peter Drucker, a world famous management consultant, in a thought provoking article "The Coming of New Organisation" (Harward Business Review Jan-Feb 1988) has given the structure of a new organization 20 years from now. His basic premise has been something like this: "The typical business will be knowledge based organization composed largely of specialist who direct and discipline their own performance through organized feed-back from colleagues, customers and head quarters. It will be an information based organization". In such an organization the levels of management would be reduced to less than half.
* To digress at this juncture would not be out of place. The knowledge explosion that is taking place all over the world has necessitated a professional from any discipline to have up to date knowledge, in other words, information. The rapid introduction of computers in India has generated a whole lot of data on very many issues. If the professional talent does not make use of this data after carefully shifting relevant from the irrelevant and transform this data into useful information, he would not be able to make use of this information effectively.
* This calls for mastering the information technology. The present day command and control type of organizations, if they have to survive, must generate profits, maintain a competitive edge in the export markets, they will have to transform with the changing times. They have to build up the information bank for themselves and upgrade the skills of personnel starting from the supervising levels to the highest so that within a period of time each supervisor or a manager become a specialist in his own way.
* Mr.Drucker in his article has enunciated the following requirements for building an information-based organization.

* Information based organizations require clear cut, simple, common objective that translates into particular action. There should be concentration on the objective, or utmost, on a few.
* Information based organization must be structured around goals that clearly state management performance, expectations for the enterprise and each part and specialists and around organized feedback that compares result with these performance expectations so that every member can exercise self-control.
* Every one information responsibility. That is, every one in an organization should constantly be thinking through what information he or she needs to do the job and to make a contribution.

The Indian business class or firms will have to look ahead to see whether one can bring about a change from the conventional command and control system to an information-based system. In latter type, the knowledge about critical type aspects would be with specialists – who are in the bottom – hierarchy who do different jobs and direct themselves.

Information-based organizations, service staff for advising, co-ordination, etc. will shrink drastically. Traditional departments will be absent. They would serve as guardians of standards, as centres for training and assigning specialists. It will require greater emphasis for individual responsibility for relationships and for communication.

Having said this, it is also easy to pick up a model and plant in Indian conditions. It poses management problems and challenges. It would be better in the fitness of things to adapt an information-based model to suit Indian industries so that opportunities for growth and specialization exist for individuals. Though it is a far-fetched dream, it is indeed round the corner.

THE ROLE OF INDUSTRIAL AND TECHNOLOGICAL INFORMATION SYSTEM (ITIS)

The role of ITIS is widely recognized, both in technology transfer and in management of industrial activity in developed and developing countries.

Its role is of paramount importance in any decision making process where the need arises to find a solution for industrial problems.

The collection, storage, processing and dissemination of industrial information requires well established formal information facilities, which, together with informal information channels, contribute to the satisfaction of the needs of diversified categories of industrial information users.

In a developing country like India where a planned approach to the creation of industrial production capacity and utilization of available technological resources is needed. It is essential to have readily retrievable information on demand, licensed capacity, details of implementation of licenses, demand-supply gap, economical scale of production, appropriateness of technological resources available, availability of capital goods and raw-materials, availability of specialized manpower and training facilities, details of earlier collaborations approved and implemented, etc. Such information would help to take optimal decisions in the meetings of the Industry Dept, Directorate of Industry and Commerce, District Industries Centre and the subject-wise administrative departments.

In view of the catalytic role of information, causing the growth of the industry through more optimal decisions taken and its ability to bring about interaction between the users and the policy makers, it is essential to treat information as a commodity. This position accentuates further by computer-aided analysis of information and making it available in an analysed or processed way to industrialists, technologists, designers and researchers.

Information that is not available adequately, accurately and timely loses its value. To make available adequate information on industry and technology it is necessary to create comprehensive industrial information system for the state as a whole. However, to collect, collate, and store all information relevant to industry and technology would be a costly solution. The need for accurate information, calls for a careful planning of the information collection procedures and practices. It is proposed to build in feedback checks and corrective methods to enable a continuous evolution of accuracy of the information system. It is well proposed in the study for the timeliness of information system through efficient computer-based retrieval techniques with a query facility. For this reason as well as to enable updating of the databases, it is proposed to have the system around Database Management Software (DBMS). Through the combination of the above, adequacy, accuracy and timeliness of information will be accomplished in a quantitative and qualitative way.

THE FEATURES OF NATIONAL AND INTERNATIONAL INFORMATION SYSTEM

National Industrial Information System

In the scenario of Indian National Industrial Information System, the Small Industrial Development Organisation – SIDO under the Ministry of Industry had mooted the idea of starting a national level training institute exclusively for small scale industries at Hyderabad in the name and style of SIET – Small Industries Extension Training Institute – The SIET has started a Special Library and Documentation Centre known as SENDOC – Small Enterprises National Documentation Centre to disseminate information to SSI entrepreneurs in India, and to train professionals and Information managers in Information storage and Retrieval system.

Small Enterprises National Documentation Centre (SENDOC)

SENDOC is at the National Institute of Small Industry Extension Training – NISIET, Hyderabad. This documentation centre was established in 1971 at NISIET. The SENDOC Library presently has about 40.000 books, nearly 25,000 reports of various kinds and subscribes to around 600 periodicals. It also has access to about 2500 project profiles. The main earnings of the Centre are from training programmes that earn about Rs.8.8 lakhs/annum. Earnings from subscription and from the sale of project profiles amount to rupees one lakh annually. The annual budget for the centre varies from 4 to 6 lakhs/annum, out of which nearly 60% is spent on periodicals, 30% on books, reports, etc; and 10% on reference works. The process of computerization is in a nascent stage. The computers are presently being used for word-processing in bringing out their periodic bulletins.

INSDOC

At national level, the Indian National Scientific Documentation Centre – INSDOC was started by Council of Scientific and Industrial Research – CSIR under the Ministry of Science and Technology, at New Delhi to cater to the needs of Scientists, R&D Centres and other users in the country. The details of the services provided by INSDOC are given in the study.

NISSAT

In the mid 60s, the National Information System for Science and Technology – NISSAT – programme had been introduced in India by UNESCO scheme to improve the Information System in Science and Technology. By the NISSAT scheme several important information centres had been started with specializations on India. The details are given in this study.

TIFAC

Technology Information, Forecasting and Assessment Council – TIFAC, an autonomous organization under the aegis of Department of Science and Technology – DST has been set up with the following objectives:

- Undertake Technology Assessment & Forecasting studies in key areas of national economy.
- Technology watch on global trends and formulation of preferred options for India.
- Establish a nationally accessible technology information system.

In pursuit of such objectives, TIFAC has brought out documents in a number of areas with the help of experts and has developed an online information system: TIFACLINE.

As an excellent example of maximizing synergistic advantages, TIFAC, Computer Maintenance Corporation Ltd. – CMC Ltd. and Delhi State Industrial Development Corporation – DSIDC have joined hands for a collaborative venture in setting up the centre for industrial information in New Delhi. The centre planned as a 'one-stop information shop' will cater to the technology and trade information needs of the potential entrepreneurs and business planners.

CII

The Confederation of Indian Industry has started "The Technology Information Centre – TIC". It is also developing it's own database. TIC services are available to the users through the existing network system.

CII offices spread across the country. In addition, if any company/organization is involved in developing unique technologies in its field or already has a technology or is interested in sharing information with others, an excellent platform is provided by TIC for disseminating the information.

NRDC, NSIC, CSIR, etc.

There are other Govt. agencies like National Research Development Council – NRDC, National Small Industry Corporation – NSIC and Council of Scientific and Industrial Research Centres

– CSIR which provide industrial information services in India. The details of them are given in the study.

In the recent past, several Information Network Programmes had been introduced by private agencies and in collaboration with the Government. NICNET programmes are working in the field of Information Technology and System in India. About all these aspects, the research study has given full coverage.

Totally, the scenario of Information System in India is looking bright and looking for a bright future.

INTERNATIONAL INDUSTRIAL INFORMATION SYSTEM

In the scenario of Industrial Information System in International level, it is well obvious that the services of the UNIDO – The United Nations Development Organisation has played its crucial role since its inception.

UNIDO

The UNIDO is providing quite efficient worldwide industrial information service. They have UNTIB – United Nations Technology Information Bank which helps for technology transfer. The UNIDO is publishing and circulating UNIDO news letter and distributing free and priced publications for Industry and Technology in different popular languages like English, French, German, etc.

APCTT

In India, UNIDO has started APCTT & TIFAC 1977 for appropriate Technology transfer. Asian and Pacific Centre for Transfer of Technology – APCTT is a leading technology transfer agency in the world to help small and medium sized enterprises – SMES. APCTT does not develop technologies but facilitates transfer of the same by establishing contacts between technology suppliers and seekers. The centre provides its clients with short but quite informative profiles of technology offers, searches along with contact details and thus making further direct technology transfer negotiation possible. The following are the important services provided by APCTT.

i) Technology information
ii) Technology promotion
iii) Matching of business partners and search for technology through co-operative agencies/worldwide
iv) Technology market assessment
v) Consultancy on technology
vi) Presentation of the company at international events and preliminary technology transfer negotiations on their behalf.

INTIB

The tasks of UNIDO information services are to provide access to ever-increasing quantities of technological information and to present it in a more attractive and easier way to use. The access to UNIDO's own information resources is provided through INTIB, the Industrial and Technological Information Bank.

The information for industry is considered by the UNIDO not simply as a matter of fashion but as a result of one of the main trends of UNIDO activities, providing necessary support and access to technology information needed by industry, and making information resources readily available in and outside UNIDO to be used for development by UNIDO member states.

The services of INTERNET, DIALOG, etc. have made great revolution in the field of information technology. The important aspects of these services are given in details in the study. The Internet and Intranet system with the fast developing telecommunication technology have added vigorous strength to the Information System in the world to cater to the needs of the users at their door steps on any specialized information.

The information Super Highway is always under strain and traffic jam. The business and industrial activities are highly benefited by the latest technology developed in the world.

Information needs of SSI Sector and the Organisations Disseminating Information in Kerala Small Scale Industries provide employment to many and they play an important role in nation's socio-economic advancement. Technical information is a vital ingredient for the small-scale industries for solving many of its problems. Unlike the heavy industries, the information infrastructures of the small-scale industries are rather very poor and their information needs are slightly different in nature.

In Kerala State, under SSI sector various types of industries are in existence and many are being commissioned. These industrial establishments are engaged in producing consumable and non-consumable goods. And some of them are under service sector industries. The major fields of production are rubber, coir, food, readymade garments, electrical, electronics, plastics, mechanical, medical and pharmaceutical items. Large and Medium industries like HMT, FACT, KELTRON,...., etc. are some of the notable government undertakings. There are some private sector industrial establishments. In addition, many SSI units are functioning as ancillary units to large and medium industries. And many of these industrial units are producing goods directly for marketing to the public.

Recently, Government of India, has announced enhancing investment limits in fixed assets in plant and machinery from Rs.60 lakhs to Rs.3 crores in small scale sector. There are about 1,26,220 registered units and 15,836 newly registered units in the state.

Industry, being a very dynamic and complex system has to be managed on scientific lines for the development in the face of competition and tremendous technological changes and innovations that are taking place. Management of industries requires recognition of economic, psychological and sociological factors affecting it. It entails planning, directing, controlling, decision making, motivating, forecasting, using variety of statistical techniques, etc. All these require harnessing and utilization of information.

Large and Medium industries like HMT, KELTRON, KMML, etc. have got their own libraries and technical information service centres to collect the required information and disseminate it to the R&D units and information seekers. Whereas the small scale industries have neither the capability to support their own information units nor the infrastructure to collect the required information.

Proper information and guidance are required for SSIs for all sorts of work and for development and diversification. To meet the information needs, the Central Govt. has established Small Industries Service Institute – SSI and National Small Industries Centre – NSIC. The State Ministry of Industries has established District Industries Centres in each District headquarters under the control of Director of Industries and Commerce – DIC at the state capital, Trivandrum. The DIC – has established a Documentation Centre at Trivandrum and disseminates information through District industries centres.

In addition, there is an Industrial and Technical Consultancy Organisation, Kerala Industrial and Technical Consultancy Organisation Ltd. – KITCO established by Industrial Development Bank of India – IDBI and other promotional agencies, Nationalised Banks and State Govt. which is becoming more popular in disseminating Industrial and Technological information. KITCO renders consultancy services for product selection and assistance in preparation of project report/feasibility studies/sick unit studies/ special studies/market survey reports and handle turnkey assignments, detailed engineering services, civil contracts, electrification and interior decoration, etc. Information may be obtained from KITCO about the procedures for licensing, registration and financial support, details of machinery and raw material procurement, foreign collaboration, technical know-how, patent information, exporting and importing, marketing, testing facilities, training, pollution control, etc.

Of course, the recently established National Information Centre Network – NICNET at different district headquarters have also started disseminating important industrial information. Apart from these, there are other agencies like Centre for Monitoring Indian Economy, Informatics India Ltd., Bangalore, etc. catering to the various information needs of the industries.

There are other agencies like Kerala State Industries Development Corporation – KSIDC, National Oceanography Laboratory – NPOL, Regional Research Laboratory – RRL, Marine Products Development Authority – MPEDA, Vikram Sarabai Space Research Centre, Trivandrum – VSSC, Central Marine Fisheries Research Institute – CMFRI etc. who are disseminating information in Kerala in addition to the British council library and the University libraries.

Unlike the large and medium industries, the information needs of SSIs are somewhat different in nature. Whereas the former is more interested in acquiring the regular published information for their R&D activities, the latter is interested in acquiring information for their routine activities and solving problems related to the day-to-day production and marketing. The small industries information centre should collect information for the possible queries and supply it on demand to the entrepreneurs. Apart from that, they should provide referral services also. These services will help the entrepreneurs, administrators and decision makers in taking suitable decisions to start new industries and for their effective management, promotion of production and quality control, marketing goods and diversifying the production in the most profitable manner.

THE NEEDS AND WANTS OF THIS RESEARCH STUDY IN KERALA

It is a well-known fact that there exists strong correlation between industrialization and economic development.

When we analyse the growth performance of Kerala in the post formative period, the results are not encouraging. The planners and policy makers are not happy with the total performance in the state.

The industrial level performance, compared to the national level development, measured by any conventional parameter has been on the low level in the state. The industrial sector is dominated in Kerala by traditional industries. The small and medium scale industries are dominant in the total number of industries in the state. In many of the traditional industries innovations and technological advancements have not taken place over the years and the existing industries are functioning at a very low level of efficiency. Both agricultural and industrial sector showed a tendency of stagnation particularly after the mid-seventies. The state is facing severe fiscal and unemployment problems.

Despite its low per capita income, Kerala has attained the physical quality of life index that is more in line with high-income economics. It is often described as the Kerala model development. However, one can easily notice some paradoxical features in the development process of Kerala. The low income and high standard of living can no longer be called as a model of development. The present analysis of the state economy reveals clearly that no country or state in the long run is able to sustain the welfare of its people without continuous injections of economic growth. The ultimate solution for the present economic problem in the state is to strengthen the agricultural and industrial sector, which are the major income sources of income. The unemployment problems will also be reduced to a considerable amount when these two sectors are improved. For this purpose, especially for the industrial growth and development, the essential infrastructure facilities should be given priorities and improved. In Kerala the infrastructure bottleneck hits industrial growth.

The infrastructure facilities to disseminate vital information to entrepreneurs especially in small-scale sector seem to be inadequate and very poor. Of late, the planners, policy makers and entrepreneurs have started realizing the essential needs of value-added information for industrial growth. There is no full-fledged information centre to disseminate the Industrial and Technological information to the users. At this juncture, the author of this research study who has been motivated by his counseling experience and close interaction with the entrepreneurs in SSI sectors for more than a decade, has started thinking seriously to take up the study for his research work to analyse the present scenario like the lacuna in information service to entrepreneurs and find out suitable system to improve the present status in the state. The author had been motivated by many of the visitors to the KITCO Library and Data Bank for reference and counseling. Besides this, he had also been motivated by the guide of this research study, colleagues in KITCO, and Library and Information professional to take up this great task and provide suitable suggestions to improve the present scenario of information facilities to entrepreneurs.

The author of the study has experienced the following needs and wants for this research study.

a. The users/entrepreneurs are running pillar to post to avail basic industrial and technological information.

b. There is no authentic and full-fledged information centre to provide industrial and technological information under one roof.

c. The existing Library and Information centres in the state are having inadequate facilities to provide information service to entrepreneurs.

d. Well-equipped library and information centres are having strict rules and regulations to allow outside users i.e. they are not easily accessible for outside users.

e. The lack of awareness of value added information is still existing with the planners, policy makers and entrepreneurs in the state.

f. There is no proper channelisation and network to make use of the available information from the service centres established in the country.

g. The present advancement in Information Technology and Telecommunication system can provide simple and user friendly system to improve the existing problems.

h. There is an improved climate to market value-added information service by which mutual benefits will be gained by Information service centres and users.

i. The Govt. and private agencies have already started working on essential information services.

j. In the world scenario, the services like INTERNET, DIALOG, KOMPASS, DATA BANKS, etc are revolutionizing the Information Age.

k. There is an urge for value-added information at any cost by the users for their decision making.

With all these needs and wants the research study has been carried out successfully.

THE COVERAGE OF THE STUDY

The study is divided into six chapters along with annexures and Bibliographical Note. In the introduction chapter, brief details are given. The significance of "the information age and information era", the role of information system, the features of National and International information system, the requirement of the study for Kerala and the uniqueness of the study are covered in the first chapter.

The objectives and methodologies are covered in the second chapter. The questionnaire designed for the survey purpose is included in the annexure for reference.

To have better knowledge and understanding about Information System, Information Technology, Standards for Information System, Government roles, etc, the author has taken the help of UNIDO guidelines and given elaborate details in the third chapter.

The study has thrown light on the existing facilities for information to entrepreneurs in Kerala and brought into attention about the lacuna in information system with the help of questionnaire, survey findings and analysis and personal interviews with experts and professionals. Also, the author has given references of published reports and theses on information system for Kerala.

Based on the finding's analysis, the author has evolved a suitable system in the fifth chapter for free flow of information to entrepreneurs in Kerala.

A SWOT analysis has been made subjectively to explore the strength, weakness, opportunities and threat of the proposed Information system for entrepreneurs. The social cost benefit analysis has also been made for the proposed information system subjectively by presenting an economy of the study in the fifth chapter.

The sixth chapter gives the summary of the report along with the findings and recommendations of the study.

The important lists, tables, graphs, etc. are provided in the annexures and appendices. A bibliographical note is also given separately.

THE SIGNIFICANCE AND UNIQUENESS OF THE STUDY

The most important significance of the study is given in details in this study.

We have seen the fast developments in Information Technology and telecommunication system and its effect in national and international level. But, however, the benefits are not reaching to the grass root level users. Another important aspect is the Local area information for which there is no proper system developed in India. Unless this area is developed, the achievement of the present Information system at National and International level may not be effective. The author of the study has given importance to the above mentioned two aspects and the study is making earnest efforts to develop a new system to achieve good amount of growth in Information system for Industry and Technology.

In the state of Kerala, obsolete technologies are still existing in industrial sector. To change the scenario, a suitable information system should be implemented in the state for which the suggestions given in the study will be more useful.

Information on all subjects is pouring out at such a fast rate that it has become impossible to retrieve it from abundant databases. It is like searching a needle in haystack or fishing for in the deep waters of the Ocean. Inter-disciplinary nature of topics for search makes the recovery of relevant information even more tedious especially in Industry and Technology. In this situation a small entrepreneur looking for some basic relevant information to start an industry is finding it very difficult. He has to run pillar to post and finally get fed up. To improve the present difficult situation, it is proposed to establish an Industrial and Technological Information System in the name and style of "IT IS" which will help to set up the Industrial and Technological Information Centre (ITIC) for entrepreneurs in small scale sector in the State. The IT IS will play its vital role with the help of a nodal agency between entrepreneurs and well-established national and international information centres. With the help of IT IS, entrepreneurs in the nook and corner of the state can have accessibility with the information centres anywhere in the world. The proposed IT IS will function with the help of Technical Consultancy Organisation – TCOs-which are already functioning in each state with the support of Financial Institutions. The IT IS will be properly established and developed by Technical Consultancy Organisations – TCOs in the state. In Kerala, KITCO Ltd. will have the opportunity to establish IT IS as it has established contact with entrepreneurs at grass roots level by its multivarious services like Entrepreneurial Development Training Programmes – EDP, Technological Clinic, Entrepreneurial Awareness Programme – EAP, Prime Minister's Rozgar Yojana Training – PMRY, Project report preparation, Detailed Engineering services, Energy audit and management services, Sick unit revival study, plan betterment services, information service, project preliminary counseling services, etc. For the purpose, SENDOC and INSDOC in the country will also contribute their maximum help.

The study highlights the economical background details of Kerala highlighting the lacuna in infrastructure facilities. One of the main causes for the poor economy of the state seems to be lack of Information facilities to entrepreneurs. The study has been motivated to explore and remove the bottlenecks in infrastructure facilities for free flow of information to users. The coverage of the study is provided in the first chapter to have a bird's eye-view of the study.

The uniqueness of the research study is the importance given to Dr.Ranganathan's modern laws of Information Science, i.e "Every information it's user" and "Every user his/her information". By the proposed Industrial and Technological Information System every entrepreneur in small scale sector in Kerala will get information accessibility and every information processed in the centre will find its user/entrepreneur. The grass root level user will be benefited. There will be an Industrial and Technological Information revolution in India just like the successful attempts made by the Government in Green revolution and White revolution.

Let us hope for the best use of the research study by planners, policy makers, entrepreneurs, corporate, information experts, etc. to achieve the information revolution to provide value-added information to grass root level users/entrepreneurs.

OBSERVATIONS

Our country is mostly rural based. There are about 5,57,137 panchayats in India and within that 983 panchayats are functioning in Kerala. The main income of our country is from agricultural sector. Our country's economic conditions would be improved only with the share of industrial sector in the Gross Domestic Product – GDP improvements. For this matter, by the past experience the role of SSI sector in the development of India has been fully recognized.

The small-scale sector has made remarkable recovery during the post liberalization period notching up a three-fold increase in export earnings during 1992-1996.

The Dept. of Small Scale Industry – SSI has in its review indicated that this sector has recorded a higher rate of growth compared to industrial sector as a whole during the recent period in the country.

In Kerala total number of SSI units stood at 1,26,220 by the end of March 1995. The Intensive Industrialisation Programme launched by the State Govt. in Feb. 1993 made this achievement possible. The units registered during 1994-95 provided employment to 73,618 persons. The total investment in the small-scale industrial units registered in Kerala as on March 1995 is placed at Rs.1367.34 crores. They were employing a total number of 7.03 lakh persons during 1994-95.

Yet, things are not going well in the industrial sector in Kerala especially in small-scale sector. In fact most of the sick units in Kerala are in SSI sector. The State is still in the industrially backward list. There are many factors considered for the cause of this status like lack of an industrial or entrepreneurial culture or industrial climate, lack of information facilities, lack of other infrastructure facilities, etc. To change the scenario many factors are to be considered and improved in the state like proper information and guidance mechanism, timely financial assistance, orientation programme to inculcate entrepreneurial culture, motivation, etc.

Time is valued in terms of money. Today, time is the cutting edge. The ways leading companies manage time in production, new product development and in sales and distribution, represent the most powerful new sources of competitive advantage. The elapsed time can make a critical difference between success and failure. The right information, in right time to the right user can save the time of potential users/entrepreneurs. Entrepreneurs require varieties of information when they get involved in the process of identifying and formulating the project, raise various resources, implement them and keep them growing. All the activities of entrepreneurs require a mass of accurate and uptodate information.

The information services are well organized in the developed world with the developments in electronics, computers and telecommunication. Although many organizations in India, both Govt. and private are in the business of providing information, they have severe limitations with regard to resources, expertise, technology and vision. Small-scale entrepreneurs themselves cannot afford to set up their own information centre. The cost of reading materials like books and non-book materials are not in an affordable status. The amount of information proliferating in the world is enormous and voluminous. No one can keep pace with the developments in their own field of interest. In such situation how can we expect an entrepreneur to start his own information centre? But he can depend on an authentic information service centre on a nominal subscription basis. And also he can procure information on need basis for affordable price. Entrepreneurs have started feeling the needs and wants of information. They are ready to pay reasonable price for the appropriate information services. With this background and scenario in information technology and information services in the nation, a research work for exploring the present status of information services in the nation and the state in particular has been started with the intention of finding a suitable information system to improve the present scenario. The author has formulated clearly the objectives of the research study. A suitable questionnaire has been designed to analyse the details and opinions from potential information users or entrepreneurs. The author has conducted personal interviews and meetings with the Information experts to seek their opinions to evolve a suitable information system for entrepreneurs. For the purpose of the study, published thesis and reports in the recent past have been referred and cited. After analyzing the results of the questionnaire survey, opinions of personal interviews, recommendations of published thesis and reports, the author has presented a suitable user friendly and economically viable Industrial Information System to potential information users/entrepreneurs.

In the study, the author has given an elaborate statement with regard to the concept of Information, Information services to Industry, their global standards, Govt. policy formulation, implementation, users needs and wants, information network, database system, etc. One of the main objectives of the study is to explore the lacuna in providing proper information facilities for entrepreneurs in Kerala State and remove bottlenecks or obstacles in the existing system for free flow of information not only to the users in city and town location but also in rural areas by implementing an information network system at Panchayat level in the state. For the purpose, a questionnaire survey has been conducted among the users/entrepreneurs to analyse the important factors like the users' basic knowledge about information and existing facilities available in state, nation and abroad.

In the survey attempt, the users were given chance to reveal the factors or reasons for not making use of the existing facilities in information service available in the state, their order of preference of standard information services in the process of setting up industries, their preference of location for the future information, sub-centres, their willingness to pay for value added information services in future, their opinion for a suitable information system and network exclusively for entrepreneurs in the state.

As a part of the study, personal interviews with information professional experts have been conducted. A special visit to Small Enterprises National Documentation Centre – SENDOC at Hyderabad, Indira Gandhi Kalpakkam Atomic Research – IGKAR at Kalpakkam, Central Electro Chemical Research Institute – CECRI at Karaikkudi have been made for the purpose. At SENDOC NISIET the author has arranged a special meeting with the information professionals and experts to seek their views and opinions to help information users/entrepreneurs at grass root level.

Many published reports, theses, and other published relevant documents have been referred and analysed as a part of the study.

The hypothesis of the study has been well defined in the study. It is better to know the concept of Information System, what is Industrial and Technological Information system – IT IS and the latest developments on Information Technology in the world and the status of the same in India. For this purpose, very clear definition and explanations are provided in the thesis and the fundamental rules and guidelines laid down by United Nations Industrial Development Organisation are provided along with the International Standard for Information Services. Also the type of standard information to be provided to the users/entrepreneurs in Industry and Technology are also given. The Govt. of India policy on information technology and services and the efforts to implement the information system from the inception till the latest NICNET system in India are clearly mentioned in the study. After stating what is information system and Information Technology and their concepts, rules, etc, the status and developments of the same in Kerala State has been analysed.

The existing facilities available to entrepreneurs with regard to Industrial and Technological Information service in the state and Nation both by Govt. and private agencies are highlighted in the study. The services established by Small Enterprises National Documentation Centre – SENDOC at National Small Industries Extension Training Institute – NISIET – Hyderabad by Small Industry Development Organisation – SIDO under the Ministry of Industry, Govt. of India, exclusively for small scale entrepreneurs during 60s have been clearly accounted in the study. The services provided under National Information System for Science and Technology – NISSAT by UNESCO Scheme to strengthen the information services in Science, industry and technology in India are highlighted in the study.

The study has covered the other important services provided by Indian National Scientific Documentation Centre – INSDOC at Delhi, and other Council of Scientific and Industrial Research CSIR information centres like Central Food Technological Research Centre – CFTRI, Mysore, Central Leather Research Institute – CLRI, Adyar, Madras, Central Institute of Plastic Engineering Training – CIPET, Madras, etc. where information centres are established under NISSAT – programme in different specialized fields like food, leather, plastic, etc. An exhaustive list of CSIR – centres providing Information service in India are given in the Annexure.

There are private agencies like Centre for Monitoring Indian economy – CMIE, Bombay, Informatics India Ltd., Bangalore and several other agencies who have already established their centres and commercialized information services in India. The study has given importance to such private agencies and covered their services.

As far as the existing information services available in the state of Kerala for entrepreneurs, the following organizations are highlighted in the report. The Kerala State Industrial Development Corporation – KSIDC, CSIR & RRL at TVM, Small Industries Service Institute – SISI at Trichur, FEDO-FACT, NPOL, CMFRI, CIFT, NSIC, Coconut Development Board, Spices Board, Rubber Board, Coir Board, Khadi and Village industry commission at Cochin, the ISRO – VSSC, TVM, the British Council Library and other University Libraries for Agricultural, Engineering and Technology are mentioned in the report.

In addition, the ministry of Industry in the state has established an exclusive library and Documentation Centre for entrepreneurs at TVM and extension services are provided to all District Industries Centres – DIC at each District head quarters. The report has pointed out the importance of such services in the state.

An another important consultancy organization, Kerala Industrial and Technical Consultancy Organisation Ltd – KITCO Ltd. established by Industrial Development Bank of India – IDBI and other important nationalized banks and the State Govt. for consultancy services for small-scale entrepreneurs in the state is given importance in the study. The KITCO Ltd. which was started in Kerala during 1972 on an experimental basis to provide consultancy services to small scale entrepreneurs has completed several studies and reports for entrepreneurs and has completed several entrepreneurial training programmes in the state for small scale entrepreneurs. On an average 20 to 25 visitors from all over Kerala make use of the Data bank and Information Centre in KITCO. It is worth mentioning that the research study has given importance to the special information service started by KITCO on subscription basis in the name and style of "KITCO information management system – KIMS". It has been made very clear in the study that the KITCO Ltd. is well known among the SSI entrepreneurs/users than other organizations in Kerala. Besides that, the KITCO Ltd. seems to be easily accessible to users/entrepreneurs. KITCO is also taking serious measures to strengthen its "KIMS" service and establish an information system in the state for entrepreneurs with the support of "Tool" Consultants, the Netherlands.

THE LIST OF LARGE PROJECT STUDIES COMPLETED BY KITCO

i) Cochin International Airport (Rs.3 billion) at Nedumbassery

ii) Cattle Feed Project (Rs.350 million) at Kallettumkara for Govt of Kerala.

iii) Rare Earth Chemicals Plant (Rs.100 million) at Udyogamandal for Indian Rare Earths Ltd.

iv) Bamboo Board Project (Rs.20 million) at Angamaly for Kerala State Bamboo Corporation.

v) Technology Development Centre (Rs.250 million) at Kakkanad for Coconut Development Board.

vi) Restoration of Maharaja's College (Rs.7 million) at Ernakulam.

vii) Ayurvedic (indigenous) Medicines Project (Rs.100 million) at Kanjikodu for Kottackal Aryavaidyasala.

viii) Civil construction and procurement for Kerala Forest Dept.

ix) Corporate Office for Cochin Refineries Ltd. at Ernakulam.

TECHNO-ECONOMIC RESEARCH STUDIES COMPLETED BY KITCO

i) Technology Profile Study of Kerala under Technology Absorption and Adaptation Scheme (TAAS).

ii) Technology Evaluation Study on Marine Food Industry.

iii) Consultancy capabilities of Kerala.

iv) Modernisation of rubber-based industries.

v) Top Industrialists Development Programme.

vi) Study on Common Facility Service Centres.

vii) Study on the prospects of Electronics Industries in Kerala.

viii) Study on Readymade Garment Industry.

ix) A Video film on selected industries.

The study has analysed the factors by questionnaire and tables present survey method among entrepreneurs/users and the facts and figures in the survey findings and analysis. The main finding of the survey is the lack of awareness of information services in the country and abroad among the respondents for which suitable awareness programmes and users education programmes are suggested in the study.

The bottlenecks or obstacles for free flow of information from the existing information centres investigated in the study are analysed and suitable suggestions to overcome or remove the obstacles/bottlenecks are provided.

FINDINGS

A new "Industrial and Technological Information System – IT IS" exclusively for small scale entrepreneurs in the state is suggested to overcome the existing problems in free flow of information from well established information centres like SENDOC, INSDOC, CSIR – centres, etc. in the country. The importance of new system suggested in the study has found out prominent solution to provide information service to entrepreneurs at grass roots level in the state. The envisaged new information system will have information centre at Panchayat level in the state. And all these Panchayat level information centres –PITIC will be connected by a net work system to Nodal centre in the state which will be linked with all national and international databases. The new system will have the facility to collect local area information through PITIC with regard to the information connected with industries, business, marketing, etc. This is the specialty and uniqueness in the proposed system.

The proposed system will not only smoothen the information service problems in the state, but also provide reasonable employment opportunities in rural areas.

In the state there is no authentic information centre available with regard to local area information. As such no attempt has been made to explore the information at grass roots level i.e. local area information. Without local area information, it is very difficult to assess many factors for decision making by Govt. Depts. and users. To remove this existing never ending problem, the study has envisaged a new system, which will not only be useful to the state of Kerala, but also to the other states in India. Though there are different information net work system like INFLIBNET, SIRNET, NICNET, DELNET, MALIBNET, etc. in the country, no one could reach to the users at grass root level in the country. Perhaps, the new system envisaged in the report will be able to succeed and improve the present status of information services to entrepreneurs for small-scale sector not only in Kerala but also in India.

The envisaged system will be useful to the Government, and other Private organizations in their planning and decision making.

And also it may attract foreign investment, because the information provided by the new system will be authentic and valuable. Investors can easily assess the market potential, machinery & raw material availability, etc. before they take any concrete decision.

To assess the potentiality of the proposed system a scientific "SWOT" analysis has been made subjectively to reveal the strength, weakness, opportunities and threat of the new system. The system seems to have more strength and opportunities and less weakness and threat.

The aim of the study is to provide a suitable and economically viable Information system and network for small-scale entrepreneurs, so that the entrepreneurs can minimize their time in hunting for crucial information for any decision making.

It is high time to introduce such a suitable information system in Kerala for entrepreneurs, because the necessity has been already strongly felt by many users in Kerala. Many entrepreneurs have given their comments in seminars and meetings that they had to run pillar to post, media and Delhi for obtaining value added information. There is a strong feeling among entrepreneurs to establish a Library and information facility in the State exclusively for small-scale entrepreneurs to provide suitable information service.

The main aim of the Govt. both Central and State is to provide more employment opportunities. For that matter the small scale industries are the best source. They generate more income as well as employment opportunities. The new information system again will create more job opportunities in the country. Govt. has started several training programmes like Entrepreneurial Development Programme – EDP, EAP, Entrepreneurial Awareness Programmes, Technology Clinic and Skill Up gradation Programmes, etc. to produce more trained entrepreneurs in the state. These training programmes are based on new trends and technology for which more uptodate knowledge is required. The knowledge is nothing but the source of information. If proper information is easily accessible by the users, then the growth is always on the positive side.

The following are the major findings of the study:

i) There is no facility to provide local area information in Kerala.

ii) A unique information system in the name and style of "Panchayat Industrial and Technological Information System" is the outcome of the research study to provide speedy and authentic information service to the end users.

iii) A nodal centre to co-ordinate PITIS with national and international information system has to be established in the state level important centre.

iv) The envisaged new information system "IT IS" seems to be economically viable and technically feasible.

v) The proposed new system seems to have less weakness and threat and more strength and opportunity as per the scientific SWOT analysis presented subjectively.

vi) The scope of the national level leading information centres like INSDOC, SENDOC, CSIR centres will improve with the help of the envisaged new information system.

vii) Employment opportunity will increase with the implementation of the new information system.

viii) Technological advancement will take place with the help of the new information system.

ix) The Government plans for the rural development will be achieved shortly with the help of the proposed IT IS in the state.

x) The industry and planning Depts. can function efficiently with the help of the new Information System – IS.

xi) The proposed information system for Kerala State could be a model to be implemented in other states in the country.

xii) On the whole, the economy of the country will be accelerated for higher growth with the improvements in SSI sectors by the help of the new information system.

xiii) The country's bilateral trade both imports and export will be strengthened with the help of accurate information facility to be provided by the new Information System – IS.

xiv) India can march along with the well-developed nations in trade and industry with the help of the rural based industrial and technological information network system.

xv) Foreign investors will be attracted by the authentic information, which will be made available by the proposed information system.

xvi) Several new and appropriate technologies will proliferate in the country due to the availability of authentic and value added information by the IT IS.

RECOMMENDATIONS

To implement the system suggested in the study, it may not be a difficult affair to the Govt. Because the cost involvement for establishing a Panchayat Level Industrial and Technological information centre will be around Rs.2 to Rs.5 lakhs. There are about 983 panchayats in the state for which a total investment of Rs.20 crores may be required. And this will be a one time investment and further only recurring expenses.

For the nodal information centre in the state, again it is suggested to take the help of Technical Consultancy organization established by Financial Institution in the state for helping small-scale entrepreneurs in consultancy services. As the TCOs have already gained good amount of experience with the entrepreneurs in SSI sectors, they may be in a better position to assess the information sources required for entrepreneurs and the cost factors in providing them. With this background, the study has suggested to select the TCOs in the state as Nodal Agent to co-ordinate the proposed information system at Panchayat level.

The following are the important recommendations of the study:

i) Govt. and Financial institutions should support to implement the envisaged information system for entrepreneurs. at Panchayat level.

ii) The consultancy organizations established at Financial Institutions and Govt. should take the lead role as nodal agent to co-ordinate the proposed information system.

iii) The apex information centres like SENDOC, INSDOC, TIFAC-APCTT, CSIR Information centres, and other important special Libraries and information centres concerned with industry and technology should extend their full co-operation by network system to the success of the PITIS and enjoy the benefits to the maximum.

iv) The potential users can be encouraged by a special subsidy to subscribe to the special information services by Govt. both central and state.

REFERENCES

1. Drucker, Peter.F. "The coming of the New Organisation", Harward Business Review, Jan-Feb. 1988; in E.F.I Bulletin Bombay : The Employer's Federation of India 9(11) : 42-43 (1988)
2. Vashisth, C.P. et al. New Horizons in Library and Information Science: Velaya Venkatappaiah Fests Chrift. Madras, T R Publication, 1994.
3. Herner, Saul. A brief guide to Sources of Scientific and Technical Information. ed 2. Virginia, Information Resources Press, 1977.
4. Helvey, T.C. The Age of Information: An interdisciplinary Survey of Cybernetics. New Jersey Educational Technology Publications, 1987.
5. UNIDO. Developments in the field of informatics in selected developing countries: Technology trends series. UNIDO, 1989.

6. NISSAT. "Information Industry Promoter – user Interaction – National Meet", NISSAT news letter 14(1): 3-10 (1995)

7. NISSAT. "Information Management for rural development: Its parameters – XII SIS Annual conventions", NISSAT news letter 12(2): 8-11 (1993)

8. Thingalaya, N.K. "Strategies for rural development: Some issue" Pigmy Review 37(3) : 1-8 (1991)

9. Raju, K.V. "Kerala's Development Experience – A Diagnosis", Monthly –Commentary Sep: 36-42 (1996)

10. Bakshi, Sadhana, "The new age of information", Madras : The Hindu Oct 15(1994)

11. Kishore, Rangashri. "Information – a powerful tool in industry", Madras : The Hindu Oct 29 (1997)

12. Podshibyakin, Valdimir. "INTIB Services for Industry and Business", Sendoc Bulletin 11: Economics and Development 21 (5) : 123-129 (1993)

13. NISSAT. "Unesco/NISSAT/Nistads regional workshop on new information technologies: Machine Translation", NISSAT news letter 11(1) : 7-8 (1992)

14. Ravi, N.ed. The Hindu speaks on Information Technology. Madras, Kasturi & Sons Ltd, 1996.

15. Herner, Saul, A brief guide to Sources of Scientific and Technical Information. ed 2. Virtinia, information Resources Press, 1977.

16. Sisikala, S. Industrial Library Systems. New Delhi, Reliance, 1994.

17. Peter,K.M. and Susy. "Information needs of small scale industries : A projected study for industries in Bangalore", Iaslic Bulletin 38 (4) : 167-168 (1993)

18. Podshibyakin, Valdimir. "INTIB Services for Industry and Business", Sendoc Bulletin, 11 : Economics and Development 21 (5) : 123-129 (1993).

5

INFORMATION NEEDS AND USE PATTERN OF VETERINARIANS

Dr. Adarsh N.Gokul

INTRODUCTION

Information gained through observation, experience and experimentation enabled the progress of the humankind since ancient times. Information or processed data transformed into knowledge through intellectualization since the beginning of civilizations. Primitive man tamed wild animals, domesticated them and selectively bred them to increase their value. Assets so gained were passed on to successive generations and this accumulated as their animal wealth. Knowledge so gained formed the intellectual capital in this field of human activity. Unprecedented growth and diversification of information is a problem in veterinary and animal science also. The complexities in information requirements coupled with information explosion and globalization necessitates reorganization, and repackaging of the information according to the needs of veterinarians.

RELEVANCE OF THE STUDY

Livestock especially cattle form an important component of Indian agriculture and can contribute directly to man's sustenance and progress. The role of livestock for mankind are the provision of income, food (milk, meat and eggs), wool, hides and skins, draught power, transport, fuel, serve as a capital reserve for bad times and provide a esthetic pleasure and social benefits like sports. Viewed as part of and as contributors to the agro-ecosystem domestic animals provide ecosystem services like manure for soil fertility, food and shelter for mankind, grazing and seed dispersal to maintain and restore nature, consumption of crop residues and by-products from processing crops (waste converters) preventing pollution. Cattle and buffaloes are the main assets of rural people, which they can trade off for cash in times of emergency.[1]

Draught animals provide energy required for land preparation, which is a vital factor for agricultural productivity. They are recognized by the UN as one of the 14 sources of renewable energy. India depends on draught animal power (DAP) for land preparation to the extent of 66% of area cultivated. Due to a variety of reasons, use of DAP is inevitable or appropriate in certain areas and conditions, such as farms of small size, water logged fields, narrow terraced fields, low resource level of poor farmers, etc. About 75 million draught animals (bullocks and buffaloes) are engaged in land preparation and small-scale rural transportation. It may be noted that DAP saves six million tones of petroleum per year, valued at 4,000 crores. Advocating DAP as a source of appropriate technology for agriculture does not necessarily mean an anti mechanization stand. In fact, mechanism can be adopted wherever it is technically feasible, economically viable and ecologically desirable.[2]

India, with about 2 per cent of land area in the world, is maintaining nearly 17 per cent of the world's human population and about 20 per cent of the livestock. Livestock-man ratio is 1:2 in India, and is less in all other countries, There is not enough pastureland to carry such a huge population of livestock. Due to lack of adequate feed, nutrition and health care, we are not able to tap the full potential of livestock. The massive demand of milk from the urban population has compelled the government to launch the operation flood program through the National Dairy Development Board (NDDB). Repeated breeding results in ill health, fertility and susceptibility to diseases in cattle. Indian cattle are really a draught variety, with milk being given a by-product status. It is apprehended that the overwhelming enthusiasm for milk production has lead to the neglect of the draught characteristics in the breeding programme. According to Dr.Balain former Head of the Animal Genetic Resources, the Ongole breed of cattle has already disappeared in India and is reportedly found only in Brazil, where it was imported from India. Dual purpose breeding retaining draught characteristic has to be encouraged. This requires a review of the existing programmes for investment and management of the cattle sector in order to achieve proper mix of milk and work from India's cattle.[3] The above grave situation calls for urgent measures to rectify the imbalance and inadequacies utilizing recent Information technology tools. Veterinary and health care systems should be strengthened by providing adequate field-based services, using scientific methods for breeding, health care, castrating, dehorning etc.

Information technology is important resource input in the process of gradual and orderly change in the development of traditional bound rural areas. India's program of reforms and economic liberalization coupled with launching of decentralized planning opens a significant market led opportunities for livestock sector. India has now emerged as the largest milk producer in the world with 74 million tones per annum. Such rapid progress was made possible by the pioneering work of National Dairy Development Board (NDDB) under the leadership of Dr.V.Kurian. The operation flood programmes and milk cooperative have changed the face of India's milk sector. Between 1985 and 1992 value of livestock output grew by six per cent a year in real terms, from Rs.196 billion to Rs.302 billion. Major share of this growth is attributed to dairy and poultry sectors. Country's livestock population continues to grow steadily especially among goats and poultry. Of the total households in the rural areas, about 73 per cent own livestock. Income from livestock sector accounts for 15-40 per cent of total farm household incomes. Small and marginal farmers account for three fourth of this household raising 56 per cent of Bovine population.

Kerala occupying just 1.18 per cent of the total geographic area of the country accommodates over 110 crops and the entire livestock population is spread over 60 lakhs small holdings. Milk production in Kerala has increased from 2.2 lakhs tones during 1963-64 to around 264 lakhs tones in 1988-1999 due to extensive cross breeding programmes on the cattle development. The percent of crossbred females has reached 68 in the state, the highest in the country.[4] Dairy and poultry sections are gradually attaining the status of sustainability in the State. They provide lucrative, subsidiary and self employment ventures to many unemployed youths. More than 75 per cent of the total egg production in the state is from backyard sector since commercial layer farming is not at all feasible due to high feed cost. Recently the state exhibits marked growth in the broiler sector.

Veterinary science deals with anatomy, physiology and pathology of animals other than man. It includes diagnosis, prophylaxis and treatment of diseases and infirmities, their relation to man with regard to inter communicable diseases and use of their milk, flesh and other products and their scientific breeding and handling.[5] Veterinarians undertake the duties of maintaining and improving the animal wealth, carry out fundamental and applied research, generate new information and disseminate the most relevant scientific knowledge to the farming community. This has become vital in the changed atmosphere of globalization where agriculture has metamorphosed into agribusiness and animal genetics into gene business. Our farming sector has changed a lot. Slogans like "Small is beautiful" coexist with the new dictum "Big is bountiful" characteristic of structural adjustments in the changing economic scenario. Veterinary scientists working in the laboratories and carrying out extension activities should receive the services of information professionals to equip themselves to discharge their duties.

Veterinarians require nascent information in diverse fields of knowledge such as animal anatomy, physiology, biochemistry, parasitology, bacteriology, virology, pathology, pharmacology, therapeutics, animal breeding and genetics, fermentation technology, farm management, marketing, nutrition, preventive medicine, zoonoses, conservation of breeds, dairy science, genetic engineering, biotechnology, various reproductive technologies and many other interdisciplinary areas including environmental science and wild life management and Information technology. New strategies for increasing productivity and investment policies of transnational corporations also should be properly reviewed in this age of globalization because any breakthrough in any area of life science may have an impact on our economy in the farm sector. Some new trends for increasing productivity via processing includes hydrolyzed milk for lactose intolerant market, development of whey residues for various industrial uses, improved cheese production and development of transgenic cows functioning as bioreactors for secretion of industrial and pharmaceutical products etc. Similar strategies in animal genetics include attempts to reduce gestation period, cloning of various bulls and cows, increasing milk production using somatotrophin (growth hormone) and production of high quality meat, preparation of doses of intestinal bacteria to increase efficiency of feed digestion etc. Recombinant DNA technology has facilitated the development of new and more efficient varieties of breeds resistant to animal diseases.

New reproductive technologies also have an impact in veterinary science and animal husbandry. From artificial insemination (AI) the scenario is changing gradually to embryo transfer (ET). Bovine fertility hormones are increasingly employed to multiply overproduction and rescue ovaries of dead ones as sources of ova.

Embryo transfer technology has even facilitated use of surrogate mothers to build herds of desirable qualities and to save any breeds or species from extinction. Other reproductive technologies such as GIFT (Gamete Intra Fallopian Transfer), ZIFT (Zygote Intra Fallopian Transfer), PROST (Pronuclear Stage Transfer), TET (Tubal Embryo Transfer), EF (Embryo Freezing) etc have revolutionized the field of animal husbandry.[6]

The Veterinarians should also browse literature in many interdisciplinary areas such as leather technology, rural development, tranquilizer gun technology, anaesthesiology and even plant genetics. For instance development of new plant varieties to increase milk yield, selection of new feed sources (e.g. single cell protein, processed wood chips with cellulose digested into glucose), preparation of feed pellets containing biological agents to increase feed efficiency, use of plant growth regulators to raise production of roughage and other techniques to improve nutritional value of feeds ensuring cost reduction. Even occupational hazards of farm labourers and employees of zoos coming under the purview of veterinarians form an important area of concern. Any emergency situation be it an epidemic of Leptospirosis, Rabies, Hydrophobia, Japanese Encephalitis or sporadic incidence of BSE (Boveine Spongiform Encephalopathy) or Creutzfeldz Jacob disease or reports of contamination of prions in human blood and blood products alerts veterinary scientists as common man with anxieties approaches him for valuable information to protect his cattle wealth and himself. Even defense studies form an area of concern. Recombinant technology enables development of weapons in biological warfare containing spores virulent microbes resistant to all known drugs and targeted against animal wealth are being developed by several countries.

Farm animal management is both an art and a science.[7] The primary objective of any livestock enterprise is to achieve maximum productivity and profitability. This involves sound application of basic scientific principles to suit the situation to perfection so that it becomes an art. India's national economy and well being is so closely knit with her livestock, that it is of great importance for India to introduce proper managerial practices of livestock, protect them against diseases and parasites and provide adequate hygiene and housing.[8] The well being of animals is the prime responsibility of veterinarians. They are called on to oversee and treat animal diseases, develop programs of preventive medicine and administer a variety of regulations related to hygiene and epidemic control.[9] They should also help owners/operators uphold ethical standards in the industry or at home.

Information is power. Readily available information alone could help veterinarians to function effectively in their interaction with the farming community or general public. The veterinarians should be provided with recent developments at their fingertip. For this a well-equipped information system is essential. To the best of the knowledge of the investigator no study has been conducted in the field in order to understand the information needs of veterinary scientists. Considering all these facts the investigator believes that it is appropriate to conduct an investigation on Information needs and use pattern of veterinary scientists in the IT environment.

TITLE OF THE STUDY

The study is entitled: Information needs and use pattern of veterinarians in the IT environment.

Definition of Key Terms

The terms, which are not self-explanatory in the title, are given below.

Information Needs

Maurice B. Line has defined information need as "what an individual ought to have for his work, his research, his edification, his recreation etc".[10]

According to Brenda Dervin" an information need is an

impediment preventing an individual from moving forward in cognitive time and space. The person is faced with a gap that must be bridged by 'asking questions, creating ideas and/or obtaining resources'. Such gaps do not occur in the abstract but arise out of particular critical events and situations".[11] Hence information needs may be described as the actual and potential needs of users for documents/information/any other services.

Use Pattern

Use pattern may be defined as the preference indicated by the information users to documents in respect of their bibliographic form, language and country of origin, age etc and information services either through citations in their own works or through requests or demands made to various information systems and services.[12]

Veterinarian

A veterinarian is a person who not only treats animals but also helps animals to remain in good health. Veterinary profession is suitable for those who love animals and has a compassionate predisposition for animals. Primary object of a veterinarian is to render service to the community by facilitating health care of animals ensuring veterinary public health, caring for sick animals and alleviating their sufferings.[13] According to the living Webster encyclopaedic dictionary of the English language, veterinarian is one who practices veterinary medicine or surgery.[14]

INFORMATION TECHNOLOGY (IT)

UNESCO consider Information Technology as scientific technological and engineering disciplines and the management techniques used in the information handling and processing, their application, computers and their interaction with men and machines and associated social economic and cultural matters.[15]

Darton and Giacoletto (1992) defines IT as systematic study of artifacts that can be used to give form or description to facts in order to provide meaning or support for decision making, and artifacts that can be used the organization, processing, communication and application of information.[16]

OECD treats Information Technology as "a term – used to cover technologies used in collection, processing and transmission of information. It includes micro-electronic and info-electronic based technologies incorporated in many products and production processes and increasingly affecting the service sector. It covers inter alias computers, electronic office equipment, telecommunication, industrial robots and computer controlled machine, electronic components and software products".[17]

Objectives

1. To examine the information requirements of users viz. teachers, scientists and researchers of the veterinary colleges, veterinarians of the Kerala State Veterinary Council, District Veterinary Centres, Veterinary Hospitals, Polyclinics, Dispensaries and other various Livestock Sectors in Kerala.
2. To study the user's approach to information in different types of information sources.
3. To assess the existing facilities and drawbacks in acquiring information
4. To design and develop a veterinary information system for Kerala.

Hypothesis I

The present infrastructure facilities in veterinary colleges, hospitals and dispensaries in respect of information in the field of veterinary science are not adequate to meet the requirements of the veterinarians in the IT environment.

Hypothesis II

The existing IT tools are not adequate and the available tools not fully utilized.

SAMPLE AND METHODOLOGY

Data from 2 Veterinary Colleges, 14 District Veterinary Centres, selected Veterinary Hospitals and Dispensaries were collected for the study. The following methodologies are used for data collection.

The methodologies used for collecting data are Questionnaire and Interview.

QUESTIONNAIRE

A properly designed questionnaire is capable of yielding valuable and highly revealing data. Under this study a well-structured and pretested questionnaire is intended to be distributed to scientists and teachers of two veterinary college and veterinary surgeons of various district veterinary centers and selected veterinary hospitals and dispensaries. Data from 2 veterinary colleges, Animal Husbandry Department, Dairy Development Department, Kerala Livestock Development Board (KLDB), Kerala Cooperative Milk Marketing Federation (Milma), Meat Products of India (MPI), Kerala State Poultry Development Corporation, Kerala Feeds Ltd. etc. were taken for the study.

Questionnaires were distributed to 109 teachers, 31 scientists, 535 field veterinarians and 435 Administrative/Executives. Of this 71 (65.1%) teachers, 27 (87.1%) researchers, 401 (75%) Field Veterinarians, 267 (61.4%) Administrative / Executives responded the questionnaire. The total response is 766 (69%) out of 1110. Apart from these, 24 teachers, 10 researchers 168 field veterinarians and 125 Administrative/Executives were interviewed to corroborate information revealed through Questionnaires. Status-wise, institution-wise and region-wise analysis were made to infer into the users actual information needs and to design the Kerala Veterinary Information System (KVIS) to satisfy the needs of various categories of Veterinarians. Based on status and nature of work Veterinarians were grouped into four categories such as Teachers, Researchers,

Field Veterinarians, Administrative/Executives. For institution wise analysis the respondents in various institutions were grouped into four heads such as Veterinarians working in Animal Husbandry Department, Kerala Livestock Development Board (KLDB), Colleges of Veterinary and Animal Sciences and Allied group. Allied group is constituted by clustering institutions engaged in production and marketing, such as Kerala State Poultry Development Corporation, Kerala Cooperative Milk Marketing Federation (KCMMF/Milma), Kerala Feeds Ltd. and Meat Products of India (MPI) for convenience of the study.

INTERVIEW

Unstructured interview was conducted. The selected scientists and veterinary surgeons of various district veterinary centers and veterinary hospitals and dispensaries were interviewed to ascertain their information needs and use pattern.

SIGNIFICANCE OF THE STUDY

The study will be helpful in designing need based information network systems, which can be used for disseminating information pin pointedly, exhaustively and expeditiously. Such a network system, which enables global technology transfer, can definitely contribute to the strengthening of the information infrastructure to support practice and research and thereby economic prosperity of our country. On the basis of this study a detailed study can be further undertaken to develop INVIS (Indian National Veterinary Information System).

ORGANIZATION OF THE STUDY

The study is organized under the following chapters.

1. **Introduction**
2. **Review of Literature** – gives a background as well as a broad over view of research methods and procedures used by earlier workers in the field of study and points out briefly the findings of related studies.

3. Genesis and Development of Veterinary Science at Global and National Level - gives an account of the origin of veterinary practices in Europe, its evolution in middle ages and growth in the modern age with special reference to the IT era. It also traces Veterinary and Animal Husbandry approaches in India since Pre-Vedic period to developments after independence and the scope of modern veterinary science.
4. **Institutional Infrastructure of Veterinary Science and Livestock Centres in Kerala** – gives a summary of Veterinary Colleges in India and discusses in detail the institutional infrastructure of various institutions in Kerala such as the two Veterinary Colleges, Animal Husbandry Department, Dairy Development Department, Kerala Livestock Development Board (KLDB), Kerala Cooperative Milk Marketing Federation (KCMMF/Milma), Meat Products of India (MPI), Kerala State Poultry Development Corporation, Kerala Feeds Ltd. etc.
5. **Analytical Study of Collected data** – Status-wise, institution-wise and region-wise analysis were made as and were necessary to infer into the users' actual information needs. Certain statistical tests were carried out on the data relating to some major areas.
6. **Findings, Recommendations and proposal for Kerala Veterinary Information System (KVIS)** – The study clearly indicates that the present Information infrastructure available for veterinary science in Kerala is inadequate to meet the information needs of various categories of users. Further the existing IT infrastructure is not properly utilized in the case of A.H dept., which is mainly due to lack of proper training in IT. So a Kerala Veterinary Information System (KVIS) is proposed.

FINDINGS

The analysis of data provides the following inferences .The

study also provides the following recommendations and proposal for the establishment of Kerala Veterinary Information System. Literature survey was mainly resorted to collect background information about the genesis and development of Veterinary Science and information on Veterinary Universities and Colleges in India.

FINDINGS AND RECOMMENDATIONS

1. The respondents from C.V&A.Sc. have higher academic qualifications compared to those from all other institutions. More than half (57 per cent) of the professionals of this institution have Ph.D. degree while only 3 (0.44 per cent out of 689) from all other institutions together have Ph.D. It is also revealed that their information needs and IT applications of professionals of C.V & A.Sc. are far greater than respondents from other institutions.
2. About one-fifth of the teachers will retire from service within ten years while about 15 per cent of other professionals covered in this study will retire within five years. The new professionals recruited will be introduced to the use of computers in statistical analysis, epidemiological studies and farm and hospital management and retrieval of information through network since VCI has included computer application as an integral component in the syllabus of B.V.Sc. and A.H. So it will be easy to give them further intensive training.
3. The study reveals the fact that 338 (44.13 per cent) belong to the age group 31-40 and that 182 (53.85 per cent) respondents of this group have 6-10 years experience in service. But majority of the respondents i.e. 234 (30.55 per cent) of the total 766 have less than or equal to five years of experience. The respondents belonging to this group are more familiar with IT tools and software packages.
4. The expertise of veterinarians in foreign languages especially in translation can be utilized effectively by the information centers engaged in translation work as some of them are

familiar in foreign language such as German (0.39 per cent), French (1.18 per cent) and Russian (1.18 per cent).

5. Veterinarians are not only users but also producers of information in the form of books, in popular magazines and newspapers and programmes in television and radio. The study reveals that 27.94 per cent veterinarians have at least one publication or mass media programme to their credit and 72.06 per cent respondents neither have publications can be utilized for electronic publishing from KVIS website and preparation of CD's for training farmers.
6. Research projects were undertaken by only a negligible percentage of veterinarians (11.75 per cent). Among various groups research activity is high in KLDB and C.V and A.Sc. as they have more qualified professionals than A.H Dept. and Allied group and so their information needs in terms of research would also be higher.
7. Research activities are more concentrated in C.V and A.Sc as 71.83 per cent teachers are actively guiding research at M.V.Sc. and Ph.D. levels and hence there will be a proportionate increase in their information needs. Only 65.66 per cent of their information needs are satisfied by various print/online/Internet/CD search.
8. Teachers show more interest in personal subscription to journals as compared to other status groups. Only less than 25 per cent of veterinarians subscribe/receive 1-5 journal. The escalating cost of the journals may be main reason for the lower percentage of subscription to journals. This indicates that libraries should concentrate more in the procurement of internationally reputed journals.
9. Teachers and researchers are forced to procure latest books and reprints of journals for enhancing their performance in teaching and research. 91.55 per cent teachers have personal collection of subject books while 54.18 per cent veterinarians

do not have subject books in their collection and 83 per cent do not have even subject reprints. This indicates that field veterinarians and Administrative/Executives have to rely more on library for most of their information requirements. The escalating cost of books may be one of the reasons that prohibit them from not going for extensive personal collection.

10. Nearly 40 per cent of Veterinarians of Kerala do not have membership in any professional bodies while about 90 per cent of the teachers and researchers of C.V & A. Sc have membership in professional bodies. The three important professional bodies in which veterinarians have membership are Indian Veterinary Association, Blue Cross Society and Association of Food Scientists and Technologists. Indian Veterinary Association has the highest number of 374 members. This high percentage of membership in various professional bodies indicate that they maintain contacts with their colleagues elsewhere through their associations and thus gain access to new sources of information and nascent ideas in order to keep themselves up-to-date in ones own subject of thrust. This validates the concept of invisible colleges generally prevalent for exchange of the latest research activity through informal information exchange.

11. Only a negligible percentage of veterinarians have shown affinity towards periodicals published in foreign languages other than English. The non-availability of journals in foreign languages may be one of the reasons for less utilization as 7.31 per cent of veterinarians have the ability to read and understand foreign languages as per this survey. Some of the teachers in CV and ASc. use journals in Japanese and German languages as the college library is receiving journals in these languages on exchange basis.

12. Library facilities are not available for majority of (66.97 per cent) of the veterinarians of Kerala. This points towards the need for a good digital library, the resources of which can

be accessed online by the veterinarians stationed even in remote areas.

13. Subject books are not at all used by more than two-third of veterinarians. Teachers rely on the library for most of their information requirement. The use of subject books by field veterinarians is comparatively less, which may be due to lack of library facilities with subject book collection. Only less than one third of the veterinary professionals borrow general books from libraries. Professionals engaged in teaching and researches borrow more subject books than general books from the libraries while field veterinarians and Administrative/Executives lag far behind in borrowing both subject and general books from libraries.
14. Majority of veterinarians are not utilizing library catalogue facility. Difficulty in the use of catalogue especially OPAC or lack of knowledge on the part of users about the correct name of the author, or the exact title of the book or about the appropriate subject headings may be the reasons for less utilization of the catalogue.
15. The field veterinarians gave their first preference to friends to find information sources as their use of libraries is much less due to the absence of libraries attached to their institutions. They may be gathering information about the new documents from their friends before visiting libraries once in a while. The teachers and researchers gave first preference to library catalogues because of their frequent use of libraries. Guide is the least preferred means to find information source.
16. The usual approaches of veterinary professionals for locating reading materials are title, author and subject/keyword. The least preferred approach is through series name.
17. Veterinarians in general prefer print media to CD. Encyclopaedias, yearbooks, abstracting journals and dictionaries are the most commonly used publications in CD.

More than one fourth of the researchers utilize abstracting journals and reviewing periodicals in CD format. Less utilization of publications in CD (12.27 per cent) are due to their non-availability, lack of gadgets and low level of awareness in IT.

18. Information needs of an average veterinarian belonging to every status group are fulfilled through on-line/Internet and CD search. Institution-wise analysis also substantiates this finding. On the average teachers and researchers spend only one to one and a half hours per week for online search.
19. Professionals of A.H. Dept. ranked the lowest in the use of CD-ROM databases. Frequency of use of CD-ROM database is higher among researchers as compared to other status groups probably because of their use of abstracting journals and subject dictionaries. On the whole 59.39 per cent of veterinarians do not use Internet. Internet use is the highest among professionals of KLDB followed by C.V & A. Sc. It is the lowest among those of A.H.Department probably due to lack of IT training. As Internet facility is available in all departments of C.V and A. Sc. one-fourth of the professtionals of the institution use it every day.
20. VET CD, the commonly used CAB CD that deals with Veterinary medicine (domestic and wild animals) is used by only 15.01 per cent of veterinarians of Kerala. Professionals of KLDB make use of Vet CD more than those of any other institution. Researchers followed by teachers use VET CD more as compared to other user groups. Non-availability of majority of CD-ROMs including VET CD in Kerala may be the reason for less utilization of these databases.
21. Regular use of computers is the lowest among veterinarians of A.H.Department; only 21.90 per cent of them use it. Of the veterinarians 69.58 per cent are not at all using computers. Professionals of the Allied group (80.95 per cent) tops in

the possession of PC at home followed by 69.57 per cent of KLDB, 52.94 per cent of C.V & A.Sc. and 50 per cent of A.H Dept. Veterinarians who do not have PC at home may be encouraged to acquire the same by providing the computers at subsidized rate through a central agency.

22. In general only 12.92 per cent of veterinarians read newspapers from Internet. The main reason for this is that newspaper in print format is easily accessible and more convenient. Lack of computer knowledge is another reason.

23. The overall analysis of the use of computers shows that 84.44 per cent veterinarians of A.H.Department are not utilizing computers. On the other hand its utilization is above 60 per cent in the case of professionals of C.V & A.Sc. and Allied group and about 59 per cent in the case of KLDB.

24. In the present age of IT wave a far higher percentage of professionals should have acquired knowledge in various software packages. Necessary changes may be made in the curriculum to include recent and important software packages. Refresher/in-service courses may be designed by incorporating the latest packages. Region-wise analysis shows that veterinarians in the central region (Thrissur, Ernakulam, Kottayam and Idukki) are more familiar with software packages followed by those of the northern region. The two veterinary colleges are located in the central region. This may be the reason for the higher position of the central region.

25. More than 40 per cent veterinarians use Internet but only half of them use it for exchange of scientific information. Among the user groups teachers and researchers rank first and second respectively in the use of e-mail.

26. Only negligible per cent (5.61 per cent) of veterinarians are members of the user groups, which are e-mail discussion groups of professionals specializing in a small area.

27. Among researchers 85.19 per cent never utilize CD-search

facility. In spite of the availability of e-mail services in the library/institute 30.97 per cent of teachers and 74.07 per cent of researchers do not utilize this facility. Internet, E-mail and CD search services are not utilized by more than 98 per cent of the field veterinarians, as they do not have a library providing such facilities. These lacunae can be filled suitably only through the establishment of a modern digital library with all amenities.

28. The analysis indicates that more than 98 per cent of the users of C.V & A.Sc library are able to locate necessary documents either fully (24.68 per cent) or partially (74.03 per cent); 96.55 per cent of professionals of KLDB locate their documents fully (6.90 per cent) or partially (89.65 per cent).
29. More than 94 per cent of professionals of C.V & A.Sc depend on library for preparation of teaching, seminars, tests, discussions etc. More than 63 per cent of field veterinarians and 54 per cent of Administrative/Executive officers do not make use of libraries, which may be mainly due to non-availability of library facilities.
30. The dependence on on-line facility and request to librarian to purchase non-available documents in the library are more or less equal, 43.75 and 41.96 per cent respectively. On-line facility is used to acquire non-available information by 80 per cent of the professionals of KLDB.
31. Overhead projector is the most commonly used equipment. While 76.06 per cent teachers use overhead projector for teaching only 2.82 per cent use LCD projector. This is due to non-availability of this equipment in the colleges. Hence LCD projector has to be procured for the institutions as teaching aid as well as for training students in IT applications. This training in slide preparation and LCD projection is essential for veterinarians to impart extension education to farmers using catching slides with animations. Being less expensive

researchers prefer transparencies and LCD for the later involves only IT skills with less expense on the part of the individual. The allied group stands first in the utilization of slide projector and LCD with 10 per cent each followed by KLDB with 6.90 per cent each. This indicates the higher use of advanced equipments in training programmes, conferences and seminars conducted by the allied group.

32. In general the use of expert systems is not popular among veterinarians of Kerala as compared to those of developed countries. Only 2.09 per cent of the respondents have familiarity with any of the expert systems. This indicates lacunae in continuing veterinary education with special emphasis on IT.
33. Bioinformatics centers are used only by less than 8 per cent of the veterinarians. However more than 29 per cent of researchers and more than 27 per cent of the professionals of C.V & A.Sc. have utilized this facility.
34. Majority (88.77 per cent) of veterinarians have not attended any of the IT training course. Hence they cannot utilize even the available IT infrastructure facilities. The percentage of veterinarians who have attended National and International training programmes in IT are only 10.71 and 0.52 respectively. Four veterinarians have undergone training at International level of which two are teachers of C.V & A. Sc. and the other two are field veterinarians of A.H Department. Among veterinarians KLDB tops in IT training of their professionals (27.59 per cent).

MAJOR RECOMMENDATIONS

1. At present there is no published consolidated work on Genesis and development of Veterinary Science, Veterinary Universities and affiliated recognized Colleges. Such a publication on this age-old profession is essential.

2. A consortia and 'user group' of 36 Veterinary College authorities is indispensable in this age of teleconferencing to discuss educational and research aspects, to improve IT applications, to meet the challenges of electronic publishing, information explosion and escalating cost of scientific documents. Consortia provide union strength to negotiate with electronic publishers and National licensees for the best possible price and rights. Consortia licensing which is widely used by the libraries all over the world is slowly picking up in India. Most of the publishers having well developed policies give more offers to libraries subscribing as consortia.
3. Necessary training should be given at the very seminal level so that most of the research scholars as well as students aspiring for higher education may make use of IT.
4. A Kerala Veterinary Information System (KVIS) with a digital State Veterinary Library and networking of Veterinary institutions/libraries in Kerala is the need of the hour as it will help to promote education and research, resource sharing, illiteracy eradication, transfer of technology to farmer and avoid large scale duplication of documents which in turn can improve the economy of libraries as well as the nation as information is power.

KERALA VETERINARY INFORMATION SYSTEM

Digital environment is becoming an integral part of our life. Today the advancements in Web, the dynamic platform for capture and delivery of information and database technology has enabled the libraries to share and publish information directly from the databases. Availability of computers with parallel processing, multitasking, parallel consultation and parallel knowledge navigation and software tools that facilitate artificial intelligence and interactivity at affordable cost, the networking technology and advent of World Wide Web have paved way for creation of digital libraries.

The studies on institutional infrastructure of Veterinary

Universities and Colleges in India and particularly the livestock centers of Kerala, the information needs and information seeking behaviour of various categories of Veterinarians such as teachers, researchers, field veterinarians, Administrative/Executives show that the present information centers/libraries in Kerala are insufficient to satisfy their information needs. All the categories of users expressed their difficulty in getting recent information tailored to their needs at the right time. The majority of the Veterinarians of Kerala who were interviewed are of the opinion to have an International Information System for Veterinary Science and to contribute our share by establishing a well-developed information system for veterinary science in Kerala as the first step. Based on the findings and inference of the study a proposal for Kerala Veterinary Information System (KVIS) is given below.

Important factors to be considered while designing a Kerala Veterinary Information System are:

* Availability of good libraries and information centers with recent IT infrastructure facilities.
* Technical manpower and
* Finance

The survey conducted among the Veterinary Institute/Libraries gives a clear picture of the existing libraries. None of the libraries are found to be self-sufficient. Moreover most of them are below the expected level of standards in collection building manpower as well as services. Libraries attached to Directorate, IAH and VB, LMTC under A.H. Dept., at the training centre of KLDB at Mattupatti, training centre of Milma at Ramavarmapuram and MPI, do not have sufficient collection and are not manned by professional library hands. In all respects the above libraries are far behind. In all the libraries there is only less than 1000 books in their collection. The only exception is KLDB where there is a collection of 3500 books. The services offered are reference & issue of books. The only Veterinary College library of the state also does not come to the standard of a well-organized library in infrastructure and the services offered. Lack of space and sufficient technical staff is the main drawback of this library. The survey reveals that Veterinary College library is comparatively good. They have a reasonably good collection and offer a number of library services to their clientele including Internet facility through ARIS cell and documentation service. Further an amount of rupees 1.5 lakhs has been allotted this year for purchase of computer by NATP project in addition to three available computers. At the same time it is not liable to cater to the needs of veterinarians as a whole as per existing rules. It is the same case with the central library KAU which possesses only very little collection of veterinary books and some CD's.

There is no networking among the veterinary college/institute libraries in the state and no union catalogues are available. Veterinarians especially those of the A.H. Dept. working in rural areas do not get any library facility. The study has also revealed that 98 per cent of field veterinarians do not have utilized Internet, e-mail and CD-search facilities, as they do not have a library with such amenities. Lack of technical manpower and finance are other factors that hampers the modernization and networking of existing libraries. Considering the need for effective and efficient information system in Animal Husbandry Sector at district and state levels the National Informatics Centre has developed a computerized user friendly NICNET based MIS.

Keeping the above conditions in mind, the existing financial set-up and taking into account the recommendations and advices of the higher officials interviewed, it is appropriate to suggest a Digital/Electronic library at Kerala State Veterinary Council, Thiruvananthapuram as its apex body, which will facilitate resource sharing and networking. The Veterinary Council of India also proposes to organize a library in its premises in order to enhance the implementation of the provisions of its Act.

OBJECTIVES OF KVIS

1. To develop a digital/electronic library
2. Strengthening of existing veterinary library system.
3. To evolve a statewide network of veterinary libraries for optimum utilization of information resources.
4. To optimize utilization of funds by minimizing duplication in all spheres.
5. To improve the cooperation in all spheres including manpower, infrastructure and the interlibrary loan services among libraries.
6. Standardization of library services and activities.
7. To facilitate intercommunication among veterinary libraries in the state.
8. To provide access to other national/international networks.
9. To prepare and market useful programmes for veterinarians.
10. To facilitate eradication of illiteracy.
11. To conduct training programmes for veterinarians, library professionals and farmers.

ORGANIZATION OF KVIS

The KVIS will have the following 4 levels of organization. They are

* State Information Centre (SIC)
* District Information Centre
* Taluk Information Centre (TIC)
* Local Information Centre (LIC)

All the centers at four levels such as State, District, Taluk and Local are charged with collection, processing and dissemination of information. They should have necessary personnel and infrastructure facilities. The user community through the user terminals can access KVIS database.

STATE INFORMATION CENTRES (SICS)

The State Information Centre, will be the apex body of KVIS. It will be appropriate to select Kerala State Veterinary Council as the right agency to organize KVIS at its Head quarters at Thiruvananthapuram, the capital city of Kerala State, KVIS has to establish a State Veterinary Library at the centre. The server, which holds the main database of KVIS, will be installed in the Kerala State Veterinary Council. The State Information Centre will be administrative head quarters of KVIS. The main database of the KVIS can be named as "KVETINFOS'. The most important duty of State Information Centre (SIC) will be the creation and maintenance of database of KVIS, its online version which can be called as VETINFOSLINE, establishment and maintenance of a good State Veterinary Library and Networking with other libraries. The proposed publications of the KVIS are KVET Index, which contain an index of publications of veterinarians, KVET CD for veterinary professionals and KVETFARM CD for farmers. The above CDs are expected to contain details about animal management, animal breeding, animal feeding and disease control practices.

The chief of KVIS will be the Director and his office will be at SIC. He can also be considered as State Veterinary Cybrarian. He should be a highly qualified professional with Ph.D in Library and Information Science and should be trained in Information Technology as he has to guide the users and conduct training programmes in IT and maintain the KVIS website. There should be sufficient professionals along with Administrative and supporting staff. The professionals should include system manager and experts in computer application, software, documentation, publication etc. The centre should be equipped with sufficient hardware and software for the maintenance of database and for networking with DIC, TIC and LIC's. As KVIS is a project to be undertaken by the Government of Kerala it can use NIC infrastructure for networking.

STATE VETERINARY LIBRARY

The state central veterinary library should be a typical digital library having linkages to various other sources of information in digital format. The major functions of the digital library are

- To manage large amount of digital contents such as thousands of images or hundreds of audio clips
- To preserve unique collections through digitization
- To enable one to perform searches that are not practical manually
- To manage contents from multiple locations
- To enable greater access to information
- To provide means to enrich the teaching and learning environment; and
- To protect content owners of information.

The digital library utilize various technologies for data capture or content creation, data storage and management, searching and accessing digital data, publishing / distributing contents over networks and rights management. The specifications of the server proposed for the digital library having approximate cost of Rs 461770/- are given below.

Server IBM e Server xSeries 232 with Dual Pentium III 1.126 Ghz.

512 KB L2 Cache

2 GB PC 133 SD RAM ECC expandable to 4 GB

4 × 36.4 GB 10k Ultra 160 Hot Swap Hard Disk

6 Drive Hot Swap bays

On board dual channel Ultra 160 SCSI controller

IBM Netfinity ServRAID 4 Lx Ultra 160 SCSI adapter

Integrated 10/100 LAN

1.44 MB FDD

40XIDE CD ROM Drive

8X/4X/32X/8X/CD RW/DVD ROM Combo

8MB AGP Video Memory

Standard 2*250W Redundant Hot-swap power supply.

15" IBM Colour Monitor, Keyboard, Mouse

3 Serial and USB Ports

Netfinity Director (System Management Software) Prefailure alert on disks, memory, processors, VRAMS and fans in conjunction Netfinity Director.

The library should also acquire software and hardware accessories at an approximate cost of ten lakhs which include additional Pentium IV computers, Network – Ready CD-ROM server with maximum drives which facilitate better security of disks, Modem, Laser printer, Scan Jet digital flatbed Scanner (with up to 2400 dpi optical resolution and 48 bit colour with auto colour enhancement feature) which can easily scan thick books for clear and sharp images and editable text and Network Laser Printer. IT Wealth Agriculture Bureau International such as VETCD and BEAST CD.

Server machines store and retrieve digital data. Relational database Management System (RDBMS) like SYBASE, Oracle, and DB2 are being used popularly for organizing and managing the digital data. The server machine has to retrieve and forward data from various resources including networks expeditiously to the users irrespective of time and geographical location. Using the software 'ADSTAR Distributed Storage Manager (ADSM) developed by IBM, the data can be automatically transferred to various storage media such as tape and optical disc.

Though the library proposed is a digital one it should have a separate section of print media, which will contain the hard copies of proceedings of seminars, conferences and training programmes for reference. This can be converted to a digital format conveniently.

The library will also maintain its own publication in print media.

DISTRICT INFORMATION CENTRES (DICs)

The next level of State Veterinary Information System is the District Information Centre. The Directorate of Animal Husbandry Department at Thiruvananthapuram and 13 District Information Centres. The main function of District Information Centre is to evaluate the information received from the Taluk Information Centres (TIC) under its purview. The information after scrutiny will be technically processed and forwarded to include in the main database of SIC (VETINFOS). The articles received for publication, index and abstracts of articles received from Taluk Information Centres have to be checked and necessary modifications/amendments have to be made before sending it to SIC. In addition to this it will also maintain a district database, which includes the information produced in the areas coming in its purview. The other important function of DICs is to conduct seminars and workshops for veterinarians and information scientists and 'Karshaka Melas', exhibitions and multimedia programmes for farmers with the help of TICs and LICs. These DICs should be equipped with sufficient infrastructure and manpower. The Directorate of Animal Husbandry Department at Vikas Bhavan will act as DIC in Thiruvananthapuram and will collect information from Dairy Development Board, LMTC, CDIO, IAH & VB, Rinderpest Eradication Unit, SLBP, DAHO office, Central Hatchery at Kodappanakunnu and TRCMPU (Milma) Thiruvanathapuram, Kerala State Poultry Development Corporation, KLDB etc. The DIC at Ernakulam district will be responsible for collecting all the relevant information from the Meat Products of India and ERCMPU (Milma) of Ernakulam region. The DIC at Thrissur district will collect all the relevant information from C.V&A.Sc. and central library of KAU, Milma training Centre at Ramavarmapuram, Kerala Feeds Ltd. etc. Similarly DICs of concerned districts will collect information from KLDB training centre at Mattupatti, MARCMPU (Milma) of Malabar region and other livestock centers in Kerala.

TALUK INFORMATION CENTRES (TICS)

Fifty eight polyclinics under A.H.Department can be identified as TIC. The TICs will be charged with the duty of evaluation and onward transmission of information received from various local information centers for inclusion in district and state level databases. TIC should also maintain a taluk level database, which contains all the information collected from LICs. The TICs should have a group of subject and centers of that taluk. In the absence of polyclinics in a particular taluk, one of the veterinary hospitals of that taluk will be earmarked as TIC.

LOCAL INFORMATION CENTRES (LICS)

All the veterinary hospitals and veterinary dispensaries under the taluk can be spotted under LICs. They are significant centres in the KVIS, as they have to conduct surveys and collect vital information at the grass root level. Details of the local indigenous breeds of animals especially livestock which are under the threat of extinction has to be recorded and informed to SICs through TICs so that they could take necessary steps to conserve them and there by maintain the germplasm of the animal wealth of Kerala. The other duties of LICs include condcting consultancy services to farmers and such details can be included as FAQs in the website maintained by the KVIS. LICs should train clientele in the proper use of KVIS. They should also organize seminars to familiarize the farmers with high yielding, disease resistant varieties of livestock. 'KVETTECH CDs' produced by KVIS will be of immense use to train them as knowledge is the key input which is very essential to improve the productivity level. Knowledge on scientific dairy management practices such as disease control, management feeding and breeding practices have to be taught. They should also be fed with information about improved milch breed, recommended quality and quantity of green fodder etc. There is an urge for flow of need based technical information to make farmers knowledgeable, which will help them to adopt improved practices. The LIC should be a local databank with all necessary information suited to serve individual farmers.

Apart from SIC, DIC, TIC and LIC the four levels of organizing centres, there will be a number of information receiving points which are known as the KVIS nodal points.

FUNCTIONS AND SERVICES OF KVIS

The KVIS database especially KVETINFOSLINE will be of immense use to all the veterinarians engaged in teaching, research, extension and private practice, pet lovers, farmers and to the entire human population as it will be dealing with prophylaxis and care, communicable diseases, preparation, preservation and consumption of egg, milk meat and their by products which are of common interest to ordinary citizens, the ultimate users of KVIS nodal points.

The individual users who are interested in utilizing the KVIS database has to register their name in the KVIS website at a nominal fee and will be allotted with a password. However this will be free for farmers when accessed from the KVIS nodal points during farmers' day and festivals.

The most important functions of KVIS are the creation and maintenance of website and database which collects all the relevant information in the field of Veterinary Science and Animal Husbandry. The information can be disseminated through print/online/CD-ROMs. The KVIS should provide information services using its database and resources. They are

- Current Awareness Service
- Selective Dissemination of Information
- Indexing and Abstracting Services
- Literature Survey
- Reference Service
- Document Delivery Service
- Translation Service

· Reprographic Service etc.

The other important services by KVIS are consultancy service to Library and Information Centres, farmers and other KVIS users, training programmes for library staff and users, preparation of technical processing tool for veterinary documents and patent information services.

Educational CDs can be developed as a replacement for animals used in some courses in pharmacology, medicine and veterinary science. This will eliminate and rampant and repeated use of experimental animals in the study of the effect of various drugs. Surgeries and obstetrical interventions conducted in various hospitals may be copied in CD for use of undergraduates.

CONCLUSION

The study give an idea about the Genesis and Development of Veterinary Science at Global and National Levels, Veterinary Universities and Colleges in India and the institutional infrastructure of various institutions in Kerala in detail.

The objectives of the study were :

1. To examine the information requirements of users viz. teachers, scientists and researchers of the veterinary colleges, veterinarians of the Kerala State Veterinary Council, district veterinary centres, veterinary hospitals, polyclinics, dispensaries and other various livestock sectors in Kerala.
2. To study the user's approach to information in different types of information sources.
3. To assess the existing facilities and drawbacks in acquiring information.
4. To design and develop a veterinary information system for Kerala.

The survey results given in chapter entitled 'Institutional Infrastructure of Veterinary Science Institutions and Livestock Centes in Kerala' and 'Analytical study of collected data' substantiate the first, second and third objectives. The last chapter entitled 'Findings Recommendations and Proposal for Kerala Veterinary Information System (KVIS)' substantiates the fourth objective by designing the Kerala Veterinary Information System.

The two hypotheses which led to the present study are :

- The present infrastructure facilities in veterinary colleges, hospitals and dispensaries in respect of information in the field of veterinary science are not adequate to meet the requirements of the veterinarians in the IT environment.
- The existing IT tools are not adequate and the available tools not fully utilized.

The results of the surveys mentioned above clearly substantiate the validity of hypotheses formulated in the study. It led to the designing of a Kerala Veterinary Information System (KVIS) for veterinary science, which will satisfy the needs of information users in Veterinary and Animal Sciences.

The findings of the present study are reasonably limited in its scope with regard to certain aspects. The study was conducted through out Kerala to ascertain the information infrastructure, user needs and use pattern of veterinarians at the micro level, which is necessary for the development of KVIS. Based on the lines of KVIS, Information System may be developed in other states after conducting user studies. Such systems can be linked to form an Indian National Veterinary Information System (INVIS). Further, it may be developed into an International Veterinary Information System (IVIS) for Veterinary Science.

KVIS, if implemented, will open up new vistas for the electronic publication of various research studies of veterinarians, which will definitely wave out the usual criticism that Indians are interested only in downloading information. It would be a right march towards application of Information Technology to veterinarians as well as farmers of rural areas and will substantiate Prime Minister

Atal Bihari Vajpayee's dictum "IT means India Tomorrow".

REFERENCES

1. Zijpp, A.J. Van der. Role of Global Animal Agriculture in the 21st Century. Asian Aus.J.Anim.Sci., 13 (S) 2000, p.1.
2. Ramaswamy, N.S.Livestock and Environment for Sustainable Development. Bangalore: Centre for Action Research and Technology for Man Animal and Nature, 1998, p.3-14.
3. Ibid. Ramaswamy, N.S.p.3.
4. Sethumadhavan.T.P. Analysis of Animal Husbandry Information in the Farm Feature Pages of Leading Malayalam Dailies (Thesis), Thrissur: College of Veterinary & Animal Science, 2000, p.1-3.
5. Encyclopaedia Britannica. London: Encyclopaedia Britannica Ltd., 1962, V23, p.116.
6. Fowler, Cary et.al. The Laws of Life: another Development and the New Biotechnologies. Development Dialogue (1-2) 1988, p.127-140.
7. ICAR. Handbook of Animal Husbandry.2nd rev.ed., New Delhi: ICAR, 1990.
8. Sastry, N.S.R et.al. Livestock Production Management, 3rd ed., New Delhi: Kalyan Publishers, 1991, p.1.
9. The Merck Veterinary Manual, 7th ed., New Jersey: Merck & Co.,Inc., p.928.
10. Lane, Maurice B.Draft definitions: information and library needs, want, demand and uses. Aslib proceedings. 26, 1974, p.87.
11. Dervin, B. Audience as listener and learner, teacher and confidante: the sense-making approach In Public Communication Campaigns, ed. By R.E.Rice and C.Whitmey, California: Sage, p.67-85.

12. Kawatra, P.S. Library User Studies: a manual for librarian and information scientists. Bombay: Jaico publishing house, 1992, p.19-34.

13. Veterinary Council of India. *http://www.nic.in/dahd/vci.htm*

14. The Living Webster Encyclopaedic Dictionary of the English Language. 6th ed. New York: Delair Publishing Company, Inc., 1980, p.1103.

15. William, James. Information technology: a state of the art report, In Information Technology, ed. By Allent Kent and T.J.Galwin. New york: Marcel Dekker, 1982, p. 342-458.

16. Darton, Geoffrey and Giacolctto. Information in the Enterprise: it's more than technology. New Delhi: Prentice Hall of India Pvt. Ltd., 1992.

17. Sasanwal, D.N. Information Technology and Higher Education. University News 38(46) 2000, p.1-6.

6

REFERENCE BOOKS IN MALAYALAM LANGUAGE: A BIBLIOMETRIC STUDY

Padmanabhan K.K.

INTRODUCTION

The history of printing begins from 2nd century AD by Chinese. John Gutenberg a German architect realized the modern technology of printing machine in 1455. It revolutionized the history of mankind. Now the book is designed as an instrument of communication. A book is a written or printed work consisting of pages guided or sewn together along one side and bound in covers.

Printing was started in India, for religious purpose as in other parts of the world. The history begins with the arrival of Christian missionaries from Portugal. 'Vedopadesm' in Portuguese language was the first book printed in India. 'Samkshepa Vedantham' 1772 is the first book published in Malayalam language which was printed in Rome.

From the point of use we may divide books into two categories i.e., ordinary books and reference books. Books which are written so that these can be read consecutively for inspiration, enjoyment or information is considered as ordinary books. Books, which are designed and consulted for, reference from time to time for a specific piece of information is called reference books.

The first reference book published in Malayalam language was by a Christian missionary Poulinose Padiri. The title of the book is 'Sentam Adigiya Malabarika' which was published in Rome in 1791. Contents of this book include hundred proverbs and their translations. This book is the second one in the Malayalam language and first proverb collection in Indian language.

As a result of intensive research and study various new subjects emerged. New basic subjects emerged by distillation and fusion of two or more subjects. Men are much interested to get new knowledge. But they do not get much time to spend for searching the books, which are needed by them. Reference books help them to acquire this knowledge. A bibliography helps them to save their time in the search of books.

RELEVANCE OF THE STUDY

The backbone of any library collection is formed by reference books and they can be considered as the lifeblood of research. Reference books are considered as the most important media of communication of information about new knowledge in any subjects. The most recent reference books are the sources of current materials that cannot be found else where. They constitute the primary medium of publishing discoveries, trends etc that do not appear in common books.

As a result of information explosion, there is a flood of literature being generated through out the world. Malayalam literature is also facing a similar flood of publications. But there is no authentic bibliographic source in Malayalam literature except the Malayalam Grandasoochi. There is no bibliography available for a particular type of publication like reference collection of Malayalam language. The reference book is an important tool for scholars and students of Malayalam language. So we are in need of a bibliography for reference sources alone. We can identify the strength and weakness of reference books from such a bibliometric study. This will give a correct picture about this field and help in identifying the weak areas in the publication of Malayalam reference books. This will lead to balanced production of reference sources in Malayalam.

TITLE OF THE STUDY

The title of the study is "Reference Books in Malayalam Language: A Bibliometric Study."

EXPLANATION OF KEY TERMS

Reference Books: Books, which are designed to consult or referred to, from time to time for a specific piece of information. Ordinarily these are not meant for continuous reading.

Malayalam Language: The language spoken in Kerala is called Malayalam language or the mother tongue of Malayalees.

Bibliometric Study: It is the analytical study of the literature using bibliometric techniques. Alan Pritchard used this term first in 1969 and he defines it as the application of mathematical and statistical method to books and other media of communication.

OBJECTIVES OF THE STUDY

The main objective of the study is Quantitative analysis of the reference books published in Malayalam language and its nature. More specifically the study is aimed at:

1. To examine the quantitative growth of reference books in Malayalam language.
2. To find out the major subject areas covered in the publication of Malayalam reference books.
3. To analyse the year wise growth of reference books in Malayalam language.
4. To identify the prominent contributors of Malayalam reference books in Kerala.
5. To find out the translation pattern of reference books in Malayalam.
6. To find out the bibliometric characteristics of reference books. The following sub-objectives were also formulated for analysis:

   (a) Publisher-wise distribution

   (b) Gender wise-distribution of authors.

   (c) Geographic distribution of publishers.

METHODOLOGY

The following methods were adopted for the collection of data.

LITERATURE SURVEY

To examine similar studies in this topic extensive literature survey was conducted. The purpose of literature review is to see the methodologies adopted by investigators in their study and to understand the outcome of those studies. For literature review primary sources such as Journals, Ph.D thesis and dissertations were consulted. The secondary sources were also consulted to review the literature, which include LISA PLUS (CD-ROM version).

For the collection of data various sources have been consulted. The most important among them was the Malayala Grandhasoochi published by Kerala Sahitya Academy, Thrissur. It is an important bibliography, which provide a comprehensive account of books in Malayalam in seven volumes. The compilation of the bibliography was started under the editorial ship of K.M Govi and A.K.Panickkar. The first volume came out in 1973, the second volume in 1974, recently seventh volume was published in 1996. A notable feature of the Grandasoochi is that first volume is exclusively devoted for literary works and the second volume for non-literary works. Entries are arranged alphabetically in the name of authors under each subject. The Grandasoochi also provides indexes for author, title and subject.

HYPOTHESES

The following are the hypotheses of this study

(1) The publication trend of Malayalam Reference books was upward year after year.

(2) Biographical sources covered the major area of reference sources;

(3) Government contribution is less;

(4) Males are the major contributors of the reference books; and

(5) English language is prominent, in the case of translated works.

LIMITATION OF THE STUDY:

This study considered only the period up to 1995. The entire study had been done within a short period of one year. Non-availability of adequate time was a difficulty faced during the study. Physical availability of literature about Malayalam reference sources was another limitation of the study.

ORGANISATION OF THE STUDY

The study is organized as follows.

1. Introduction
2. Review of Literature
3. History of Publishing of Reference Books in Malayalam: An Overview
4. Reference books in Malayalam: Bibliometric Analysis
5. Findings and conclusion

REVIEW OF RELATED STUDIES

Review of related literature forms an integral part of any research report. It helps to find out what is already known and what is still unknown and untested. It also helps to avoid the duplication of research. A careful scanning of the literature on related studies will help the researcher in understanding the studies of similar nature and the methodology followed. A total number of 29 related studies have been reviewed in the present study, which includes General, Library and Information Science, Science, Journal, Thesis and Dissertation.

Ivank Djaja (1978) in his work studies the national library of Serbia in new premises and now has an open access of 20,000 reference volumes. The Library aims to possess publications covering all fields of human knowledge and is enriching its reference collections, by purchasing national, current and retrospective bibliographies; printed catalogues of the world's great libraries; international and national encyclopedias; and reference series. It has 500 titles of current secondary sources and several hundred volumes of monographic reference works. Publications are arranged by using UDC classification scheme. (1)

Heng and others (1979) in their article classified and annotated a list of 136 Chinese reference books published in Taiwan in 1977 and 1978. Reprints of old works have been omitted except revised editions with supplements for reference. Statistical reports issued by government departments and periodical reference materials are not included in this list. (2)

The paper presented at the annual conference by Alan Amstrong (1982) of the Library Association Industrial Group, 22 Mar 81, looks at the short and long-term future of the publishing of reference books in the UK. Predicts little change in the near future and suggests that the influence of electronic publishing will not be overwhelming (3)

Eugene Psheehy (1984) in his article on a project of the reference departments of the Columbia University's Butler and Lehmman Libraries, observes that the purpose of this study was to provide a selection of recent scholarly and general works of interest to reference workers in university libraries. The list does not claim to be well balanced nor comprehensive. Categories include bibliography, archives, dictionaries, government publications, dissertations, biography, linguistics, literature, film studies, photography, folklore, sociology, political science, law and history. It also contains a brief account of new editions of standard works, continuations and supplements. (4)

Bakewell (1989) in his work 'Reference book for indexers' gives details of about 200 reference books which are of use to indexers. Listings include bibliographies, thesauri, press guide, dictionaries and encyclopedias, gazetteers, newspaper and periodical indexes. (5)

Nancy R. Johnson and others (1990) were challenged with the task of keeping the reference collections current and useful. So the reference staff at the Medical College of Wisconsin sought the opinions of their colleagues at other medical school libraries as to what they valued most in their reference collections. 39 libraries responded to the questionnaire, listing 213 titles as essential for every reference collection and 130 titles as gems or tools that may not be well known, but were personal favorites. There was consensus among the responding librarians for recommending many standard reference tools. However, there were also a variety of tools mentioned by only 1 librarian. The compiled lists offer medical school libraries some valuable suggestions for developing their reference collections. (6)

Mizoo Itabashi (1991) conducted a survey of reference books useful for Japanese pharmaceutical and medical librarians. Beilstein's Handbook of Organic Chemistry is known in Japan as the main work on organic chemistry. It is now available on-line. There are many published lists of Japanese reference books, including one for life sciences. Discusses dictionaries of medical and pharmaceutical terms, glossaries and chemical dictionaries. Considers the following specific works: Ikagaku Daijiten, Nanzando Ugaku Daijiten, Illustrated Steadman's Medical Dictionary, Eiwa Igaku Yogo Daijiten, Medical subject Headings, English – Japanese – English, ed, Yokogawa Yaj\ Kugaku Daojiten, Yakumei Kensaku Jiten, Seikagaku Jiten, Iwanami Joho Kagaku Jiten, Kagaku Gijutsu 35 Mango Daijiten, Nihongo Daijiten. It is important to scrutinize dictionaries and encyclopedias to assess ease of use. [7]

Cheng, Leun and Wu, (1993) conducted surveys on the publication of reference books in Taiwan between 1972 and 1988, as a continuation of Tze – chung Li's study in 1974. The number of reference books published in the period was 4,079; social science materials accounted for 38 percent and science / technology materials for 23 percent. Presents an annotated list of significant reference works issued from 1972 – 1987, categorized in five different subject areas: general works, social sciences, humanities, history and area studies, and science and technology; selection of entries was based on the materials most often used in libraries served by the authors. (8)

University of Calicut has brought out its Silver Jubilee publication, titled New Frontiers of Knowledge edited by Adiyodi (1993) in which efforts have been made to asses the knowledge generated by the University of Calicut during its 25 years existence. The knowledge output comprises 6026 publications and 474 in house doctoral theses.

A number of findings and conclusions were reached out of which a few of them are given below.

1. Faculty of language and literature with 2,175 titles tops the list in publication and faculty of science with 192 units is ahead of others in doctoral thesis production.

2. In the faculty of science, Zoology tops the list with 773 publications and 77 doctoral theses.

3. History and economics are the top players in knowledge generation in the faculty of Humanities. Psychology, Philosophy and LIS form the second position and Anthropology the third.

4. Publication showed a progressive increase in number from 1968 to 1992.

5. The most productive teachers and researchers in each faculty in university of Calicut from the point of view of knowledge generation have been identified.

6. A study of authorship pattern of publications showed that single authorship was the most common pattern in all faculties except sciences, engineering, Medicine and Dentistry all of which in a broad sense are experimental sciences relying on team work.

7. In the 25 year old University of Calicut more men (342) than women (132) have qualified themselves for Ph.D. The extent of gender disparity has been analysed in doctoral awards in different faculties and subjects. (9)

Philiph John (1994) in his PhD thesis investigates about the early scholarly publishing in Malayalam. The study spread light over the elements of which enabled the progress development, and history of scholarly writing in Malayalam. The study concentrates on prose writing through analyzing their languages. The author tries to give a definition to the scholarly literature and distinguishes it from the creative writings. The characteristics and the objectives of the scholarly publishing are given in the thesis. The investigator gives details of each of the books, which were published at early periods. He points out that majority of the early literature were translations from other languages. The study also discloses a variety of scholarly literature in Malayalam and gives a list of publications.(10)

In a study Ashok (1994) has made an effort to find out the trend of bibliographical activities in Malayalam. It contains a survey of the various bibliographies in Malayalam, brought out by different institutions and individuals over the years. The results show that less attention has been paid to the systematic organization of the information sources in Malayalam. None of the bibliographies was found to be comprehensive and up to date except Malayalam Grandhasoochi. Therefore the study suggests the need for preparing a current, Malayalam bibliography. (11)

Beena (1994) in her article, 'Book Publishing: A Bibliometric Approach', analyse the trends in the publishing of books in Malayalam from the beginning of printing to 1990. By giving the subject wise and year wise distribution of Malayalam books in science, social science and humanities, comparison is made between the book production in the library and non library fields. Identifies the major publishers of Malayalam books. The growth pattern of books over the years is also given. [12]

In the article entitled 'Malayalam Publishing Today' (1995), DC Kizhakkemuri tries to find out the reason, for the slow paced growth in Malayalam book industry. The article tries to give the history of books beginning from the introduction of printing in Malayalam. The role played by Sahitya Pravarthaka Co-operative Society (SPCS) in the publishing of Malayalam book is described. Major publishers in Malayalam books are discussed and the year wise growth of books is given. The author also discusses the effect of electronic media on the reading habit of public. [13]

Moosath (1997) in his article Vaijanika Sahityam, analyses the scholarly literature in Malayalam since its beginning. He analyses the books and their authors. It observes that most of the books printed are in mathematics, accounting and economics. The author also discusses the magazines that are devoted specially to popular science articles. The contributions of famous writers like C. Achutha Menon, O.M Cherian, M.Rajaraja Varma and Dr.K.Bhaskaran Nair are also discussed in this article. The author stresses the need for using Malayalam language as the official language so that the science can reach all the people. [14]

Dinesan (1997) conducted a bibliometric study of the publication of Kerala Sastra Sahitya Parishat during the year 1977-1997. The major objectives of the study were to assess the trends in book publication by KSSP, to assess the quantity of books published by KSSP and to find out the occupation or field of activity of the authors of books. It was found that the number of books published by KSSP is maximum during the period 1977-1979 (18.62%) and it was minimum during the period 1992-94 (7.16%). The maximum number of books belonged to general science and fiction (14.56%). It was also found that college teachers were the major contributors

(32.94%). The subject matters of the books published was related with the activities of the organization. The study suggested that an annotated bibliography of books published by KSSP had to be compiled as a means of bibliographic control of science literature. (15)

Moosad (1998) in another article tries to describe the attempts made in the publication of scholarly literature in Malayalam. The article stated that the book "Horthus Malabaricus' is not a Malayalam publication. The establishment of Book committee is discussed in the article. The author tries to deal with most of the famous writings of that time. He observed that the subject areas in which majority of the works were written are Mathematics and Geography. The author critically analyses each of the books. [(16)]

Damodaran (1998), portrays the contributions of P.T. Bhaskara Panicker to the scholarly literature in Malayalam. The article establishes that P.T. Bhaskara Panicker is the man behind the development of scholarly literary tradition in Malayalam. P.T. Bhaskara Panicker gave notable contributions in the establishment of Sasthra Sahitya Parishad, which is primarily meant for the popularization of science. The author points out that P.T. Bhaskara Panicker had given more than hundred books and several articles to the scholarly literature. P.T. Bhaskara Panicker's contributions are remarkable in the field of encyclopedia publishing. In the opinion of the author, the main feature of P.T.Bhaskara Panicker's works is the simplicity of language and the style of writing. The author makes an effort to summarize the lifetime contributions of P.T.Bhaskara Panicker in scholarly literature.[(17)]

In his article entitled 'Vijana Sahitham Malayalathil', Benjamin (1999) attempts a survey of the scholarly literature, and writers in Malayalam. The article begins with the description of works written in the early 20th century. The author investigates each type of publications like dictionaries, encyclopedias, books and periodicals. The contributions of institutions like Kerala Bhasha Institute, Sastra Sahitya Parishad, Kerala University and STEPS are also mentioned in this article. The prominent authors in the scholarly literature field like Kesari Balakrishna Pillai, Dr.K.Bhaskaran Nair etc., were also mentioned. The study points out the need for original works in Malayalam rather than going for translation. (18)

In the editorial entitled 'Vaijnanika Sahityam Valarchayude Pathayil', Thampan (1999) assess the growth of scholarly literature based on the publication of Kerala Bhasha Institute. He points out that the majority of books, which are sold out in the year 1998, were mainly scholarly publications. The most sold out book in 1998 was the 'Veda Shabtha Ratnakaram' by Dr.D.Babu Paul. The reference books such as dictionaries, general and subject glossaries etc. were in great demand. The author says that the prime objective of the Kerala Bhasha Institute is to extent the modern science and technology information to the people. (19)

Smitha (1999) conducted a bibliometric study of doctoral thesis of M.Tech and sponsored projects in Regional Engineering College (REC), Calicut. The study covered the doctoral thesis of faculty members working at REC in the year 1998, M.Tech project submitted by post graduate students during the year 1987-97 and the sponsored research works completed by the faculties during 1987-97. The objective of the study was to analyse the year-wise productivity and to find out the years, branch and subject field in which maximum research work was done. The findings showed an uneven distribution of doctoral thesis and M.Tech projects in all branches of Engineering. Male researchers were found dominating. Maximum research output of doctoral thesis was found to be in the year 1998 (10.61%) and that of M.Tech projects in the year

1995 (18.67%). Maximum research productivity in the form of sponsored projects was found to be in the year 1997 which was 27.65% among the 47 projects. [20]

SCIENCE LITERATURE

Prabhakaran (1999) in his article entitled Sastra Sahityam Malayalathil calls attention to the fact that, science literature publishing in Malayalam is not very old. According to the author this is because of the slow growth in the language, education and the telecommunication technologies. The article points out that it is the prime duty of the science writers to create awareness among the people about the right way of using modern science. The author deals with the early books, which were written, in Sanskrit language in subjects like Theology, Astrology, Architecture and Medicine. The author suggests that popular articles should be used as an effective tool for creating awareness among the public. [21]

Namboodri (1999) portrays the growth of science literature from the early periods of 19th century. It is stated that the first, science book written in Malayalam is 'Yogamritham' in 1861. The author analyses the early literature in Malayalam. Many early titles are listed in this article. It is observed that most of the early works were in subjects like Mathematics, Medicine, and Astronomy. The author critically analyses the activities of Kerala Bhasha Institute and its contribution to the scientific literature in Malayalam. The article also draws attention to the lack of original writings in Malayalam. [22]

LIBRARY SCIENCE LITERATURE

Musib (1986) conducted a study of the growth pattern of periodicals in Library and Information science. His study shows a continuous growth in the number of new periodicals for the last

150 years. This study shows that there are 1967 periodicals published from 78 countries. [23]

Majeed (1991) studied the growth of LIS literature in India during 1980's. This study was to identify the important contributors of LIS literature in India. The authorship pattern was also received. The study revealed that the distribution of the published literature among various fields of LIS was lesser. The quantitative and qualitative growth of literature in India during 1980's was found to be in a sluggish pace. [24]

Anand (1991) analyses literature published in professional journals in the field of Library and Information Science, both published and cited in the 'Journal of Documentation' from 1980 through 1989. Makes out various features of the journal such as institutional affiliation, collaborative authorship, sex-wise distribution, geographical location of the contribution, as well as leading contributors of the journal. It also describes the nature of contribution and research strategies adopted by different authors. The Journal of Documentation has been one of the most reputed journals in the field of librarianship. Majority of the contributors belonged to UK. More than 70 percent of the contributors have given tables, charts and appendices. More than 75% of the contributions that appeared in the journals were of applied nature. There was a heavy concentration on subjects grouped under information, management, processes techniques and tools. [25]

SOCIAL SCIENCE LITERATURE

Beena (1994) in her study 'Social Science Books in Malayalam: A Bibliometric Analysis' reveals the characteristics of social science books in Malayalam. An effort is made to identify the areas in social science disciplines in which there is need for publication of books. Using the various bibliometric variables the titles are analyzed. The extent of translations to Malayalam from other languages is also studied. Major publishers of social science books in Malayalam are also located. Findings of the study shows tremendous growth of publications in social science after the independence. The study throws light on the need for effective bibliographic control in the Malayalam books in general and social science books in particular. (26)

JOURNAL LITERATURE

Tahar (1989) attempted to develop a brief profile, to quantify the literature and to identify the list of core journals in the field of Islamic studies. He examined the level of degree of subject and geographical dispersion of journals in the field. He identified 24 core journals in this field. The important findings of the study were,

1. The inclination was towards Islamic studies 56%.
2. Non Muslim Countries produced 88.6% of journals relevant to the Islamic studies.
3. Bradford's law of scattering was found to be applicable in the field of Islamic studies. (27)

Jalaja (1995) conducted a bibliometric analysis of science journals published from India. The study was based on Indian Science Abstract and the objectives were to find out the core journals, authorship pattern, institutional affiliation and year-wise productivity. The study revealed that the joint authorship was dominant in old subject except in Engineering. Analysis of reference showed that most of the research works are being pursued in Universities and other higher educational institutions. Geographical analysis revealed that the contribution from abroad were more in applied science. The references existed in four forms- Journal articles, Patents, Standards and Thesis. Productivity of subject in general shows a trend of exponential increase. (28)

The review of literature shows that attempts towards publication of books and journals are increased. Some studies points out the need for proper bibliographic work in the field. It may be noted from the review of literature that a number of studies were carried out by different individuals, institutions and agencies. Most of them are focused on bibliometric studies on various subjects. However, it is noted that a study on the Malayalam reference books is yet to be made. The present study is an attempt to bridge the gap that exists.

BIBLIOMETRIC ANALYSIS

For bibliometric analysis each and every publications (reference books) was found out with the help of Malayalam Grandasoochi, Desiya Grandha Soochi and publisher's catalogue to collect the bibliographic details of Reference books. For assigning subject headings DDC scheme was used. The collected data were recorded in slips. The standard size catalogue cards (7.5 x 12.5) were used for recording data.

In each slip the Title of the book, authors name, editor, collaborator, name of translator, place of publication and year of publication are recorded. Then they were analysed under each variables.

The reference books show the development and progress of languages. The reference book is an important tool for scholars and students and its significance is very high in every day life of individual in the to academic field. The major purpose of the study was to analyse the "Reference books in Malayalam language published from the origin of printing of Malayalam books to 1995 by using bibliometric techniques. In order to provide the background of the study several reference sources were consulted to get an idea of the nature of the reference sources, year-wise distribution of reference sources, gender wise contributors of reference sources, publisher wise distribution, translation wise distribution, and source wise distribution.

DISTRIBUTION OF REFERENCE BOOKS

During the study period, 2963 reference books were published in Malayalam language. Biographical sources, Encyclopedias, Dictionaries, Bibliographies, Proverb, Quotations and Yearbook are the major reference books published in Malayalam language. Most of the reference books were mainly published in the area of Biographical sources (85.15%). This means that the literature contribution in the field of biographical sources become very rich and also reveals the cultural enlightenment of the Malayalam language through decades. But the representation of other sources was comparatively very less.

YEAR-WISE DISTRIBUTION OF REFERENCE BOOKS

The "Sentem Adigiya Malabarica" is the first reference book in Malayalam published from Rome in 1791. The decade 1981-1990 was the most productive period constituting 23.32 percent of the total books published. But the period witnessed continuous variations up to 1951-1960. From 1961-1990 there is a steady deviation in the production of reference books. So the year wise distribution of reference books was not in a balanced condition.

GEOGRAPHICAL DISTRIBUTION

The geographical distribution analysis was very important in this study. Thirteen probable geographical areas were identified. About 2963 reference books were published mainly in Kerala and out of states like New Delhi, Mangalapuram, Madras, Bombay, Madurai and Pune. In addition to this a number of books were published from different parts of the world viz, Rome, Moscow,

Singapore, Kuwait and other countries. Kerala State is the leading contributor of the reference books and New Delhi and Madras contributed highest number of books from outside Kerala.

DISTRICT-WISE DISTRIBUTION

The district wise analysis of the reference books in Malayalam language shows that Kottayam district stood first in the publishing of reference source during the study period. Trivandrum and Trissur districts occupied the second and third places respectively.

YEAR-WISE DISTRIBUTION OF BIOGRAPHICAL SOURCES

About 2523 biographical sources in Malayalam were published. The rate of production in each decade changed from source to source. It can be noted that the highest number of biographical sources were produced in the decade 1981-1990. During the study period till 1900, all biographical sources published were under the category of biography. As far as the decade is concerned, from 1901-1910, the contribution of biographical sources increased considerably. The period 1911-1920 enriched the area of autobiographies, biographies and letters. During the decade of 1971-1980, 1981-1990 and 1991-95, witnessed the comprehensive contribution of all the categories of biographical sources.

Biographical sources-source wise distribution:

Autobiography, biography, speeches and letters, are the biographical sources published in Malayalam language. The autobiography and biography are the leading biographical sources. The period 1981-1990 was the most productive period in the case of autobiographies, constituting 29.55 percent. Biographies are the leading item among the four - and it shared, major part among other sources. The decade 1981-1990 was the productive period in the case of autobiographies, constituting 29.55 percent. The decade 1981-1990 was the productive period in the case of biographies (20.57 percent). 1981-1990 was the most productive period of the speeches. The decades 1981-1990 and 1991-1995 were the most productive period of letters.

Gender wise contribution of Biographical sources:

The Gender wise distribution reveals that, males are the major contributing group in this regard. It means that males dominates in the publication of the biographies throughout the study period (it is 94.69 percent). Female contribution is comparatively very less, 5.31 percent throughout the study period. The most important factor is that, their representation is very less. But anyhow along with these limitations female contribution is valuable and significant.

YEAR-WISE DISTRIBUTION OF ENCYCLOPEDIA

It is very important to find out the year wise distribution of encyclopedia in Malayalam language. It can be noted that, the decade 1981-1990 was the most productive period that is 47.39 percent of the encyclopedia was published.

SUBJECT-WISE DISTRIBUTION OF ENCYCLOPEDIA

The general encyclopedia shared the major part of the publications. The encyclopedia on agriculture is comparatively very less. The other branches like encyclopedia of religion, literature, medical science, science, history and children literature etc, have more or less a good collection.

YEAR-WISE DISTRIBUTION OF BIBLIOGRAPHY

The decade 1971-1980 is the most productive period constituting 42.11 percent. The bibliographical sources were published from the year 1931 onwards. After the ten year period of 1941-1950 no bibliography were published. It also shows an alternative trend in the publications of bibliographical sources. 31.5 percent bibliography is published during 1981-1990.

SUBJECT-WISE DISTRIBUTION OF BIBLIOGRAPHY

For the purpose of the study, subject wise bibliographical sources were classified under the heads of general, journal, literature, religion and science. General bibliography is the major significant contributing area (47.36%). The bibliographical sources with regard to literature are the second important one (22.69%). This showed the vividness of the bibliographical sources in different areas of Malayalam language.

IMPORTANT CONTRIBUTORS OF BIBLIOGRAPHY

Sahitya Academy is the major leading contributor of bibliography in Malayalam language (34.21), The Department. of Education is the second leading contributor - about 18.42%. The publishers like Bhasha Institute, D.C.Books, K.S.S.P, CLS etc had published one bibliography each respectively.

YEAR-WISE PUBLICATION OF DICTIONARIES

245 dictionaries were published in Malayalam language. 25.70 percent of the dictionaries were published in the period 1981-1990. This means that, the decade 1981-1990 was the productive period of publishing of dictionaries. The period 1971-1980 was the second important decade in publishing dictionaries in Malayalam language (14.29%). There is continuous growth in publication of Malayalam dictionaries until 1990 except the decade 1951-1960, but after 1960, a sudden increase has witnessed.

YEAR-WISE DISTRIBUTION OF DIRECTORIES

The decade 1961-1970 was the most productive period. 1921-

1930 was the decade in which the first directory was published in Malayalam. For the next two decades, no directories were published. At present, the trend of directory publishing is not in a better position. So we can understand the fact that, the contribution of publication of directory was very less. This means that it is difficult to get information about Govt. institutions, current working status and programmes.

TRANSLATION FROM OTHER LANGUAGES

Majority of the translations were from English language (55.11%). In addition to this, various foreign languages such as Russian, French, German, Chinese, Latin, Italian and Arabic were also translated to Malayalam language. Along with these foreign languages, number of reference books were translated from oriental languages like Sanskrit, Hindi, Bengali, Urdu and vernacular language like Tamil.

PUBLISHERS-WISE DISTRIBUTION OF REFERENCE SOURCES

The Sahithya Pravarthaka Sahakarana Sangham is the leading publisher, and Kairali Childrens book trust is the second one. The D.C Books, P.K Brothers, Christian Literature Society, National book stall, Vidyarthimithram, Prabhat Publications and Current Books, Chintha publications and Malayala Manorama are the other major leading publishers followed by the SPCS. The state Institute of Education is the first among the government publishers. But it is not coming under the first ten leading publishers rank. The private institutions are found publishing majority of the reference books. The higher quality in design and content as well as the modern market management are the major reason behind their success.

PUBLISHER-WISE DISTRIBUTION OF ENCYCLOPEDIA

The Bala Sahithya Institute and Dept. of Encyclopedia are the major productive publishers of the encyclopedia. The Sahithya Pravarthak Sahakarana Sangham and the Kerala Sastra Sahithya Parishad respectively, are the other leading publishers of encyclopedia.

PUBLISHER-WISE DISTRIBUTION OF DICTIONARIES

There are 245 dictionaries published in Malayalam language. The Sahithya Pravarthaka Co-operative society (SPCS) have 13 dictionaries. Kerala Bhasha Institute is the second leading publisher of the dictionaries. Vidyarthi Mithram and Assisi are important publishers of dictionaries.

LANGUAGE-WISE ANALYSIS

About 245 dictionaries were published in Malayalam language including monolingual, bilingual and multilingual. About 40% are monolingual dictionaries 18.77% Sanskrit dictionaries were also published in the category of monolingual dictionaries. The English-Malayalam, Malayalam-English, Hindi-Malayalam, Malayalam-Hindi, Arabic-Malayalam, Sanskrit-Malayalam, Suriyani-Malayalam, Urdu-Malayalam, Russian-Malayalam, German-Malayalam, Latin-Malayalam, Kannada-Malayalam and Portuguese-Malayalam, etc are the bilingual dictionaries published (35.91%). 6.13 percent multilingual dictionaries were also published and representation was not satisfactory when compared with monolingual and bilingual dictionaries.

PUBLICATION OF GOVT./GOVT. SPONSORED INSTITUTIONS

The participation and contribution of govt. institutions in

the publication of references were comparatively not in a better position. Majority of the reference books in Malayalam were mainly by the gift of private publishers. This means the lack of interest of the government publishing companies with regard to reference sources. This situation is very unfortunate, so Government institution needs a new vision and mission. In addition to these, we need an initiation from governmental level on this issue. So a comprehensive policy and planning is necessary for the fulfillment of new projects along with sufficient financial aid.

The analysis of the study on the basis of hypothesis is significantly positive in the first hypothesis i.e., publication of reference books were increased year by year. This trend is progressive consecutively in the post-independence period. This also reveals the influence of development of Malayalam language after formation of the Kerala on the linguistic basis. The study also shows that majority of the reference sources were mainly published in the form of biographical sources. Among them autobiography and biography constituted the maximum.

There are number of books translated from many foreign languages. Among them, English is the prominent one. The hypotheses are significantly proved by the outcome of the study. The gender wise distribution of Biographical source reveals that males are the major contributing group, which means that the male dominance is higher in the publication of the biographies. This reveals that male dominance is significantly positive and supports the validity of the hypothesis. Publisher wise distribution of reference sources shows that, private companies are the leading publishers. The hypothesis, government participation is less, is significantly positive. This reveals the lack of initiative and interest of the Government publishing agencies in this area.

CONCLUSION

The reference books show the development and progress of language. The reference book is an important tool for scholars and students and its significance is very high in every day life. The major purpose of the study is to make quantitative analysis of the reference books in Malayalam language published from the origin of printing of Malayalam books to 1995. In order to provide the background of the study several reference sources were consulted to get an idea of the nature of the reference sources, year wise distribution of reference sources, gender wise contribution of reference sources, publisher wise distribution, translation wise distribution and source wise distribution.

The study highlights the strength and weakness of reference sources in Malayalam language. The year wise distribution of the reference sources was successful. But contribution is not in a poised condition. The biographies, autobiographies, dictionaries, directories and encyclopedia are the major reference sources. The biographical sources covered the major area. In encyclopedia we have rich collection. Dictionaries have occupied a prominent position. Female participation is very less in the publication of biographies. The role carried out by Government agencies in the publication of reference sources was less than that of private publishing companies. Any way our reference sources are valuable and rich, throughout the developmental stages of language. But more initiation in this direction is necessary.

SUGGESTION

The study also points out the following related areas for the further research

1. Comparative analysis of growth trends of Malayalam literature and reference sources.

2. Role of Christian missionary in the productivity of reference sources in Malayalam language.

3. Impact of state reorganisation on the growth of reference sources in Malayalam language.

REFERENCE

1. Kesavan, B.S History of printing and publishing in India: A story of cultural awakening, New Delhi, 1968.

2. Govi, K.M "Nammude Reference Sahityam", Kottayam, NBS, 1992.

3. Devarajan.*G, Ed*. Bibliometric studies: New Delhi, Ess Ess publication, 1997

7

INFORMATION NEEDS AND USE PATTERN OF COLLEGE TEACHERS

Vasudevan Namboori K.R.

INTRODUCTION

Libraries have a long history starting from those of ancient Alexandria and the Christian theological libraries in the medieval period and the university libraries in Oxford and Cambridge. The role of libraries in the academic field is an accepted fact all over the world. The following statement shows the importance of the library in the higher education field. It is worthy to start with an often quoted statement by the University Grants Committee of United Kingdom in its report of 1921.

"The character and efficiency of a university may be gauged by its treatment of its central organ – the library. We regard the fullest provision for library maintenance as the primary and most vital need in the equipment of a university"[1].

The importance of libraries had been recognized even by the colonial masters of British Empire. The starting of universities and the establishment of public libraries in important cities in India like Calcutta, Bombay and Madras are not worthy in this context. R.K.Narayanan has expressed the aesthetic and educational importance of libraries in a poetic language:

"The faint aroma of gum and calico that hangs about a library is as the fragrance of incense to me. I think the most beautiful sight is the gilt-edged backs of a row of books on a shelf. The alley between two well-stocked shelves in a hall fills me with the same delight as passing through a silent avenue of trees. The colour of a binding-cloth and its smooth texture gives me the same pleasure as touching a flower on its stalk. A good library hall has an atmosphere which elates. I have seen one or two University Libraries that have the same atmosphere as a chapel, with large windows, great trees outside, and glass door sliding on noiseless hinges"[2].

Information is a vital resource in all educational activities. College teachers are supposed to be involved in teaching, research and publication activities. Information needs of college teachers have certain special features because their approach to information is different from others.

INFORMATION NEEDS OF COLLEGE TEACHERS

Information needs of college teachers are typically different from other professional groups due to several reasons. They are:

College teachers are working in an environment different from other types of teachers (eg. University teachers, school teachers and elementary level teachers). College is a place where grown up students carry on their education. The students in this level are in a transition stage from complete dependence to full freedom in academic life. Students were under the strict control of teachers up to the intermediate level in academic and social activities. In the intermediate level, students had special training in the special subjects as well as languages in an average level. Such training will be helpful to make the students aware of the taste and interest inherent in their mind. So when students come to the degree level, they have already taken a decision about their field of study. At this stage comprehensive as well as deep study in the chosen subjects are expected. So subject specialization seriously starts from the undergraduate level. Here the role of the teacher is that of a subject specialist. But due to the plurality of subjects at the degree level, as well as lack of orientation in the subject field, even without a specific request from the part of the students the teacher has to co-ordinate different components of the educational systems and introduce them before the students. The different components like class room lecture, field work, laboratory, library and other external media must be introduced before the student. It is especially relevant in the context of India, because our school system is comparatively lacking in basic facilities like library services, laboratory facility and social interaction. So the teacher has to take special interest to make them aware of the different components of the educational system and the benefits of each of the component for independent learning.

Another important aspect of this problem is that the spirit of learning is to be imparted among the students. Learning is a process that needs a sense of goal and achievement. The teacher has to initiate the spirit of independent learning in the minds of the student for a socially relevant subject. Here the teacher should be a guide, friend as well as philosopher for the students. The basic purpose behind all these initiatives from the part of the teacher is to make the student a socially adaptive person with a large heart as well as developed head.

The college teacher is expected to be a subject specialist, leader of the students in extra curricular activities, guide in research oriented projects, a source of inspiration, personal guide and a respected friend and evaluator for the student community. The complex nature of the role of the teacher is clear from the above description. The teacher is supposed to be constantly updating himself for fulfilling these diverse duties assigned to him. So he needs timely and exhaustive information service in different subjects fields related to him.

These information needs can be summarized as follows:

INFORMATION NEEDS RELATED TO TEACHING

Most important duty of a college teacher is classroom teaching. The teacher needs timely and continuous information services related to teaching. The information needs of teaching can be summarized as:

Subject information:

The latest developments in the subject field should be available to the teacher in order to make him competent and effective in timely updation of the topic. All the relevant data, information and knowledge must be available to the teacher in time.

This kind of information service regarding the subject field includes primary, secondary, and tertiary sources. Primary sources are current periodicals; Government documents, reports of seminars and symposia etc. Secondary sources are indexing journals, abstracting journals, monographs, bibliographies, encyclopaedia, dictionaries, and textbooks. Tertiary sources are directories, bibliography of bibliographies, treatise and pathfinders etc. A teacher requires all these types of information in order to update himself in the relevant subject/subjects. The physical media of information may be either print or digital and the sources of information can also differ from situation to situation.

The teacher is supposed to do three kinds of activities related to curriculum. They are: (1) Current knowledge about the curriculum, (2) Updating of the curriculum & revision of curriculum. (3) Make the evaluation of the students proper and scientific.

The teacher has to adopt all the channels to update himself for these purposes.

INFORMATION NEEDS OF THE TEACHER FOR RESEARCH PURPOSE

Research is the second most important activity that a college teacher is supposed to undertake. Research is an outcome of original thinking and study related to a particular micro subject or topic. There are different types of research activity.

INFORMATION NEEDS OF COLLEGE TEACHERS FOR VALUE-BASED EDUCATION

Values are as important as subject knowledge in the education process. The character and ethics of the teacher is important in this respect. The teacher is not a mere subject expert but must be a source of inspiration. The teacher should be able to instill noble values to the next generation through teaching as well as action. A good teacher and a bad character is not at all compatible to each other. So the teacher is expected to be a good citizen himself and must be able to inspire others in that line. A teacher without reading cannot be a good teacher. There are two ways of inspiration; inspiration through interpersonal relations and inspiration through reading of good books. In the Indian tradition, 'sat sang' (the company of the noble persons and reading of good books), comprises of the two noble paths for right education. There is a spiritual and social dimension in this mission. The eternal values of human civilization cannot be challenged out of mere fancy. The age old civilization of human beings has evolved out of much filtration and experimentation. So the importance of reading is very much part of the civilization itself. Education and reading are some what synonyms in the eastern and western tradition. So there is no need to emphasis the importance of reading in the college level. The real significance of a proper library services is a prerequisite for any education process. All the education commissions in the post independence India have emphasized the need for proper library facility. They include the university education commission (Dr.S.Radhakrishnan, 1957), the Education commission

(Dr.D.S.Kothari, 1964), the committee on national policy on library and information science (D.P.Chattoopadhaya, 1986), the UGC committee (Prof.R.C.Mehrotra, 1987.) can be considered in college environment. The teacher can do independent research in a particular topic. He can also lead group research either as a teamwork of teachers or as a guide in the research projects assigned to the students. Research always may not lead to an award of a degree and all research activities cannot expecting any immediate practical application. One of the important aspects of research in the college environment is the creation of scientific attitude among the students. There are different types of researches like solo research, team research, relay research etc. The teacher must be competent enough to lead the students in research activities. For this purpose he must have thorough in research methodology as well as subject knowledge. An effective information service is a pre-requisite for this. As we mentioned earlier all the primary, secondary and tertiary sources of information should be accessible to the teacher so as to lead research endeavour in the college environment.

INFORMATION NEEDS OF COLLEGE TEACHERS FOR CO-CURRICULAR ACTIVITIES

The importance of co-curricular activities cannot be underscored at the college level. The real intention of the educational process itself is the evolution of complete personality already inherent in the child. As Swami Vivekananda said "Education is the manifestation of divinity inherent in the student". For this purpose mere classroom study is not sufficient. The student must be exposed to the real situation encountered in human life and make him able to respond in the right manner. Socially oriented activities must be included in all the degree programmes. There are different social organizations working in the colleges of Kerala like National Service Scheme(NSS), Junior Red Cross, Career Guidance Cell, Blood Donation Forum, Planning Forum, Readers Forum, etc. The teachers are supposed to give effective leadership in all these activities.

The teacher should have the practical knowledge and genuine interest in social activities in order to make the programmes successful. The teacher should be well informed about the aims and objectives of each of the programme. Proper reading and information service is a must for all these activities.

A good collection of classics and moral and ethical works including religious scriptures is an important component in all educational centres. The works on modern philosophical movements also is to be made available in the college library collection. The information value of epics or scriptures or other classics cannot be measured by mere mechanical devices. The role of the library is very much direct and crucial in value education. 'The sphere of wisdom' is above the level of knowledge and so our ultimate aim is 'that wisdom' in all educational programmes. The teacher must be a voracious reader, so as to become an inspiring personality.

TITLE OF THE STUDY

The title of the study is information needs and information use pattern of college teachers in kerala: A study

DEFINITION OF KEY TERMS

INFORMATION NEEDS

Information means data or information, knowledge related to any thing either subjective or objective. It may be described as the conscious or unconscious efforts from the part of a person or a group of persons to know or to get a data, knowledge or wisdom for that person or group of persons for any purpose. The information need may not be always perceived by the conscious mind. Basically it is a search for new things or ideas, at least to the persons who find it out as a new addition to his conscious mind.

INFORMATION USE PATTERN

Use pattern means the style of using. The style may be different for different persons. The use pattern includes concepts like style of searching for information, source of searching information, preference of materials, interaction with the information system etc.

COLLEGE TEACHERS

The teaching community of arts and science colleges all over Kerala.

KERALA

The state of Kerala in the Republic of India, one of the south Indian states where high literacy as well as population density prevails.

STUDY

Study means examining all the details of a problem or situation, in order to find out what happened or what is happening.

HYPOTHESES

The following hypotheses have been formulated for the study.

HYPOTHESIS I

The information use pattern of college teacher has definite relation to the characteristics of college teachers.

HYPOTHESIS II

The information infrastructure and services provided in the college libraries are inadequate to satisfy the information needs of college teachers in Kerala.

HYPOTHESIS III

There is a positive correlation between the information use and productivity of college teachers.

HYPOTHESIS IV

The information technology has only a limited impact on the information use and information use pattern of college teachers in Keraia.

HYPOTHESIS V

There is a section of college teachers who contributes substantially at national and international level in terms of literature output.

OBJECTIVES

With the hypotheses spelt out, the investigator is now in a position to define the objectives of the study. The following objectives have been set out for the study.

i. To determine the characteristics of college teachers, (status, qualification, experience, field of specialization, nature of work, activities and achievement etc)

ii. To determine the information needs of college teachers in Kerala.

iii. To examine the information use pattern of college teachers. (nature and type of information required, motives of using information; purpose of using information, sources of information used, time spent in information gathering; use of computer network; use of library)

iv. To asses the productivity of college teachers in terms of publications.

RELEVANCE OF THE STUDY

User survey is a systematic collection of data concerning information use, preference of sources, depth of use, method of use, intention of use, satisfaction of use at a given time or over a given period. Compared to other methods, the user survey is found more suitable for collection of data regarding what all materials and services are expected by the clientele of the library and how far they are satisfied by them.

User studies refer to "Any systematic examination of the users (and, if possible of non-users) of services and systems" (Bawden, 1990). Satisfaction of the user needs is the ultimate objective of the services and systems[3].

User studies focus on information needs of users and use of information covering a wide range of information sources and channels. It is systematic study on information requirements of users so as to enable a meaningful transfer of information between users and information system. For a need – based information service, user studies form a pre-condition[4].

The user group under consideration in this study consists of the college teachers of Kerala, working in different affiliated colleges in Kerala, both Government and Private.

The study will be helpful to identify the information needs and mode of interaction of college teachers with the college library systems. The result of the study shall be helpful to identify the problems related to academic back up services of college libraries. The study will also assess the publication output of college teachers. This shall be the first study of its kind investigating information needs and use pattern of college teachers in Kerala.

The findings of the survey may be considered as a means for future developments in the field of college education in Kerala. It may help in laying down a policy for the development of college libraries, in Kerala state. The findings may also help in developing a programme of action for the development of college library and information systems in Kerala.

METHODOLOGY

The problem for the study, and different assumptions to be

tested in the study merged out of the personal firsthand experience with the field under study. His long and varied experience as a college librarian provided him a total perspective of the area, and the problem inherent there in this was supplemented by constant surveys of the important empirical investigations reported in journals and specialized publications. The review of the area with which he started, enabled him to point out some of the major dimensions of the problem which needs a more detailed discussions with the college teachers and experienced librarians to make the study with greater precision. A thorough examination of the available college library records, statistics and rules framed for the functioning of the library helped him to finalise the study.

Methodology of the study has been discussed under the following four heads.

1. Data Sources
2. Sampling
3. Statistical procedures
4. Method of analysis

1. Data sources

A close examination of the objectives of the study enabled the investigator to fix the data sources. The following are the sources of data as used in the study:

I. Questionnaires administered to representative group of teachers of a representative set of colleges.

II. Relevant records, statistics, rules and regulations and registers relating to libraries available in the offices of different official bodies controlling the working of college libraries such as, Directorate of Collegiate education, Trivandrum. Records in the colleges under study and authentic literature on the subject of study.

III. Personal observation by the investigator of the organization, administrative practices, functions, facilities and resources of the college libraries and the degree of utilizations of libraries by teachers of the colleges under study.

The details of the sources used for this study are presented below:

1. Questionnaire to the college teachers.

Name of the investigator and address, has been given in the questionnaire for communication purpose. This questionnaire consists of four sections. The first section is general which has ten questions relating to the bio data. Name of the teacher, name of the college, designation, and other bio data including experience in teaching, academic qualifications, and field of specialization, present topic of research or teaching etc have been included in this section. The next section has 28 questions related to various aspects of information use and use pattern.

This section deals with preference of sources of information, dependence on different collections including personal collection for gathering information and knowledge, style of information seeking, journals used, personal satisfaction of information users, problems or short comings in the present information system, categories of reading materials preferred, reading habit, number of periodicals subscribed, newspapers subscribed, number of books borrowed from the library, adequacy of library collection in the college library, help or assistance from the library staff, physical form of catalogue preferred, need for translation, frequency of visit in the library, awareness about new arrivals, photocopy facility, satisfaction about the services of the library, survey on home library etc have been included in this section.

Third section has only 2 questions. They are related to details of publication activities of individual respondents.

The fourth section is about the digital sources and availability of digital sources in the college library as well as at residence. This section also contains a question about the individual preference about the type of source (ie digital versus print media). The last question invites suggestions of the respondent regarding the improvement of college library.

2. Sampling

A sample of twelve colleges three from Calicut University and eight from Mahatma Gandhi University and one college from Kerala University has been selected. The details of these colleges are given in table 1.

Table 1.1: List of the colleges taken as sample.

Sl.No.	*Name of the college*	*Location*	*Urban/Rural*
1	St.Thomas College	Thrissur	Urban
2	St.Mary's College	Thrissur	Urban
3	St.Theresas College	Ernakulam	Urban
4	University College	Thiruvananthapuram	Urban
5	Nirmala College	Muvattupuzha	Rural
6	Newman College	Thodupuzha	Rural
7	St.Xavier's College	Vaikkom	Rural
8	Henry Backen College	Melukavu	Rural
9	B.P.S.College	Piravom	Rural
10	S.S.V College	Perumbavoor	Rural
11	Carmel College	Mala	Rural
12	D.B. College	Thalayolaparambu	Rural

Besides this, random samples of college teachers from different colleges have been included for the study and it will give an overall picture of the information needs and use pattern of college teachers.

III RECORDS AND LITERATURE RELATING TO COLLEGE LIBRARIES

A large number of records relating to college libraries available in the offices of the colleges under study, University of Kerala. Director of collegiate education, Trivandrum have been examined. The records include book circulation statistics, accession register periodical stock register, book issue Register library rules etc. A thorugh study of the articles published on the topic of investigation and related areas in standard journals (both Indian and foreign), and proceedings of conferences and seminars on the subject of study was made. The specific reading materials referred to are indicated at the appropriate places in the report and a bibliography is given towards the end of the report.

IX FIELD OBSERVATION

The investigator visited 6 of the colleges under study and spent hours for personal observation of library functioning and users interaction with the system and facilities and utilization of libraries by the college teachers. These visits also provided opportunities for discussions with the librarians, teachers, principals on college library situations and services.

STATISTICAL PROCEDURES

Correspondence analysis

One of the goals of correspondence analysis is to describe the relationships between two nominal variables in a correspondence table in a low-dimensional space, while simultaneously describing the relationships between the categories for each variable. For each variable, the distances between category points in a plot reflect the relationships between the categories with similar categories plotted close to each other. Projecting points for one variable on the vector from the origin to a category point for the other variable describe the relationship between the variables.

An analysis of contingency tables often includes examining row and column profiles and testing for independence via the chi-square statistics. However, the number of profiles can be quite large, and the chi-square test does not reveal the dependence structure. The Cross tabs procedure offers several measures of association and tests of association but cannot graphically represent any relationships between the variables.

THE METHODS OF ANALYSIS

The data collected through various sources explained above were entered in the computer with all details. Later, the information related to the organization of college libraries, adequacy of library resources and facilities and use of the libraries by teachers were consolidated, in such a way that they could be easily used for computation or other qualitatives, were analysed to throw light on the objectives of the study. In the case of quantitative data, suitable tables, figures etc were developed to facilitate their interpretation. In other cases qualitative interpretations were resorted.

LIMITATION OF THE STUDY

The study shall be confined to college teachers working in arts and science colleges of Kerala. All professional and Fine Arts colleges have been excluded from the purview of the study. Due to lack of time and other resources the study has been limited to selected twelve colleges from Calicut, Mahatma Gandhi and Kerala Universities.

User survey with the help of questionnaire was conducted only among the users available in the college during a few months forming part of calendar year 2002. Interview method was applied to a random sample from among the academic community. Interview method was also applied to a random sample of college librarians and college teachers.

ORGANISATION OF THE DISSERTATION

The dissertation is organised and presented as follows.

Chapter I: Introduction

In this chapter the problem is introduced. The objectives, hypotheses, significance of the study etc are given.

Chapter II: User Studies and college teachers: A review of literature

Gives an overview of the college education system in India, and describes the various user studies in academic libraries carried out so far that are relevant to the present investigation.

Chapter 3: Background of the study:

College education in India and Kerala and the role of library and information services to the college teachers.

Describes history and development of the higher education in India especially at the college level. The genesis and development of higher education system in India are outlined. The present state of college libraries in relation to their information infrastructure and current needs of college teachers are discussed in detail.

Chapter 4: Information requirements and use pattern: An analysis

In this chapter the data collected through questionnaire, interview and observation methods are analysed and interpreted.

Chapter 5: Summary of findings and conclusions

In this chapter the important findings and conclusions are narrated.

APPENDICES

a) List of colleges in the sample

b) Format of the questionnaire used

c) Interview schedule to the college teachers.

d) Interview schedule to the college librarians

FINDINGS AND CONCLUSION

The main purpose of the study was to find out the information requirements as well as information use pattern of the college teachers in Kerala state and the efficiency of the library system prevailing in the state. To carry out the study, the following objectives were formulated.

1. To determine the characteristics of college teachers, (status, qualification, experience, field of specialization, nature of work, activities and achievement etc)
2. To determine the information needs of college teachers in Kerala.
3. To examine the information use pattern of college teachers. (nature and type of information required, motives of using information; purpose of using information, sources of information used, time spent in information gathering; use of computer network; use of library)
4. To examine relationship between information use pattern and characteristics of college teachers.
5. To examine the capability of college library systems to cater to the information needs of college teachers.
6. To asses the productivity of college teachers in terms of publications.

With a view to frame the work and methodology for the

study, the review of literature on user studies and academic libraries was made.

As the study focuses on the teachers of the affiliated colleges in Kerala State, it was felt that the details of the education system in India as well as Kerala, highlighting the historical background, evolution of colleges and universities in India and the development of academic libraries particularly of college libraries are necessary for the study. Therefore a detailed analysis of these factors are given from available sources.

With this background information, user surveys were conducted using questionnaire and interview methods. The observation method was also adopted for the investigation. An analysis of the data collected through the combination of techniques is given.

MAJOR FINDINGS

The major findings from the analysis are summarized below.

1. Teachers give more value to personal interaction for information seeking. The majority of teachers selected the personal interaction as the first source of information while only a minority of teachers selected the documentary as the first preferred source of information.

2. Teachers generally prefer the subject experts for information and its availability. The study revealed that majority of teachers selected subject experts as the first preferred facilitators of information while a minority selected the librarians or the library staff as the facilitators of information.

3. The library system is comparatively inadequate to fulfill the information needs of teachers. The study revealed that 47.08 percentages of teachers are of the opinion that the library system is incapable to cater to the information needs of teachers while 41.7 percentages of teachers considered the library

system as capable to cater to the information needs of teachers.

4. Teachers generally prefer outside librarians rather than college librarians for expert guidance.

5. Digital source of information has only a limited impact on academic community. From the analysis of the questionnaire, it is found that only 1.77 percentage of teachers selected the internet as the first preferred source of information while CD-Rom has been selected by only 0.44 percentage of teachers. The analysis shows that internet services have been selected by 7.55 percentage of teachers as a source of information while CD-Rom has been selected by 4 percentage of teachers. The analysis shows that the digital media has only a limited impact on the academic community. Most of the preferences given by the respondents as per the analysis are second, third and fourth preference for internet and only 4 teachers indicated internet as the first preferred source. The CD-Rom databases come in the bottom of preferred sources as very few people selected it as a preferred source of information.

6. The information flow of college teachers are mainly confirmed to intra institutional level rather than state or national level.

7. Abstracting journals are preferred to indexing journals.

8. Library catalogue as well as publishers and book seller's catalogue are given equal importance by the college teachers.

9. It is revealed from the survey that most of the teachers adopt self effort as the mode of searching for information.

10. The analysis of the data revealed that the majority of teachers considered the library resources inadequate to their information needs. The majority of respondents (63.55%) reported it as the major difficulty encountered by them in their information related activities.

11. The majority of teachers participated in the survey reported

that they depended mostly on books for gathering information. 85 percentage of teachers considered that books were the reading material that they used to a great extent for their teaching-learning process.

12. Periodicals are the second most used reading material by the teachers. There were 89 teachers (41.9%) who reported that they used journals as the reading materials to a great extent.

13. The survey indicated that internet is an accepted source of information by a minority. Only 20 percentage of respondents who considered the 'Internet' as a reading source that they depend to a great extent.

14. CD-Rom is not at all popular as an information source among the college teachers. Only 4.4 percentages of teachers reported it as a study source that they used generally.

15. The majority of the teachers as per the survey are satisfied with the learning facilities available for teaching purpose in the college library. 66.66 percentage of teachers reported that the information services offered for teaching purpose by the college library was satisfactory.

16. The majority of the teachers participated in the survey are of the opinion that the facilities available for research activities in the college library is not satisfactory, 56 percentage of teachers reported that they are not satisfied with services provided by the library for research activities.

17. The analysis of the data indicated that most of the teachers considered the text book as the most important instruction tool, 72.88 percentage of teachers considered the text book as the most important material for instructional purpose.

18. The investigation indicated that reference works are the second most preferred document for instructional purpose. 18 teachers

(8%) selected the reference works as the first preferred source of material for instructional purpose while 95 teachers (42%) considered it as second only to text books and 38 teachers (16.8%) as third preferred source for instructional purpose.

19. Internet has been selected as source of information for instructional purpose by a small percentage of respondents, 1.33 percentage of teachers selected it as a first preferred source for teaching purpose.

20. Journals are considered as a reading material of low priority for teaching purpose, 3.11 percentage of teachers selected it as a first preferred material for teaching purpose.

21. The analysis of the data proved that an overwhelming majority of the teachers are in favour of library orientation programmes for college teachers. 82.06 percentages of teachers favoured library orientation programmes.

22. The analysis of the data revealed that majority of the respondents are utilizing the assistance of the librarian or library staff for various information related activities like locating the book (75%) searching the catalogue (55%), getting the current periodicals (60%) and to get information from the reference works (44%).

23. The majority of the teachers (53.33%) reported that they are not getting any assistance from the librarian or the library staff for research activities.

24. The analysis of the data revealed that On-line Public Access catalogue (OPAC) is the most favoured physical form of catalogue among the college teachers, 37.33 percentages of teachers favoured the OPAC while 35.55 percentage of teachers were in favour of card catalogue, and 19.55 percentages of teachers were in favour of book catalogue in the college library.

25. The analysis of the data indicated that majority of the teachers are in need of translation service from national and international languages for their academic activities, 51.55 percentage of teachers felt the need for translation in their information gathering process.

26. The analysis of the data revealed that the college teachers generally visit the library reasonably. The majority of teachers visit the library every day as per the analysis (64.88%), 17 percentage of teachers reported that they visit the library 'at least once a day'. A minority of teachers stated that they visit the library at least once a week, 9.33 percentage of teachers reported that they visit the library 'occasionally'.

27. The survey indicated that the overwhelming majority of teachers were aware of the new arrivals in the college library, 67.55 percentage of teachers reported that they were informed of the new arrivals in the college library. Among them 56.57 percentage of teachers were getting the information through the display of books and journals, 28.28 percentage of teachers were getting the information through the library staff, 15.13 percentage of teachers were getting the information about the new arrivals through their colleagues.

28. The analysis of the data revealed that most of the teachers are not satisfied with the book collection available in the college library, 60 percentage of teachers reported that they were not satisfied with the collection of books available in the college libraries.

29. The analysis of the data revealed that college teachers generally appreciated the dealings of the library staff, 82 percentage of teachers thought that the dealings of the library staff is satisfactory to them.

30. The availability of ample space in the reading hall was investigated in the survey. A good number of teachers (38.66%)

reported that the space available for reading hall was inadequate while 34.6% of teachers are of the opinion that the space available for reading hall was adequate.

31. The investigation made it clear that teachers are generally satisfied with the number of books issued to them in college libraries, 76.8 percentages of teachers expressed their satisfaction over the number of books issued in the college libraries.

32. The investigation made it clear that the college teachers are satisfied with the period of loan fixed by the library for books, 80 percentages of teachers were satisfied about the period of loan allowed for home lending to the teachers.

33. The investigation made it clear that teachers are not satisfied with the periodicals available in the college library, 62 percentage of teachers were of the opinion that the periodicals subscribed in the college library were inadequate for their information needs.

34. The analysis indicated that majority of teachers are computer literate, 66.22 percentage of teachers reported that they are computer literate.

35. The investigation indicated that majority of teachers are not having computer facility at their residence, 66.22 percentage of teachers reported that they were not having computer facility at their residence while 32 percentage of teachers reported as having computer facility at their residence.

36. The analysis of the data indicated that only 23.5 percentages of teachers were having internet facility at their residence, while 71.11 percentage of teachers reported that they were not having Internet facility at their residence.

37. The study indicated that 68 percentage of teachers are having a home collection of books varying from 100 to 7200.

38. The analysis indicated that there is a minority among the teachers who are actively involved in research and publication activities.

39. The investigation indicated that the percentage of teachers among the productive group having publications in international journals is about 40.38.

40. There is a minority of teachers who are highly active in their publication activities. The analysis shows that 27% respondents contribute to 60.73% of papers published in the journals at national level. The majority of the papers published in the journals at international level (67%) are contributed by 11% of respondents. This proved that a small percentage of teachers are highly productive in terms of number of papers published at international level.

41. The analysis of the data indicated that majority of teachers (66.22%) were having functional knowledge of information technology.

42. The study shows that only a tiny minority of respondents (3.11%) were having a personal collection of books more than 1000.

43. The study revealed that the largest number of papers (19%) were published by the teachers in the faculty of chemistry, the second place goes to zoology (16.74%) and the third place goes to physics (14.97%) in terms of papers published in national and international journals.

44. The study revealed that the majority of papers (64.75%) are published by science teachers in national and international journals.

45. The study indicated that the respondents from humanities (18.49%) occupy the second place in number of publications.

46. The study revealed that the social science had been placed

in the third rank with 16.91% of total published papers.

47. The study indicated that the male teachers contributed the vast majority of papers (73.2%) in national and international journals while the female teachers contributed 26.89% of the total.

48. The study indicated that the lion share of papers are published by Ph.D holders (74.44%) while M.Phil holders contributed 15.85% of the total papers. The P.G holders contributed 9.69% of total literature.

49. The study indicated that substantial contributions of papers in journals at the international level (90.62%) have been made by the Ph.D holders while the M.Phil and P.G holders shared an equal percentage of productivity (4.68%).

POLICY SUGGESTIONS

Based on the results of the study, the investigator formulated a perspective development plan for the college libraries in Kerala. The problems are identified and remedial measures are suggested wherever possible as follows:

1. Lack of coordination between individual colleges and universities as well as colleges and directorate of collegiate education on matters related to book selection, staff training and resource sharing.

The department of higher education may set up a standing committee to draw the broad policy formulations on matters related to college libraries with due representation from academicians, university officials, librarians and educational administrators.

2. Unscientific staff pattern of college libraries. The trained staff in the college libraries is not adequate. The gradation system itself is unscientific as well as outdated. There is only fully qualified person in the college library. But there

is no qualified person in many of the college libraries. The Semi-professionals are acting as librarians in many of the colleges.

The existing staff pattern of college libraries may be refined on the basis of the recommendations of 'Expert Committee on College Libraries'.

3. Individual teachers in many of the colleges are doing book selection without proper deliberation. There is no consultation about the position of existing collection, the area where the collection is weak or outdated. So an unbalanced collection is created in the college libraries in the long run. The textbooks are given overdue emphasis which makes the collection to be outdated within a short period. There is no periodical updating of reference collection. Reference books are not at all considered in many colleges for a long period. The utilization of U.G.C funds are also being done in haste and without proper consultation. The lack of time for acquisition of documents due to the short period available for utilization of funds is one of the reasons. The practice of the distribution of funds to individual departments with out any consultation with the librarian makes the process unscientific. The outdated norms insisted on by the Government for the purchase of books is another reason. There is no clarity regarding the purchase of non book materials like CDs and audiovisual cassettes from the part of U.G.C This leads to the total neglect-book materials.

The U.G.C should revise its guidelines regarding the utilization of funds for books and journals with special reference to sharing of resources for each type of materials like textbooks, reference books, non-book materials and journals.

4. The reference service is not carried out in most of the college libraries due to several reasons. They are

a) The shortage of current documents in reference section for this purpose.

b) The lack of trained staff for this purpose

c) The lack of awareness among the users.

Training programmes may be organised for the semi professionals to enable them to become competent for information services. Special grants for reference collection may be allotted to the colleges. There should be enough emphasis on the utilization of library and information facilities and there should be classes on bibliographic instruction and user education for the teachers in orientation and refresher programmes conducted for the teachers by academic staff colleges.

5. The furnishing of reading as well as the reference section is not considered in most of the college libraries. The inconvenience in seating arrangement and lack of reading facility makes the library unattractive to the users. Many of the college libraries also lack enough light and fans in the reading hall.

A percentage of U.G.C fund allocation may be specifically given for modernization of libraries. Individual colleges may be encouraged to mobilize private funds for this purpose.

6. Many students consider libraries as a place for discussion, combined study and reading for private. This unhealthy trend creates problems of indiscipline as well as loss of books.

Students study centers may be opened out side the library to facilitate combined study and reading of private books.

7. Library fee is not revised from time to time to compensate for the rising expenses the costs of books and journals have increased three fold while the increase in fee is negligible.

The library fee may be revised with context of the current level of inflation.

8. Lack of proper relation between the class room and the library. The college system still continues to be teacher centred and class room oriented. Other learning process ends up in the classroom with a lecture. Students are not properly motivated and guided to have advanced and independent reading.

The class room lecture may be adjusted with reasonable time gap for self study and library reference.

9. Lack of library orientation among the teachers as well as students is a major problem. The lack of awareness about the bibliographic tools as well as source of information is an obstacle in the use of library resources.

Library orientation programme for college teachers may be made compulsory. Another suggestion is inclusion of library orientation lectures on orientation programmes.

10. The system of department libraries in colleges is a major obstacle in the proper utilization of library facilities. The department libraries are generally monopolized by the teachers and there are no proper system for the circulation of books or reference facility. The lack of knowledge in library science by the library assistants and the lack of awareness among the teachers about the library norms make the problems more complex.

Department library should be centralized and act as a part of the general library.

11. Lack of modern communication facilities like telephone, computers and other gadgets make access to the library difficult.

Modern facilities like telephone and computers should be provided to the college libraries.

12. Many college libraries have not classified or catalogued their collection and so it is difficult to retrieve the required documents.

The technical process like classification and cataloguing can be carried out with the help of interested students with a reasonable remuneration, wherever huge collection is remaining unclassified and catalogued.

13. The negligence of the library authority regarding the proper functioning of the library.

The importance of library services may be demonstrated by the librarians through the active services and at the same time the role of the libraries in learning process may be popularized by the professionals through social contacts.

Library orientation classes may be made compulsory for all students up to under graduation.

14. The concept of libraries as the centers of recreational reading only and no information value is given to the libraries due to the lack of proper library consciousness.

The information value of libraries has to be demonstrated with the help of current awareness service as well as reference service.

15. Many of the top officials in the education department have been trained in the present system which gives very little attention to self learning or reading and so they are reluctant to accept the value of libraries in education.

The library associations and other professional teachers associations should take the initiative to make campaign for the promotion of reading and self learning.

16. The reluctance of the establishment to consider the librarian as an academician and so the resultant problem of professional recognition.

The library professionals should try to acquire qualifications and engage in publication activities to enhance the status of the profession.

17. The lack of library consciousness among the general public and its reflection on the academic community.

The library associations and teachers associations should take the initiative to promote the public library movement with acceptable standards.

18. The shortage of dedicated professionals among the librarians and the resultant problems of professional image.

The new entrants to the profession should have qualifications at par with that of college teachers. The existing staff should be encouraged to acquire statutory qualifications.

19. Lack of coordination between the library schools and college libraries and the resultant problems of lack of facilities for continuing education for the library professionals.

The library schools should take the initiative to provide continuing education programmes to the library professionals. There should be convenience for acquiring higher qualifications through the part time registration or distance mode.

20. Lack of suitable literature related to the modern trends in the functioning of academic libraries and the resultant problems of widening knowledge gap.

Starting of new journals for the study and communication to the matters related to the college libraries in general with special emphasis on Kerala.

21. Lack of professionally qualified officials at the higher education level as well as collegiate administration to take care of matters related to the college libraries.

There should be an official in the rank of deputy director to handle matters related to college libraries. He must be a person hailing from library profession.

22. Lack of active and dynamic professional associations for

the college librarians and the resultant problems of non-representation of library professionals in academic and professional maters related to higher education.

The professional associations should be more active in the interaction with the higher education establishment to improve the status and quality of library professionals.

23. The rivalry between the individual professionals which often leads to spoil the reputation and well being of the profession.
24. The communication gap between the college libraries due to distance as well as psychological barriers.
25. The compartmentalization of librarians on the basis of grading and the resultant problems of professionals disunity.

The grading system may be abolished and qualified librarians may be appointed in all colleges with salary and status of college teachers as implemented in other states.

26. The incomplete and unscientific implementation of U.G.C scheme in the college libraries and the resultant problems of professional dissatisfaction.

The U.G.C scheme should be implemented in to and all the qualified librarians may be included in the U.G.C scheme as recommended by the expert committee on college libraries.

27. Lack of library consciousness among the educational administrators including the college principals.

The matters related to libraries may be discussed at the principal's conference under the auspices of collegiate education department.

28. Lack of research on the users and resources of college libraries.

The user studies may be conducted by the college libraries as well as by the faculty for identifying problems related to library use and use patterns.

29. Lack of coordination between the college and university libraries.

The university libraries are in a better position with more staff and resources to undertake information service in a wider area. The documentation activities as well as current awareness service of the university libraries may be available to the college libraries for utilization.

30. The absence of a central organization to study the matters related to college libraries.

There should be a research centre on matters related to the efficient functioning of college libraries and the changing information needs of academic community.

30. The college libraries may initiate the activities that can be implemented at the grass root level and more social interaction and commitment will improve the situation to a great extent.

31. The college libraries may initiate the activities that can be implemented at the grass root level and more social interaction and commitment will improve the situation to a great extent.

32. Overemphasis on classroom teaching due to the traditional pattern of education and the resultant problem of indifference towards self study and reading.

More emphasis should be given to assignments and project works instead of more frequent written examinations which are mostly memory tests.

33. Non-representation of libraries in academic bodies at the university level.

There must be an elected member from the constituency of college librarians in the university senate and syndicate.

34. The lower status of library profession due to several reasons like unqualified staff, professional indifferences, lack of continuing education etc.

The professional quality of college librarians must be ensured through insisting on qualifications to new entrants in the college libraries.

35. The overemphasis given to commercial use of information technology and the resultant problems of non-availability of information technology infrastructure for library purpose.

36. Lack of credible and efficient software for library application

The department of higher education should recommend a set of standard library software from which the individual libraries may be encouraged to select one.

37. The unaffordable cost of library software and the resultant problems of reluctance from the part of library authorities to implement library automation schemes.

38. The lack of awareness about the benefits of library automation among the top level management.

39. The insufficient money and manpower for library automation.

40. Lack of interlibrary loan facilities and resource sharing.

The college libraries of a locality form a mutual agreement for resource sharing and library cooperation.

41. Low priority given to the libraries by the college authorities.

Implementation of the report of 'Expert Committee on College Libraries'

42. Lack of continuous and uninterrupted power supply.

43. Lack of bibliographic instructions at the high school and college level and the resultant problem of lack of library consciousness among the students and the teachers.

There should be library instruction programmes from the high school level.

44. The declining trend in the reading habit of the general public due to the influence of T.V, radio and Internet.

The reading habit of the teachers and the students may be encouraged through the emphasis given in the syllabus for aesthetic and recreational reading.

45. The impact of globalisation and the resultant problem of commercialization of education.

Giving more emphasis in general education through the public schools and arts and science colleges can prevent the commercialization of education. The degeneration of education may lead to the total collapse of the value system.

46. The indifference of Indian business groups in the promotion of reading and culture.

The exemplary examples of western business groups like Carnegie, Rock feller and Microsoft in educational philanthropy may be popularised here also.

47. The lack of interest on the part of intelligentsia to the promotion of libraries.

The initiatives of intelligentsia in the activities of library movement have to be ensured by the library professionals through interactions.

48. The decline of Malayalam language and literature and the resultant problem of shortage of suitable reading materials and the degeneration of culture.

The beauty and greatness of Malayalam language and literature and the rich cultural heritage of Kerala has to be preserved through original research in this area and the popularization of the results.

49. Degeneration of political, family and personal values in the society.

The challenge of cultural invasions can be countered only through original thinking and reading.

50. The imitation of western customs and culture without proper study of knowledge.

The dangers of imitation and cult formation have to be countered through the popularization of knowledge among the public and the in depth study of different cultures by the intelligentsia and popularization of the result.

51. The decline of spiritual values among the individuals.

    Popularisation of reading and original thinking.

52. The isolation of intelligentsia from the social activities.

53. The trend of sensationalism in the popular media.

The sensationalism created by the media and the degeneration of values can be countered only through promotion of reading and original thinking.

REFERENCES

1. Shannon, C and Weaver, W.(1949). The Mathematical Theory of communication. – Urbana : University. Of IIlinois Press, p.5
2. Chen, and Hernon, P. (1982). Information Seeking : Assessing and Anticipating User Needs. New York: Neal-Schuman, p.10.
3. Devarajan, G (1995) Library and Information Users and Use studies – New Delhi: Beacon Books, p.7-11.
4. Bavakutty, M. (1988) Libraries in Higher Education – New Delhi : Ess Ess Publications, p. 1-3.

8

ROLE OF LIBRARIES IN SOCIETAL DEVELOPMENT AMONG RURAL WOMEN

Dr. S.S. Jagnayak

The progress of a country mainly depends upon the education of its citizens. Education can be of two types-formal and informal. Formal education is strictly adhered to textbooks. But after 1966, the trend in the educational sphere has changed from the formal to informal one. The changed system of education has demanded a network of libraries. Libraries play an important role in moulding the character of the people of the country particularly public libraries. So reading habit has to be created and encouraged in children from their early stages onwards. Academic libraries are mainly established to cater to the academic needs of the people. But for all around development, a wide and unfettered reading is essential i.e. general types of books are also needed which can be provided only by public libraries. Public libraries are established not only for the distribution of books but also for conducting extension activities, which include mainly socio – economic and cultural activities. These extension activities mainly focus on the socio-economic and cultural development of the public.

'Education provides people with an opportunity to effect on the critical, social, economic, moral and spiritual issues facing humanity. It contributes to national development through dissemination of specialised knowledge and skill. It is, therefore, a crucial factor of survival. The national strategy of education has to ensure the availability of highly educated trained and motivated manpower for dealing with the challenges, which are inherent in modernisation, and globalisation of economy. India has to be able to compete with the most advanced countries in many fields of production' [1]. In this context, public libraries play a prominent and paramount role

THE PUBLIC LIBRARY AND THE RURAL COMMUNITY

There is a reflex relation between library and the community. Libraries do not function in vacuum but they function in societies and their functions are determined by social forces. When social conditions change, the function of the library also changes . 'The modern public library is a living force in the society where it functions with potentialities to determine its shape and quality. At the same time, it is also a product of that society. So, the library may be described as a social institution as well as a vital societal force'.[2] The public library possesses all the features of a social institution viz. social origin, social objectives, interrelations with other institutions, the ability to adapt itself to new social order and functional organisation.

Being a social product, the public library has certain functions to perform in the rural community such as acquiring of documents related to the needs of the rural society, giving reliable and essential information , helping the productive drive of the rural mass, giving intellectual recreation, developing rural social homogeneity, socializing the individuals, cultivating of friendship, giving people the opportunity to mingle with others belonging to different classes, castes, religion, political parties etc, helping people to learn social behaviour and helping to promote socio-cultural, educational and economic activities suitable to rural community.

As a social product, the library has to fulfil the social needs of the rural community and it cannot remain as an isolated rigid institution on resisting the various changes, which affect the daily life of the people. As Ogburn puts 'the library is a part of our social fabric and cannot remain independent and immutable amid social change, but as one of the social institutions, it must adapt itself to the social order as it changes.[3]

It has been remarked that a public library has ' a social mandate'[4] to serve the whole community where it functions. The rural community needs library as a vital, creative and active social force for its advancement. J.H. Shera's comment is important in the context of public library in the rural society. He points out 'the library is one element in the total communication system by which a society is held together and culture is created and maintained' [5]. 'The developments in the fi‹ld of communication of information, support and accelerate a symbiotic relationship between the community and the library. A public library is a community centre around which the cultural life of the community revolves [6]. Actually a public library in a rural set up exists and functions just like a bow and arrow.

It is well known that the 'library has an obligation to mobilize all its resources and those in the community in order to help people get all necessary information with which to make intelligent decisions and lead more enlightened lives[7]. Public library in rural community is designated as a community resource centre, entrusted with social and educational functions. The Malmo Seminar concluded, 'it is axiomatic that a library should be adapted to the environment it is designated to serve; that its contents should be suited to its users; and that its services should accord with a clear, pre-established programme ...... It is certainly useful for the librarian to be acquainted with the population's ways of thinking, expressing itself and reacting; as also with the various forms of symbolisation to which it is partial. Otherwise he may find, to his surprise, that his clearest recommendations which, to him, carry the greater conviction produce an effect that he had by no means anticipated'. [8] George Beaton remarked 'it is difficult to predict what kind of library service is needed until you are definite about what the requirements of your users will be'[9]. This indicates the forms or methods of library services should be appropriate and match with the cultural traditions, ways of thinking and conduct of people.

It is reported 'significant differences exist' between urban and rural areas – in lifestyles; attitudes and values, in information needs and in delivery system needs '[10]. Rural people are less educated, poor, having less effective social organisation and burdened with structural economic inequality.'[11]. To reduce the above disabilities, libraries should have systematic dissemination of survival information to specific social groups.......'[12]. So, rural library services should focus attention to relevant information such as skills, resources, raw materials, market facilities, policy of the government services and programmes of the local authorities etc.

It has been pointed out 'an important function of a public library is to improve the economic level of its community by the provision of not only books, periodicals etc. but also of commercial, technical and other related information. In rural areas and particularly those in the Third World, the most urgent economic problem is to improve the production of agriculture. Yet, in many countries the farmers are not yet ready to use books and other printed sources of information. What they need is verbal advice and encouragement. Again, a substantial proportion of population in these countries are illiterate or at least not sufficiently literate to enjoy and profit by reading normal library material. It is idle for the librarians to disregard the limitations of his service'[13]. In this context, the libraries in rural areas have to give due importance to improve the living standards of the people particularly of their economic development. So, a public library in a rural locality should give focus to not only educational development but also economic development. But most of the rural public libraries are mere centres of book issues. This trend has to be changed and a local public library must be a centre for socio-cultural, economic and recreational facilities. It has been observed that any profession 'as a social phenomenon, must interact with its environment'[14] From the interaction with society arises the concept of responsibility. That is, by social responsibility one means that the library profession is accountable to the society, which indicates that the librarianship is responsible to develop appropriate methods of service to deliver library services to the community.

The library should become a centre of information dissemination to the community. It should give advice and guidance to the illiterate and mere literate people on varied matters of their occupational interests and problems of daily life. The Information and Referral service mean that it should become the focus of library services in the context of village community. Useful information on specific issues and problems is directly helpful to the people.[15] The public library should become the centre for promotion of information culture. It has been explained as 'the promotion of an information culture and activities designed to foster from childhood, the habit of seeking information and using it as a problem solving resource- both at home and in the school- would be a useful approach to the improvement of information resources especially in the developing countries[16].

Libraries in the rural community should be an agency for social education which must encourage and support the use of group services, out-reach programmes to deliver library services to the 'difficult to reach' groups, demonstrations, discussions and co-operative activities with other institutions in the organization of library services. That is why it has been pointed out libraries are primary institutions for the educational advancement of the people. As such they are one of the agencies of social education and stand in close...co-operation with groups and institutions of educational importance'[17].

The library's role in adult education as a centre for information dissemination is of paramount importance. Adult education is taken to mean those forms of education which are undertaken voluntarily by mature people and which have as their aim the development without direct regard to their vocational value, of personal abilities and aptitudes, and the encouragement of social, moral and intellectual responsibility with the framework of local, national and world citizenship'[18]. The contribution of adult education is economic development and social and economic changes are accepted widely today. That is why, it is remarked, 'we may define adult education as the effort put forth by a mature person to improve himself by acquiring new skills, information, understanding, attitude or appreciation, or the effort of any agency to prevent the opportunity and encouragement to mature persons for improving themselves or their community'[19]. And also as 'adult education is a process whereby persons who no longer attend school on a regular and full time basis undertake sequential and organised activities with a conscious intention of bringing about changes in information, knowledge, understanding, skill appreciation and aptitudes; or for the purpose of identifying and solving personal and community problems'[20]. UNESCO has been prominently advocating the idea of using public libraries in adult education promotional activities since 1949. Public library is described as a practical demonstration of democracy's faith in universal education as a life-long process. The public library manifesto of UNESCO pointed out clearly 'the role of public library as a living force for education, culture and information and as an essential agent for the fostering of peace and understanding between people and between nations' [21].Thus, public library can be considered as an agency in the local rural community to improve the people socially, economically culturally, educationally and politically.

The public library as a social institution, works for greater enlightenment of the people and gradually creates a climate in which it can flourish, but the level of enlightenment, which the community possesses at any particular time, conditions its development as an efficient institution. As such, a society gets the library it deserves and reciprocally the library is a measure of the society's level of enlightenment [22]. Society needs libraries in order to make the records of the human adventure available over long periods by giving them protection. The more sophisticated the society and the more complex its social organisation, the more it needs the libraries. Library itself is a social creation[23]. A library becomes a potential force in the social and cultural life of the community. Through various dimensions, the library can play a pivotal role in enriching the rural people multifaceted.

The present day rural libraries in Kerala play a prominent role in all arenas of social life. The libraries could play a pivotal role in the educational scientific, industrial, social and economic development of the country, which came to be recognised only in the middle of the present century. After independence, as part of industrialisation and high literacy rate, libraries too received encouragement from the government for its growth and development. Libraries play a very significant role in building up a healthy and progressive community. 'The public libraries have established themselves as an indispensable element in the life of the community. A well-organised library system can deeply influence the future development of the society.'[24]

THE RURAL PUBLIC LIBRARY AND THE DEVELOPMENT

Public libraries exert prominent influence in developing people and society socially, educationally, economically, culturally and politically. These developments happen because of literature available through the library and other extension activities related to the concerned areas. Development means an all round improvement of an individual i.e., socio-cultural, educational, economic and political. According to Rogers and Shoemaker, development means ' a type of social change in which new ideas are introduced into a social system in order to produce higher per capita income and levels of living through more modern production methods and improved social organisation'[25]. According to Mexico Declaration, developed nation means 'one whose people are well informed, cultured, efficient, productive, responsible and possess a sense of solidarity'[26]. Shiv R. Mehta pointed out development in the following words, 'development means people. Development in the new perspective has been referred to as an overall process of transforming men and societies leading to a social order in which every human being can achieve moral and material well being. It has also been referred to as a whole, an integrated value-loaded cultural process encompassing social relations, education, production, consumption and well-being. Thus, development involves the giving up or modifications of a number of old habits, beliefs, attitudes and values and the cultivation of some new ones, which are necessary to live in the modern times'[27]

Public libraries in rural areas are centres for social reconstruction and these are not centres for revolution but for development, which could bring people of all categories to become balanced, integrated and satisfied persons and valued citizens. These are indispensable agents for bringing enlightenment, encouragement, inspiration and efficiency among members of the community. A public library in a village is a dynamic agency with specific objective of developing them in its entity. According to S.R. Mittal, the objectives of a village library are. [28].

i. Disseminating authentic news and information.
ii. Providing motivation for learning, reading and writing and helping in maintaining, enhancing and feeding literacy among people.
iii. Helping to keep alive and enhance the cultural heritage
iv. Increasing vocational competence in raising the technological level of a village occupation.
v. Promoting information for various factions of the village population wherever they exist.
vi Helping village institutions and organisations to improve their programmes

vii Developing aesthetic sense and refined taste

viii Helping people to spend their leisure time profitably.

Public library contributes a lot for the educational development of the village folk. Through books and other literature as wells other educational extension activities, these libraries do a commendable work in this regard. Books and other literature provide information and knowledge, which enlighten the minds of the readers. This helps them to develop their character and personality. That is why, it is pointed out 'education is a process of meaningful interaction between a person and a stimulus resulting in changed behaviour beyond the level of simple reflex'[29] F. W. Ward regarded education as a means to social progress Pestalozz gives, education should aim at the harmonious development of all faculties. Herbert Spencer asserted that education should prepare the individuals for a well-sounded life in the society [30]. Library, no doubt, a medium for informal education and without which educational development of the people in a village community is seldom possible. Modern era is characterised by the encouragement of informal education and this is possible only through the network of libraries. In village, the mass education is essential which can be done only through village libraries as other types libraries viz. academic libraries are not in existence. Academic libraries are mostly concentrated in urban centres and these are mainly meant for students and educated mass. Books and other literature suitable to the village folk can be accumulated preserved and distributed only by the public libraries. So, a public library in a village is a heart of that area for the development of education of the simple rural folk. 'Whether a country is an affluent advanced or a developing one, acquisition of knowledge is the very basis of progress and strength . The library preserves knowledge and kindles thoughts and ideas'.[31]

Public libraries act as social institutions for the rural folk, where illiterates are educated with the aid of pictures, stories, demonstrations, discussions, lectures and readings from the Epics and other literature of our country and where the neo-literates helped to widen their knowledge with the use of selected books an various subjects; and education through literary classes is imparted to women and children also through magic lantern, puppet shows and theatre[32]. National Board of Adult Education Committee on Post-literacy and Follow-up Programme headed by J.P. Naik recommended a strong base of printed materials for the neo-literates. This has to be supplemented by vocational courses like cooking, sewing, pump repair, seed identification, fertilizer use, poultry development etc. All these activities need books for guiding the neo-literates. Thus, he implied active role of rural library particularly in educational development[33]. Since, illiteracy in the rural areas is comparatively higher than in urban areas, it would be possible to educate them through lectures, discussions, debates, film shows, folk dances, exhibitions, puppet shows, kirtans and reading out books to them[34].

Rural libraries can act as a centre for cultivation of habit of reading. That is why, it is pointed out 'though the ability to read does not necessarily ensure the formation and development of the reading habit, it goes without saying that illiteracy and lack of will to read, are the stumbling block to any such formation. Two broad aspect of the problem are [1) the society's ability to guarantee at least well maintained nursery and primary education for all children and (2) the adult illiterates. Since, children are the book consumers of the future, the promotion of reading habit among them in both rural and urban centres must play a crucially important role in educational, social, economic and cultural planning and development. Libraries and books are, in fact, effective tools inserting national solidarity and understanding. In literacy training, they act as ideal centres for helping the neo-literates to maintain and develop reading skills'[35] Library is one of the most effective tools to make available the materials for education to all people and it has the potential for the intellectual betterment of citizenry. 'Reading is a help for education and it provides information, status, spiritual satisfaction, emotional release and pleasure. It is also significant for the creation of intellectual, moral and aesthetic values. The library is the only institution, which is fully engaged in the creation of the reading habit'[36].

Nittala V. Ratnam And B. Bhaskara Rao used social development or social infrastructure development in a comprehensive sense to embrace the components viz. social services and social amenities or facilities [37]. In this sense a village library plays as a centre for social service programmes and facilities. It also acts as an agency for learning to conform to group standards, customs, traditions, and more and also to develop a sense of oneness, interaction and co-operation. It is remarked that, 'social development means the increase in the ability of get along well oneself and others.'[38] In villages, a public library creates national solidarity and work for curing evils like poverty, illiteracy, superstitious beliefs, child marriage, drunkenness, dowry system, communalism, regionalism, crime against women etc through dissemination of information and other activities such as debates, seminars, lectures, discussions etc. Substandard life styles of the families in the rural areas are changed by the provision of vocational, academic, career and recreational materials as well as other technical and professional literature suited to take intelligent decisions such as home management, child care, family adjustment and other equally important topics. Thus, 'its role is that of a medium of mass communication and acts as a social institution which inculcates fellow feeling. It imparts the essence of discipline, which gives strong foundation for the social behaviour of the people. The pivotal role in the process of searching for ways to improve the quality of life belongs to library.' [39]

Cultural development means development in artistic and intellectual activities. Culture is 'artistic and intellectual activities'[40]. Public libraries can play influential role in cultural development of the rural mass. Public libraries, through its various cultural activities, can contribute considerable impact on the development of the cultural aspects of the people. Culture, according to Edward

B. Taylor 'that complex whole which includes knowledge, belief, art, morals, law, custom and any other capabilities and habits acquired by man as a member of society' E.V. Roberty regards ' culture as body of thoughts and knowledge both theoretical and practical which only man can possess'[41] Public libraries help to create progressive as well as scientific out look and retain the basic values of our ancient culture. By providing various cultural activities, a public library can induce among people a high moral in character, enthusiasm, literary creations and an attitude to become better citizens of the country. In a nutshell, these social institutions can create revolutions in the cultural life of the people. Culture is often regarded as learned ways of behaviour. Gillin and Gillin have pointed out 'culture is the cement binding together into a society its component individuals .... human society is people interacting; culture is the patterning their behaviour.'[42] A rural library provides a boost to bind people together into a society and pattern their behaviour through its multifaceted cultural activities. The activities of the public library in this regard include indoor games, film shows, music recitals, dramas, sports, seminars, debates, quiz programmes, elocutions etc. which unfold and develop the potentialities needed for cultural development. Actually, public library is a cultural medium of the people through which they receive necessary stills to blossom their hidden potentialities for overall cultural development.

Economic development is one of the aims of rural library system. Okun and Richardson explains economic development as 'a sustained secular improvement in material well being which may consider to be reflected in an increasing flow of goods and services'[43]. All round development of the community and its economic progress cannot be achieved with out an effective public literary system. In every economic development activities, it can contribute something i.e, for agricultural development, industrial development, health, nutrition and social welfare, community development programmes etc. Distribution of books and other literature in the concerned areas are indispensable for the development of various economic aspects and an effective public library can do this efficiently. Literature related to daily needs, agriculture, industry handicrafts, health, hygiene, maternity and child welfare, home economics etc. are a must for village development. In the Third World, particularly of its rural areas the most urgent economic problem is to improve the production of agriculture'[44]. 'Information on a variety of farming problems like soil testing, availability of ground water, drip irrigation, seeds, manure, natural farming, harvesting, crop storage, tree planting, pesticides, horticulture, fish culture, dairy farming etc. should be provided to farmers. Programmes sponsored by agricultural colleges, universities and concerned departments should be secured and made available to farmers' [45]. This can be effectively done by public libraries in rural area. So, its importance in this regard cannot be neglected or forgotten.

Political development means acquisition of knowledge regarding political system and awareness concerned various political institutions, particularly the state. Democracy as a political system has become politically the most fashionable today. Sardar Panikkar says, 'democracy is, in fact, not merely a form of government, it is a complex of social, economic and political factors effecting the relationship of the state of the individual, guaranteeing essential freedoms, personal liberty, freedom of expression of organisation and of governing activities' [46] . In this sense, political development in the modern context is the acquisition of knowledge regarding democracy. The library in a rural setting provides facilities to the literates and even to illiterates to get knowledge required to participate effectively in democracy and thus be better citizens of the country. The knowledge thus got from the library helps them to be aware of the activities of the government and political parties which retract them to be dumb cattle. Several activities of the library such as discussions, debates, seminars, film shows, quiz programmes etc. are also helpful to get this knowledge.

THE PUBLIC LIBRARY AND THE RURAL WOMEN

Rural women are backward in all respects than urban women. Lack of facilities to improve their knowledge regarding various aspects as well as the limited chances to be come forward make them backward. Most of the women in rural areas are under the chains of traditionalism. They are confined in four walls of the kitchen. There is a famous dictum 'men for the field women for the kitchen'. This was the case of the women for the past few centuries. But educational technological, cultural, economic, social and political changes forced this deplorable section to respond strategically to the changing environment. But, it is not absolutely correct to say that they have broken the chains once hey were under particularly regarding rural women. This is mainly because of educational backwardness which is the result of hesitation to undergo education due to several reasons such as the domination of men, responsibility of family particularly kitchen work, vested interests of male folk, double standard of morality, traditionalism, customs etc. particularly in rural areas. Gradually, the state of women is changing due to the spread of education. The increasing education not only brings changes in the philosophy of life of women but also provides new avenues of employment to them. Those who are educationally and economically independent demand more freedom in family affairs as well as other arenas of social life. In this regard, public library in the village can contribute a lot by the provision of educational materials.

Women are a significant group in the village. They have special needs in the domain of health and child care, food and nutrition, cooking, family planning and welfare, kitchen gardens, dairy development, handicrafts and cottage industries to supplement their family income.' [47] Library in a village is the best medium for the dissemination of knowledge regarding the above aspects. Women in a village are often reluctant to go to a public library, which serves both the clienteles i.e. men and women as men usually dominate it. In this situation, a library specially for women helps them a lot as they can overcome the social stigma related to women. It is quite natural that women in a village are not in a position to behave freely with men as they are traditional bound. So, a public library specially for women catering the particular needs of them is highly essential.

'The housewives are by nature dependent on information of every type to run their households. Their information need may thus be to assist their children's education, to prepare well balanced diet for the family members, to retain their health etc.' [48] Public libraries are the best resource centre for the distribution of literature regarding the above subjects. J. J. Thabali's study clearly indicates the need for woman libraries. He says 'majority of the housewives depend on oral information handed down by their parents, in-laws, friends, neighbours as well as colleagues, to run their households. To some extent they also get information from the media and some of the housewives visit the library'[49]. Most of them depend relatives and friends for the information mainly because of the lack of public libraries specially for women. The rural library has a pivotal role to satisfy the information needs of women. That is why P.N. Kaula puts 'rural library authorities.. Should take care of the book needs of..... women' [50].

Indian feminist leaders have realized that their efforts are meaningless unless it attempts to make a change in response to the demands of education and health care among the lives of 80 percent of women who are self-employed and their basic concerns are access to clean water, animal fodder and cooking fuel.[51] Public libraries for women in villages are essential to fulfil this goal. 'By defining women as primary domestic workers and the sexual and reproductive property of men and by assigning priority to man's paid employment, the society devalues educational attainment and economic and social contributions of women' [52]. This attitude can be changed by public library system specially meant for women. Through dissemination of necessary knowledge regarding various evils to devalue women, the attitude of women as a weaker section can be changed. Various programmes through village women libraries can be conducted to empower women and help to lead a responsible and respectful life in the society. Library is the best medium to improve the status of women in family and society. Economic independence, self confidence and personal achievement motivation are a few tools that serve women well in negotiate their status in the family with their husbands and other family members. For this, education and information are important aspects. And women public libraries can play a very prominent role in educating and giving reliable information to enhance their status.

Rural women are suffered by several shortcomings, which include educational, social, political, economic and cultural, due to various reasons compared with urban women. Majority of these women are poor and away from opportunities needed for their development. To empower this section of the rural society, a well established public library system is of high need. A women library in a village can contribute a lot positively to change their present status. Special women libraries can provide knowledge and other extension activities to improve their status. Special women libraries can be attracted by women in the particular village as these are manned and run by women alone. Librarians and other authorities of these libraries are women and so they know the real problems and strengths of the women, which help them to direct activities suitable to their overall development. To improve and empower women, special women libraries are a must, as other general public libraries cannot take so much interest in the women's development.

THE LIBRARY DEVELOPMENT – A HISTORICAL PERSPECTIVE OF LIBRARIES IN DIFFERENT COUNTRIES

There is evidence regarding the existence of Libraries as early as 2,700 B.C. The history of Sumeria showed the evidence for that as their writing was inscribed on tables made of soft clay.

Babylonian history gives the existence of libraries, which were located in temples and Palaces. There were number of private and government libraries existed in Assyrian and Egyptian civilization, which were housed in temples.

The 'Classical Age' or 'the Golden Age' was characterised by the production of sizeable number of books on history philosophy, religion, literature and science, which later formed the basis of libraries. The first public library was founded in Rome in 37 B.C. A good number of monastic libraries existed in Germany in the ancient period. State libraries were the important libraries before 1939 in Germany. 18th century was characterised by many new developments in the field of libraries in France and by the middle of 18th century many monastic libraries were converted into public libraries. There were about 12000 rural and about 100 municipal libraries existed in Sweden before 1970. The library of Plague in Czechoslovakia had more than 1,00,000 volumes and several libraries sprang up in major cities of Czechoslovakia before 1939 itself. The libraries in Leningrad, Odessa, Kharkov and Keev have been developed as central libraries after1917 in Russia. Even in the early 15th century, libraries in the form of town and church libraries, learned society libraries, monastic and cathedral libraries were existed in Great Britain. The first public library came up in the later part of 15th century, which was the Guildhall Library of London. British Museum is the National Library of England started in 1753, which was opened to the public in 1759. There were number of libraries in United States in latter part of the 17th century. The public library established in 1852 in USA became a model library, which influenced the future policy of libraries and public library movement in America.

INDIA

In the matter of development of public libraries, India is about 100 years behind the developed democratic countries of the world. Libraries were started in ancient and medieval India by the patronage of the emperors, by the capitalists and other scholars of that period. The learned Brahmins memorized became 'living' or 'ambulatory' libraries that were the real source of knowledge for the young generation. The religions – Jainism and Buddhism – encouraged in making and copying of religious manuscripts to spread and propagate their philosophy, which gave birth to monastery libraries. The famous universities like Nalanda, Taxila and Vikramashila had magnificent libraries with a massive collection of manuscripts.

There were small libraries also existed attached to various temples and mathas spread all over the country for the use of all people. These libraries were housed in palaces, mosques, makatabas, khanqah, madrasas and other educational institutions during the Sultanate period. Mughal period characterised by the efflorescence of library movement in the country.

The Calcutta Library established in 1784 was made open to the public in 1820. The Madras Library Society was formed in 1812. The year 1900 is a milestone in the history of public library movement in India as the Calcutta Public Library became the National Library of India. Another landmark in the history of public library development started from the year 1937. By this time strong people's demand for libraries had emerged in the country. In 1939-40, the Government of Bombay appointed a Library Development Committee which provided a base for the establishment of regional libraries, district libraries, town libraries and rural libraries..

Madras Library Act (1948) provided a boost for the organisation of public libraries in the State. The second development after independence was the provision of the scheme for improvement of library service in the First Five Year Plan. The objective of the scheme was to cover the entire population of the country with free public library service. Different schemes were started to develop public library system in India in the following Five Year Plans. In 1966, the Ministry of Education, Government of India constituted a National Advisory Board of Libraries to advice Government regarding recognition and planned development of library services. The year 1972 was a turning point in the development of public libraries in the country due to the establishment of Raja Ram Mohan Roy Library Foundation to initiate the development of rural libraries in the country.

During the period of 1970s there were library laws only in the States of Tamil Nadu, Andhra Pradesh, Karnataka, Maharashtra and West Bengal. Tamil Nadu has passed the Libraries Act in 1948 and established State Library Authorities in each district. As on 1991-92, the State had 2663 libraries. Under the provisions of the Karnataka Library Act, central Libraries have been set up in the State level, city level and district level. As on 1994-95, there were total 3738 libraries in Karnataka. Andhra Pradesh Library Act was passed in 1960. The State has a State Central Library, panchayat libraries, village libraries and book deposit centres. Besides, regional libraries, district central libraries and branch libraries exist in the State. As on 1994 there were total of 4329 libraries exist in the State.

The Maharashtra Public Libraries Act of 1967 makes provisions for grant-in-aid, building and equipment, grants to non-governmental libraries, grant-in-aid to library associations and libraries of the research and library institutions. There were total of 5643 libraries in Maharashtra as on 1995-96.[53] The Madhya Pradesh Library Association was formed in 1957 and the State has a State Central Library, regional, district, sub-divisional and village libraries. The number of libraries functioning in the State are 15933 including the regional libraries, information centres, district libraries, private public libraries and gram panchayat libraries.[54] Attempt for enacting a legislation is going on in Uttar Pradesh since 1949 and Dr S. R. Ranganathan has drafted two bills in 1949 and in 1958. The State has established a library cell in the Department of Education in 1980 to look after the matters of public libraries. There is a State Central Library, government public library and about 250 voluntary organisation libraries in the State [55]. The library movement in Himachal Pradesh started with the establishment of a State Central Library at Sloan followed by 11 district libraries. Government action for starting libraries was started in 1952. Here school libraries are also used as public libraries after school hours. There is one State Central Library, 11 district libraries, 15 community central public libraries, 1 state public library and 101 senior secondary school public libraries in the state during the year 1989-90. In Arunachal Pradesh , there is a Central Library at Itanagar, 7 block and 14 circle libraries. There are total 82 libraries working in the state. Bihar government's libraries are under the supervision of Commissioner of Education. During 1985-86, there were 4498 libraries functioning in the state[56]. Gujarat has 7,589 libraries which are divided into government public libraries, grant-in-aid public libraries and 300 book service centres. A State Central Library was started in 1967 by the government of Haryana and Haryana Library Act was passed in 1989. The State of West Bengal could enact a library legislation in 1979 and the State had total 2421 libraries including State Central Library, district libraries, central libraries and rural/area/primary unit libraries. In Orissa, 1116 libraries are functioning under Department of Culture, 39 library cum reading rooms and 69 information cum reading rooms. In 1962, Rajasthan Library Association was formed and 42 libraries and 18 reading rooms are functioning in the State. The public library services in Assam started during the First Five Year Plan. There are 217 libraries functioning in the State. The Government of Goa has constituted a State Library Advisory Board in 1983 and total 132 libraries function in the state. The State of Jammu and Kashmir has 85 public libraries one research library and two small children's libraries. In Manipur, Imphal Public Library was started in 1983 and Manipur Library Association was formed in 1987. Manipur Public Library Act was passed in 1988 and the State has one State Central Library, 5 district libraries and 101 voluntary organisation libraries. Meghalaya has one Central Library, 4 district libraries and a few libraries by voluntary effort.[57] In Mizoram, a State Central Library, 3 sub divisional and

200 village libraries are functioning. The Birch and State Central Library in Tripura was taken over by the Government in 1953 and made a State Central Library in 1973. The Central State Library in Chandigarh was started in 1955. The Punjab has a State Central Library, one town library and 13 district libraries. The Directorate of Public Instruction controls the full-fledged government libraries.

As far as concerned to Union Territories, public library development is not commendable. At present, there are 10 zonal libraries, 11 public libraries 8 information centres and a few libraries run by voluntary organisations in Andaman and Nicobar.The Central Library in Lakshadweep is located in Kavarathe and entire territory was covered by public library service. Delhi Library Association was formed in 1953. A library bill was drafted in 1954. The Education Department in Pondicherry has 64 branch libraries in rural areas.[58]

There are more than 3,126 public libraries are working in towns and 5,57,137 in villages in India and exact availability of data regarding public libraries are not available today and this is essential for building up an efficient public library system in India. Even after 50 years of independence, only 8 states have enacted public library legislation which, no doubt, showing the disinterest and apathy of the Governments towards public library development in India. On the whole, the development of public libraries in India has been creeping.[59]

THE PUBLIC LIBRARY DEVELOPMENT IN KERALA

The history of public library movement in Kerala is older than any other states in Indian Union. Kerala is the land of libraries. The attraction towards books, aptitude for reading and interest for book collection were past and parcel of well-to-do Keralites from ancient time onwards. The three constituent parts of Kerala viz. Travancore, Cochin and Malabar had different kinds of public libraries catering to the needs of the reading public in small way. In the later part of the 19th and beginning of the 20th century, these libraries were the centre of the activities of freedom movement. Under the auspices of these workers, what is called 'open University' by arranging services of lectures on topics of cultural interest pertaining to Malayalam, which benefited for the socio-cultural educational and political development of the public.

The three former constituent parts of Kerala had their own history of public library movement. The Sate of Kerala had formed in two successive stages – merging of Travancore and Cochin in 1949 and Travancore–Cochin and Malabar in 1956. The public library development in Kerala had been compartmentalised into each of these areas.

The public library movement in Travancore emerged with the initiation of Trivandrum Public Library in 1829 which was started by the direct involvement of Col. Hans Sloan,[60] the founder of British Museum. In 1898, the government took over this library and opened for public use since 1899. It became State Central Library in 1958 and functioning under the Department of Education. Another major attempt in the library movement in Travancore started with the establishment of Suguna Poshini Library in 1880 which could not survive for more than two years. Another milestone in the development of public library was the founding of Kottayam Public Library in 1882 by Sir. T. Rama Rao.[61]

Some of the important public libraries in early time are the Jnana Pradayani Library, Neyyattinkara and the Mundenkavu Sankaravilasom Library at Chengannoor (1910), Y.M.C.A. Library at Keezhkara (1911), Sree Chithra Thrunal Library at Trivandrum and Raja Varma library at Oachira (1913), Lalithavilasaom Library at Padmanabhapuram and Kandiyoor Jnanapradayani Library at Mavelikkara (1916), and Bharathavilasam Library at Karapuzha (1919)[62]

Another boost to public library development in Travancore was the provision of grant-in-aid for libraries in 1917 under the condition that these libraries should provide free book service to the public[63]. The Travancore Educational Reforms Committee Report of 1932 helped the government to organise 78 libraries in rural areas attached to government primary schools[64]. Besides, a few libraries were existed with village uplift centres[65] and municipalities prior to 1949.

The first All Travancore Library Conference was organised by Jnanapradayani Library in 1925 followed by another conference of Sree Chithira Thirunal Library in 1933 which resulted in the formation of first library association known as All Travancore Library Association.

The library development in Cochin started with the establishment of Ernakulam Public Library (1869) followed by Trichur Public Library (1873). The government of Cochin started number of rural libraries during the year 1926. Government of Cochin had a Department of public libraries to look after the library matters. In 1946, there were three types of libraries – public libraries (17), major rural libraries (5) and village libraries (224). A meeting was held under the chairmanship of T.K. Krishna Menon in 1949 which was an important event in the history of public library development in Cochin area.

In the Malabar area, social and political workers started many reading rooms which turned to become libraries in course of time. In Malabar, Municipalities and other local bodies mainly initiated the movement. The Calicut Public Library was established in 1890 by the Calicut Municipality. From 1900 to 1956, the libraries in Malabar area were libraries organised by Municipalities and Panchayats, libraries organised by Local Library Authority (LLA) and libraries organised by voluntary effort. The Fourth All India Library Conference was held at Madras in 1927 which inspired to start an association called Samastha Kerala Pusthakalaya Samithi. Another conference called Malabar Vayanasala Sammelanum was held at Kozhikode in 1937 resulted in the formation of the Malabar Vayanasala Sangham in 1943, its name was changed into Kerala Granthalaya Sangham[66]

After 1956, when Malabar region was bifurcated into three small districts namely Palakkad, Kozhikode and Kannur, three local library authorities were created which established district central libraries, branch libraries and deposit centres throughout the districts[67]. At the time of formation of Kerala, the Malabar had 500 libraries in addition to the LLA libraries .

KERALA GRANTHASALA SANGHAM

The year 1945 is a landmark in the history of public library development as the seed of Kerala Granthasala Sangham was sown. In 1947, the All Travancore Granthasala Sangham was registered under Travancore Company Act of 1939 which became the All Travancore-Cochin Granthasala Sangham in 1948 when the two states- Travancore and Cochin were integrated. With the formation of Kerala state in 1956 with Malabar, the Sangham titled as Kerala Granthasala Sangham with the principle aim of establishing a network of libraries through out the state so as to enlighten and encourage the rural population in their social, cultural and educational persuits[68].

Sangham's initial contribution was the pressure on the government to hand over libraries attached to government primary schools in the Travancore area to the Sangham and with the co-operation of the local people. It established village libraries in all centres where these libraries existed. Besides, the Sangham got village uplift libraries in certain areas of Travancore and these were also re-organised to function as public libraries. All public libraries in Cochin area including those of government were handed over to Sangham. By 1956, the Sangham had about 1500 libraries. After the formation of Kerala state, the Sangham extended its activities to Malabar area also and got 500 libraries, which were not covered by Madras Library Act. By the Act of 1989, the libraries under LLAs were also attached to the Sangham. Through the Sangham, the government distributes annual grants to libraries and presently these are graded into six i.e A to F. In 1977 , the government dismissed the Central Administrative Committee of the Sangham and power is given to a Central Board which affected the public library development of Kerala adversely for a period of 15 years. Public Library Act was passed in 1989 and constituted an apex body known as State Library Council through democratic way and got all power concerning public libraries of Kerala in 1994.

KERALA PUBLIC LIBRARIES (KERALA GRANTHASALA SANGHAM) ACT

Many public library bills were presented during various governments in 1971 , 1974,1977,1985 and 1989 and last one only could complete the legislative process and became law. It was exactly on 16th May, 1989 and brought out Kerala Public Libraries (Kerala Granthasala Sangham) Rules in 1991. As a result of the provisions in the Act, there are 3 levels of body viz., the State Library Council, District Library Councils and Taluk Library Unions which should be organised through representatives elected from various affiliated libraries of the Sangham. The State Library Council has also ex-officio and nominated members but not having power to elect office bearers. The Act provides three types of libraries viz grant-in-aid libraries, public libraries to be established by State Library Council, District Library Councils and Taluk Library Unions, libraries functioned under government for the use of the public and libraries run by local bodies.

RESEARCH SETTING KERALA

Kerala, the southern most state of Indian union possesses highest rate of literacy, lowest fertility and child mortality rates among other states. The introduction of free primary education during the regime of Maharaja Sree Moolam Thirunal (1985-1924), democratic traditions of western culture through English education, British Indian institutions and the activities of the state and private agencies, development of Malayalam language all contributed to increase the literacy level and reading habit among the people of Kerala[69].

'The status of women in Kerala has been described as higher and different from the women in the rest of India. Several reasons have been ascribed for the situation in which literacy and education have been cited as the most significant. When one looks the general literacy and educational standard of women in other states can easily understand that the literacy and education of women in Kerala are very high[70]. Even in 1947, the rate of literacy of females in Kerala was 36%[71]. According to 1991 census, it was 86.2%. This is high compared with other states in India. That is why the reading habit and use of libraries among women in Kerala are high.

Almost all the public libraries in Kerala are affiliated with Kerala Granthasala Sangham and this affiliation is needed to get grant. The objectives of Kerala Granthasala Sangham at the beginning are[72].

i. to work as the apex body for all libraries in the state
ii. to contribute for the improvement of existing libraries
iii. to provide all possible assistance for the promotion of adult education
iv. to avoid neo-literates from falling again into illiteracy and provide facilities for the educated to read and acquire knowledge
v. to conduct night schools
vi. to make effort for starting a library department in the state.
vii. to provide training courses to library workers
viii to undertake publication activities necessary for library workers.
ix to work for the development of Malayalam
x. to start central library in each taluk
xi. to work for the development of other associations, companies etc. having similar objectives and take their controls and rights.

There are more than 5000 public libraries working in the

state of Kerala. The total number of public libraries getting grant from Kerala Granthasala Sangham as on 2000-2001 are 3693. The following table gives district wise number of public libraries getting grant from the Sangham including women libraries.

District	Number of libraries
Trivandrum	398
Kollam	352
Pathanamthitta	183
Alappuzha	141
Kottayam	279
Idukki	181
Ernakulam	203
Thrissur	379
Palakkad	197
Malappuram	267
Kozhikode	354
Wayanad	95
Kannur	525
Kasargode	139
Total	3693

(***Source :*** Data from Records of Kerala Granthasala Sangham)

THE WOMEN LIBRARIES IN KERALA

There is no evidence for the massive movement behind the organisation of Vanitha Libraries (Women Libraries) in Kerala. But even before 1917 women libraries existed in Kerala. By the request of Sri. Krishna Vilasom Vanitha Library at Balaramapuram, Trivandrum, a rule was announced in 1917 by the then Queen of Travancore. The rule was that the Headmistress of the primary schools in the concerned areas should do the checking of the vanitha libraries for grant. This rule was published in the Gazatte of April, 21st of 1928. This evidence gives the special importance given to vanitha libraries in the early period itself.

Women libraries are organized by the initiative of local women. After attaining a minimum standard, the library gets the affiliation of Kerala Granthasala Sangham. These libraries are functioning, as other public libraries, by the income getting from the subscription of the members and other public contributions besides the grant from the Sangham. If Panchayat desires, it also gives contributions in the form of newspapers, periodicals etc. or cash to the library. Sometimes, the local leaders are the active workers of these libraries and they become the president, secretary, treasurer etc.. In other cases the laymen become the office bearers and they gradually come out as local leaders due to the initiative and active participation taken in the work of libraries. Thus, these libraries are helpful for local leadership also.

At present there are 35 women libraries working in the state of Kerala.

The following table gives district wise number of women libraries in Kerala

District	
Trivandrum	5
Kollam	5
Pathanamthitta	3
Alappuzha	-
Kottayam	3
Idukki	3
Ernakulam	10
Thrissur	-
Palakkad	2
Malappuram	1

Kozhikode	1
Wayanad	-
Kannur	1
Kasargode	1
Total	35

(*Source :* Data from Secretary, District Library Councils)

Despite these women libraries, most of the public libraries in Kerala have separate women's wing. This section provides book suitable to women's need and other socio-cultural activities are also conducted specially for the women. In fact, before 1975 itself, the Sangham started to work among women illiterates to make them literate and to make attachment to the libraries. It is pointed out that Kerala Granthasala Sangham was much concerned about the increasing number of illiterate and poor women in the state. To serve their needs, the Sangham decided to start 1000 women's literacy centres attached to libraries. A plan to this effect was also submitted to the government of India. Even before this, efforts were being made to attract women towards libraries. It was very rare among the women who take books from libraries and read them. So, Sangham started the above programme to attract more and more women to libraries. The women's wing in the libraries conduct discussions, seminars, conferences etc. under the auspices of Sangham to make illiterate women literate and ensure their attachment and participation in the library activities.[73] Recently the Sangham started a scheme to distribute books among rural women known by the name Rural Women Book Distribution Scheme.

THE RURAL WOMEN BOOK DISTRIBUTION SCHEME

Sangham conducted a survey to find out the reading habit of the people of Kerala. It is found that there is no considerable decrease in reading habit of the people even at the juncture of electronic media and cable TV's and Malayalees in general read literature at least one hour per day. On the basis of this that the Sangham initiated this scheme of distribution of books among rural women. The aim of the scheme is to make interest and bring housewives and women labours in the world of reading. It was initiated during the golden jubilee of Indian independence and initiated in 50 libraries as a first step. Now, this scheme is being extended to other libraries also.

This scheme is started in the libraries where number of books are more and are functioning well in rural areas.

As a part of this, there is a committee consisting of 9 women including local leaders and other experts in various fields and the distribution of books is done by a woman librarian who get Rs. 500/- as allowance from District Library Council. The woman librarians distribute books in a particular day in a week. Besides, seminars and classes on new books and programmes on health and environment protection, social awareness, family welfare, agriculture etc are conducted by taking participation of the members of this scheme and also provide facilities to come together and express their talents in arts and sports.

The following table gives the number of Rural Women Book Distribution Centres district-wise in Kerala

District	*Number of Rural Women Book Distribution Centres*
Trivandrum	8
Kollam	7
Pathanamthitta	6
Alappuzha	7
Kottayam	5
Idukki	5
Ernakulam	12
Thrissur	8
Palakkad	7
Malappuram	8

Kozhikode	8
Wayanad	3
Kannur	10
Kasargode	4
Total	98

OBJECTIVES OF PUBLIC LIBRARIES (INCLUDING WOMEN LIBRARIES) IN KERALA

The objectives of the Public Library in Kerala are [74] :

1. to cultivate reading habit among people.
2. to widen the habit of reading newspapers so as to enable them to get knowledge regarding various aspects happening around them.
3. to arrange talks and seminars of learned men and scholars.
4. to conduct film shows, dramas, thullal, kathakali etc. based on education and recreation to encourage arts.
5. to formulate programmes for adult education and the study of subjects like Hindi and put into practice.
6. to start night schools and other study centres.
7. to provide encouragement for socio-cultural and moral development of the people.
8. to build up a healthy and civilised human race beyond all sectarian attitudes including religious and caste discrimination.
9. to take radio rural forum programmes.
10. to create separate children section.
11. to create women's section and
12. to prevent neo-literates from falling again into illiteracy.

FUNCTIONS

The public libraries including woman libraries have separate sections such as arts and sports wing, young men's association, mahila samajam, women's section, balajana sakyam, young farmer's club, science club, grama sasthra samithi, vijnana vedi, literacy councils, employment seeker's association etc. These libraries through these sections conduct several educational, socio-cultural, economic and political programmes to enrich people.

Educational programmes of the library, generally, include book display, book exhibition, talk, discussion, newspaper reading programme, nursery school, adult education centre , S.S.L.C. condensed course, free tuition programme, vacation class, science corner, literacy council, reference materials etc.

Socio-cultural programmes include construction of houses and roads, thatching of huts, road repairs, cleaning markets and other places, medical camps, anganwadi, crèche, kitchen garden etc. Besides, lectures, talks, debates, seminars, film shows etc. are also being conducted. Provision of radio, T.V and programmes like music recitals, dramas, sports, quiz programmes, mock assemblies, elocutions, special function related to literary men, indoor games, picnic and pleasure trips etc.. are also the part of their programmes.

As part of economic programmes, these libraries provide scholarships, information regarding employment, governmental welfare measures, loan facilities as well as provision of chitty programmes, giving on rent of chairs, curtains, hall etc. Lectures, talks, seminars, camps, exhibitions etc. regarding agricultural development of the people are also part of the library activities.

PANUNDA MAHILA SAMAJAM VANITHA GRANTHALAYAM

The present study was conducted in this library which is situated in Kannur, one of the northern districts of Kerala. It is a part of the former Malabar which has a hoary past in the independence movement. The area of Kannur has 2966 Sq. Kms. and female population is 1152889, ie. 51.20% of the total population. The general literacy rate of Kannur is 91.48% which is not low compared with other districts of Kerala. The female literacy rate of Kannur is 87.65% (Source : Census Report 1991)

HISTORY

The force behind the inception of this library was Panunda Mahila Samajam which was established on 30-06-1972 and registered on 31-07-1974. Before looking into the history of the library it is essential to have a glance on the activities of the Samajam. Since the beginning onwards, the Samajam undertook several welfare activities for the uplift of poor women and children of the community. In 1972, the Samajam started care-feeding programme for the poor children followed by the establishment of a Balwadi, 53 poultry units in 1976 and a garment making and plastic wire works were also established for providing self-employment to poor women. In 1976,22 kitchen garden units and in 1978,22 goat rearing units were set up. Then, the Samajam provided 5 diary units and a crèche for 25 beneficiaries of the locality. During 1979-80 it had started a women condensed course for those who failed in SSLC examination and 5 batches have been come out successfully. Vocational Training (Type – writing) course was started in 1980 and two batches had undergone training. An adult education centre and a post-literacy centre is working efficiently with Samajam. A printing press and a book binding unit were started with the financial assistance of the Central Social Welfare Board and is working well at present.

The Samajam has a building of its own at a cost or rupees one lakh with the assistance of the Ministry of rural Development, Government of India and it was opened on 6-9-1984.

Another boost behind the inception of the library was the interest shown by the women and children associated with the Samajam in reading books which were sanctioned to the literacy centre and post literacy centre of Samajam started in 1984 and also collected by the Samajam members. Thus, by the initiative of the members of the Panuda Mahila Samajam, a woman library was started on January 26, 1984 by the title 'Panunda Mahila Samajam Vanitha Granthalayam.

By the advice of the then Secretary of Kannur District Advisory Board of Kerala Granthasala Sangham, the authorities of library applied for affiliation. Thus, the library got affiliation from Kerala Granthasala Sangham on July 25,1986. It is the first woman library in the district of Kannur. The library was inaugurated on July 31 , 1986.

CONSTITUTION

Under the presidentship of Smt. Kausu, a committee consisting of 9 members was formed on June, 26,1986 for efficient working of the library. The following were the members of the first committee :

1. K. Kausu – President
2. K. Vanaja – secretary
3. P.C. Suseela - Vice President
4. P. Vasantha - Joint Secretary
5. Sailaja – Member
6. K. Thankam - Member
7. A. Santha - Member
8. C. Savithri – Member
9. T. Sathi - Member

The committee elected according to the bye- law conducts the activities of the library. The committee meets in first week of every month and review the activities of the last month. And also organise and conduct activities for the next month. The members actively participate for the progress of the library without any discretion based on caste, class, creed and politics. This is the case from the beginning onwards of the library.

The library is functioning in the Samajam building. The building is a two storied and has enough facilities for the smooth functioning of the library. The library gets Rs. 6000/- per year as grant from Kerala Granthasala Sangham. Other sources of income are membership fee and monthly fee.

ACTIVITIES OF RURAL BOOK DISTRIBUTION SCHEME

This is a scheme for the women in general and women labourers in particular to make them members of the library. This scheme was sponsored by Kerala Granthasala Sangham which was implemented in this library from February 1986 to February 1987. As a part of this scheme 200 families were selected from nearby areas and distributed books needed to them in a particular day of a weak. This scheme helped a lot to improve reading habit as well as interest to library among women of the community.

Agricultural Book Corner

After getting the affiliation, the library immediately started this corner and got agricultural books of the Institute of Languages, government of Kerala free of cost. Besides, with the help of officers of agricultural department, the library started kitchen gardens and nurseries among the population. And also conducts seminars and film shows regarding scientific agriculture which induce interest among women in the field of agriculture. At present this programme is working efficiently.

Forestry Book Corner

By the initiative of this corner, the library under the auspices of Thalassery Social Forestry started a seed nursery. The members of the library, Samajam and balavedi participated effectively and distributed plants among the people. This scheme is going on successfully at present also.

Balakairali

The library has a centre for children named balakairali. This centre gives importance to the need of children. The books, discussions and classes are being provided to them. Various experts take classes on different subjects needed for the proper development of the children. Various children's magazines journals, books and other literature are available in the library suitable for them.

Socio - cultural Activities

The library conducts various socio-cultural activities such as road repairs, cleaning of important places, medical camps, seminars, debates, discussions, lectures, music recitals, arts and sports activities, film shows, indoor games, quiz programmes, Kadhaprasangams, elocutions, picture drawing and so on.

Economic Activities

The library provides information regarding self-employment, bank loans and loans of other institutions, saving schemes, new products, market prices, scientific agriculture, kitchen garden programmes etc. The library has a good resource of literature regarding various subjects needed for economic development.

Educational Activities.

The library has a reference centre having several costly and rare reference books. Besides, various academic books needed for students are also available. Seminars, discussions, talks, lectures etc suitable for educational improvement of the women are being conducted. Library has a good collection of fiction and non-fiction books.

The following table gives other facts regarding library.

Total number of members	Total visitors in a day	Distribution of books per day	Working days in a year
300	100	50	300

Books in different languages	Number
Malayalam	6159
English	296
Hindi	26
Total	6481

Type of books	Number
Fiction	3915
Non-Fiction	2566
Total	6481

BYE-LAW OF THE LIBRARY CONSTITUTION

Aims & Objectives :

The library shall strive to promote reading habit in women and children to promote their creative abilities such as literary and historic talents; try to achieve their cultural and hygienic conditions and inculcate among them a sense of self-reliance. The Library shall work for promoting more employment opportunities for women and give guidance for family welfare schemes to the housewives; to work for the socio-economic and cultural uplift of the backward classes; to conduct Adult Education Programme and Post Literacy Programme.

The Library shall strive to inculcate among the members love for each other, friendship and give and take policy irrespective of their caste, religion or political affiliation. The library shall conduct seminars, camps and study tours with this aim in view. Contact the various departments of the government and if need be raise funds by organising public entertainment programmes

Membership :

As per the norms laid down by the Karala Grandhasala Sangham, all eligible women and children under the age of 15 will be given membership in the Library. The children are not empowered to cast their vote in the election of the Governing Body.

The membership fee for a woman is Rs. 5/- and a child Re 1/- Annual subscription for a woman is Rs. 2/- and the children is Re. 1/- and those who fail to remit this their membership stands cancelled.

Composition

All members of the Library form the General Body. The General Body elects the Governing Body. The Governing Body consists of President, Vice President, Secretary, Joint Secretary, Librarian and a few members. The minimum number of the members in the Governing Body can be 11 and the maximum number 15. The number of the members is left to the option of the General body.

The above Governing Body and the General Body of the library will be running the Library according to the instructions and guidelines of the Kerala Grandhasala Sangham and the Panunda Mahila Samajam. The Library is established by the Panunda Mahila Samajam purely for the women and children and nourished by the Samajam is under the complete control and patronage of the Samajam.

Meetings

The Governing Body should meet at least once in a month and approve the income and expenditure of the previous month, report and check out the actions for the ensuing month. The General Body should meet once in a year and approve the Annual Report and the expenditure and income for the year and elect the office bearers for the coming year.

Governing Body

There will be a maximum 15 members in the executive including President, Vice-President, Secretary, Joint Secretary and a Librarian.

President :

The President shall be administrator of the library. The President shall preside over the General Body meeting and the Governing Body meeting. In the absence of the President, Vice President shall discharge the duties of the President.

Secretary :

The Secretary is authorised to make all correspondents and maintain records. The Secretary is responsible to the Governing Body for the maintenance of records, accounts and the properties of the Library. The Secretary is empowered to admit new members subject to the approval of the General Body. She should maintain proper receipts and vouchers of convene the meeting. The balance amount if any should be deposited in bank in the joint account of the President and Secretary. All documents executed for the library shall be in the name of the president

Librarian :

Librarian should distribute books on the specified days and time. She is responsible for getting back the same. Those who fail to return the book are liable for prosecution. The Librarian shall take the stock verification once in a year.

Quorum :

The Governing body can be met if 1/3rd of its members are present and the General Body if 1/3rd of the total members or at least 20 members are present.

Liquidation :

In the event of the Library being liquidated it will be amalgamated into another registered organization.

REVIEW OF RELATED STUDIES

In developed countries, this problem has received attention. Some of the researches done in the field may briefly be mentioned as under:

Bertha T Hirschstein made a sociological study of the Aquilar Branch of the New York Public Library in 1933. This was a case study about the clientele, the library's activities and examination of the relevant literature. Some of the important conclusions reached in the study were the use of the library was directly proportional to the distance from the library and the delinquent boys read more fiction than other general readers.

Bernard Reuben Berelson made an analysis of the Role of Communications in Determining Public Opinion in 1941[75]. He examined the effects of newspapers, magazines and radio on the public opinion. He found that the people accepted the arguments which supported their own views; and they were aware of the arguments emphasized by the communication media.

Jesse Hauk Shera[76] worked on the Foundations of the Public Library in New England, 1629-1855, reviewed the history of 'social and circulating libraries' and the economic, social and cultural climate of that period. He concluded that public library was born when the economic condition of the cities was strong enough to support it.

Sidney H Ditzion[77] studies the Social History of the American Public Library Movement in New England and the Middle States from 1850 to 1900. He found that the social, cultural and political background of the movement and the gradual transition from private to public libraries. He also traced the role of public library in mass education. He concluded that for the self- realization of the broad masses of the people, both the institution and methods were conceived.

Julia Elizabeth Sabine made a study of the Social and Cultural Background of New Jersey, the other Middle Atlantic States and the city of Newark as Antecedents of the Newark Public Library. She described that the early Newark settler's ideals of formal education and self-improvement, expansion of commerce and industry, Lyceum movement created urge for self-education and legislation for free education were the important contributing factors.

The Division of Research Techniques of the London School of Economics made a sample survey of the London Boroughs of Bermondsey, Tottenham and Wandsworth during 1951-52[78]. The study was to investigate the readership figures for the various classes of newspapers and periodicals and also their interest, content etc. on the extent of book-reading of any kind and on the characteristics and main sources of books they read.

A few studies have been conducted in Britain and United States. This includes the study of Brian Groombridge[79] , Bryan Lukham[80], Barry Totterdell and Jean Bird[81] ,Joseph Wheeler[82], Leon Carnovsky and Lowell Martin[83] and Bernard Berelson[84]. These studies were stimulating and helped to know the situation of libraries in those countries. These studies have only a limited value for the present investigation because of the drastic difference between the library situation in Asia and European and American library situation.

In 1979 [85], Chin studied the information needs of citizens of New England region. The study aimed to ascertain the information requirements of the general population, identify the source of information, explore the role of the library in citizen's information seeking process and investigate the use and non-use of libraries. It was explained in the study that libraries, at least, in New England, are not viewed as an important source provider by the information-seeking public. It seems that libraries are utilised by only a limited segment of society largely professionals and technical workers as well as students and housewives.

There was another study in 1990[86] on 'What Public Libraries

Have to Offer, Collection Building in the Field of Women's Information' by Kain W. Schade Van Westrum. He found that the women's support groups frequently complained of the difficulty of locating information in public libraries because the subject is relatively new and material is scattered under several headings throughout the library.

Another interesting study was in 1991[87] by E.A. Chatman on 'Channels to a Large Social World : Older Women Staying in Contact with the Great Society'. The study showed that the respondents were not revealed as users of the public library because they have in-house library and choosing to purchase reading materials and perceiving library items to be of little interest.

In India, on such an important problem little attention has been paid and no significant work has been done. There are books on library science which are of professional nature and a few scholars have also worked on the utilitarian aspects of the library. But a few people have given interest to study the community problems, community interests and the educational needs which the library serves. The first sizable survey of a public library in Asia was done in respect of the Delhi Public Library in 1955[88]. This study was to find out how far it had met the social and cultural needs and how it had fitted into the social life of that city. Apart from the specific problems which may be peculiar to Delhi City and the socio-cultural variations, this study was evaluatory on nature. The project-evaluation was in terms of certain specific objectives which the Delhi Public Library was expected to fulfil.

Some other studies on Indian Villages have been conducted by M.N. Srinivas [89], A.H. Somjee[90], S.C. Dube[91] and the publications of Sussex[92] group on village studies which were helpful to know the problems of conducting village studies . These studies were conducted in line with particular discipline and as such they were not of much importance in the present context.

M. Kumar and B.S. Biradar [93] conducted a study 'Uses of

Mass Media and Public Library by the Rural Community' (1998). This was a questionnaire survey to assess the uses of mass media (newspaper, radio, T.V) compared with the use of public libraries by the people of Siganamane Gram Panchayat area of Shimoga Dist., Karnataka. The study revealed that a majority were not interested in the duration of the library opening hours, and also that the location of the library was as inconvenient.

K. Sarada[94] conducted another study in 1976 on 'Library Facilities for Women in Andhra Pradesh Public Library system.'. The review covers three districts of Andhra Pradesh although the situation is considered to much the same in other districts. Enrolment of women in public libraries is extremely low, the reasons for which include the social and religious legacy of India. Special branch libraries for women are available but their number is totally inadequate. More mobile units equipped with motor vehicles, rather than cycle-rickshaws are necessary particularly in rural areas. Book selection is another problem with too little attention paid to such subjects as child care, hygiene and family planning.

L. Moore[95] conducted a study 'The Provision of Women's Reading Rooms in Public Libraries' (1993). It traces the history of the provision of separate reading rooms for women in public libraries from the 19th century, when a common view was that access to public libraries to educate women, distract them from household duties and undermine parental censorship and the gradual phasing out of women's reading rooms as society's views changed.

Some other recent studies conducted on this subject were of Dr. Shrinath Saha! Dr. K. Sharda and Dr., S. S. Jagnayak. The hypotheses of study of Dr. Shrinath Sahai [96] was that there is a general apathy of the people towards library, there is a relation between the reader's personality and the nature and content of the literature they read. The readers in India still follow the traditional reading pattern and they have not yet developed taste for the modern scientific and technological subjects to a marked extent; library has a big role in moulding the reading pattern of the people, etc. It brings out social and economic background of the people using the library, and the extent to which they are representative cross section of the community in general. In more concrete term, this study explained the extent to which the library meets the educational and recreational needs of the people, the role it plays as a medium of mass communication and functions as a social institution providing fellow-feeling, imparting essence of discipline and effecting the social behaviour of the people.

Another study was of K Sarada (1982)[97]. The objective of the study was to analyse the village community and its basic component groups, identification of the information needs of the village community, a descriptive account of the Branch library in the village, efficacy of the Branch library in meeting the information needs of the people, etc. It also focussed to analyse the Branch library in general and the village and not concentrating to the development of the women through women's library.

A very recent study was of S. S. Jagnayak[98] (1992), the objectives of the study was to find out the extent of the reading habit, educational attainment, agricultural development, economic development, social and political development and attitudinal change of the rural people. Here, the study concentrated on rural people and library in general and not particularly to the rural woman library and the development of rural woman through these libraries. But, the present study was fully concentrating on the role of women libraries in the socio-cultural, educational and economic development of rural women.

METHODOLOGY

India is, generally a rural country and people residing in these areas are less advanced than the people in urban centres particularly the women population. Various institutions are important aids to development and as such special library service particularly for women is of highly needed than in towns for their all-round development. Until and unless the information regarding social, cultural, economic, educational, political as well as health are made available and incorporated in the lives of these rural women, one cannot expect a progress that is lasting and secure. This can be done very efficiently by only a network of women libraries in rural settings.

The functions of the public library is to assemble, preserve and make easily and freely available to all people the printed and other materials that will assist them to educate themselves continuously; keep pace with progress in all fields of knowledge, become better members of home and community, discharge social and political obligations; be more capable in their daily occupations, develop their creative and spiritual capacities; appreciate and enjoy works of art and literature; make such use of leisure time as will promote personal and social well being; and contribute to the growth of knowledge.[99]

The problem has been selected for several other reasons. The rural setting is a viable unit for research studies as well as such studies have become a valuable part of research investigations in social sciences. The effect and impact of libraries on women and the interaction between women and library could be discerned and examined with greater accuracy in the village. For a state, which enjoys high percentage of literacy and reading habit of women, there is not better forum like library and its extension activities for contact with large number of women. Kerala is the land of libraries and a peculiar feature of these institutions are that they act as a cultural centre of the community at large. Besides, women in rural areas are not coming forward in various areas of social life and libraries especially for women help them in this regard. No systematic and scientific effort has been made so far to find out the part played by women libraries for the development of this section. So, a study like this will be helpful to find out the extent of its impact on women.

THEORETICAL BASIS OF THE STUDY

In general, there is no discrimination against women in Kerala in the matter of formal education. However, we find that compared to men, women do not make the best use of the libraries and their services for their continuing education. There are cultural inhibitions. In general, women above 20 do not visit libraries in person in rural areas. They get books through the male members or children. Similarly, they do not attend the seminars and discussions organized by these libraries. In other words the 'liberating influence' of the libraries are not being optimally utilized by the rural women folk. It is also a fact that men do not encourage women in this respect. Hence, gender discrimination and cultural inhibitions and practices will provide the theoretical background of the study.

OBJECTIVES OF THE STUDY

1. To find out how far these rural libraries have improved the reading habit of women.
2. To assess the extent of social development made by these libraries to rural women.
3. To assess the cultural development of rural women due to the libraries.
4. To find out the extent of economic improvement of rural women by these libraries.
5. Efficacy of the rural vanitha libraries in meeting the information and educational needs of women.
6. If there is no discernible development, then to find out the reasons.
7. To find out the views on the use of the library and the problems encountered by the women folk.

HYPOTHESES

1. The reading habit of the rural women have improved considerably.

2. The libraries have contributed much to the attitudinal change of rural women.
3. The libraries have increased the interest and participation in cultural activities of rural women.
4. People are economically benefited from the resources and different programmes of the library.

CONCEPTS

Educational development

Educational development for the present investigation is the increase of reading habit and consequent development in the personality of the individual.

Social development

Social development for our purpose is the increase of participation in social activities and consequent change in the attitudes towards social issues.

Cultural development

Here, cultural development means increase in the attendance and participation in cultural activities and consequent improvement in the capabilities and habit of the individual.

Economic development

It is the increase in the income and production and the reduction in the expenses of the individual.

CONSIDERATIONS FOR STUDYING SAMPLE POPULATION

The population for this study consists of women who had access to Library and representing the rural population in Kerala. The focus was to identify a Vanitha library and the selection was made in the Kannur district, in North Kerala. The selection of the population to be surveyed, was based on the following factors:

1. Women belonged to the age group 15 years and above
2. The population groups selected conforms to the general distribution pattern of religion, caste, income strata and occupation of the state.
3. The age and family structure of women surveyed was representative of the general population in Kerala.
4. 50 % of the respondents should be members of the library and have regular reading habits. The other 50% consists of non-members.
5. Only women belonging to lower and middle class will be included in the sample.

Based on the above considerations of the samples, the variability due to other socio-economic indicators were minimized. All the parameters of social, cultural, educational and economic status to be studied was normalised to be dependent upon the library use and reading habits.

SAMPLING DESIGN

On the basis of the preliminary study conducted in libraries in Cheruvakkal, Akkulam, Kariam and Powdikonam, a stratified random sampling design was adopted. 48 members and 48 non-members were selected from Panunda mahila Samajam Vanitha Granthalayam, Kannur . And thus total 96 respondents were selected and interviewed.

UNIT OF STUDY

The unit of study was the rural library with its circle of women readers. Therefore, attention was paid on the following aspects.

i. A brief history of the library.
ii. The present status of the library – facts and figures about the library like the number of books, the category of books, the number of members, the number of daily visitors , the

number of books issued daily., the number of working days per year, working hours, grant-in-aid amount, other sources of funds.

iii. Socio-cultural and extension activities etc.

iv. Whether the librarian has formal training in library management or not.

v. The organizational set up and the present office bearers.

vi. Bye-law etc.

Besides, there was a schedule for assessing the impact. Data was also collected from literature available in various libraries, Kerala Granthasala Sangham etc. Authentic persons in the field were met and collected data through observation also. In sum, the study focused on library as a development institution in the rural areas and its impact on the women folk in respect of their socio-cultural, economic and educational development.

QUANTITATIVE TECHNIQUES

The control group consisting of 48 women provided the bench-mark data regarding the socio-cultural status of women, who are not influenced by the institution of library. The experimental group which is being exposed intensively to the influence of the libraries which have multi-faceted programmes to identify and measure the impact through statistical devices. An interview schedule consisting of questions related to the different types of impact with a four point scale attached to each question (nil/low/average/high) were used for collecting data from the selected respondents. There was also questions to collect information about their reading habits-frequency, type of reading materials, intensity of reading, whether notes will be taken down, the utility of information acquired, whether they share the information with others in the family etc.

The data collected by the survey was computerised and analysed using SPSS Ver. 7.00 software. The proforma were edited by the project Director and obvious inaccuracies were rectified before data entry. The errors in the data entry were eliminated by suitable programme validation and consistency checks. Quality control was maintained by cross checking the data input with the original proforma randomly. The analysis was done to review the socio-economic status and the impact of library on socio-cultural, educational and economic development of women. Based on available data, various hypotheses about the population were tested. The statistical analysis methods included computing the frequently tables. After identifying the distribution of data, cross-tabulation studies with correlated variable and multivariable analysis was done to establish possible causes of problems and the consequent effect on the population. Pearson's coefficient of correlation and regression index were evaluated to confirm the statistical significance of the result. Based on the trend of population behaviour the hypotheses made were subject to chi-square or students T-Test wherever applicable and p-values determined to validate the inferences of the study. The Project Director correlated the statistical results with the observation during the survey and possible reasons were identified.

ANALYSIS OF DATA

The economic and social development of the rural women in Kerala has been characterized by some important achievements like :

1. Land re-distribution and increased agricultural productivity due to better utilization of small land holdings.
2. Population control and improved health & family welfare standards.
3. Female literacy and empowerment of women which is reflected in the various socio-economic indicators of development.
4. Participation of rural population in mainstream political and cultural activities of the State.
5. Opportunities for education, social interaction and decision making in the family

The term ' status' denotes the women's position in society. Any change in the status can be brought about by :

A. Availability of resources

B. Utilization of resources

C. Socio-economic milieu that promotes transformation.

Research in women's studies does not appear to have defined the term ' status'. In this study the status has been quantified with the help of indicators such as :

I. Access to Library and community and family support to using it's services

II. Library information and continuing education through general awareness

III. Awareness of women regarding the resources and programs to contribute towards family income

IV. Participation in self development and community improvement programs

V. Awareness about social problems and opportunity to engage in social service

VI. Economic benefits and social recognition

In the discipline of sociology literacy, socio – economic and educational status can be understood as the relative privileges and access to information. The relative power in society attained through education, personal income and participation in community activities is translated into better self esteem and economic benefits for the family. As first part of the study the selected experimental and control samples will be analysed for matching parameters. The control group consisting of 48 women will provide the benchmark data regarding the socio-cultural status of local women in the Pinarayi panchayat, of Kannur district of Kerala. Descriptive statistical measures like frequencies, mean and measures of dispersion will determine the representative nature of the experimental and control groups. Once it has been established that the two groups represent random sampling plan, then the only variable that differentiates the two groups is the influence of the vanitha library. The experimental group, also of 48 women will be compared with simple statistical devices like averages, percentages, ratios and correlations to establish the role of public libraries in the status of women.

PROFILE OF SAMPLE POPULATION - EXPERIMENTAL AND CONTROL GROUP

Experimental Group - Members of the Library
N = 48
AGE DISTRIBUTION

Age (in Years)	Frequency	Percentage (%)
10 – 20	15	31.25
21 – 30	13	27.08
31 – 40	11	22.92
Above 40	9	18.75
TOTAL	48	100.00

Mean Age = 27.98 Years S.D = 12.5

Marital Status

Age	Married	Unmarried	Separated	Widow	Divorced	Total	%
10 – 20	6	9				**15**	31.25
21-30	6	7				**13**	27.08
31-40	3	8				**11**	22.92
Above 40	2	3		3	1	9	18.75
Total	**17**	**27**		**3**	**1**	**48**	**100.00**
%	35.40	56.25	0.00	6.25	2.10	100	

Level of Education

Caste Level of Education

	1	2	3	4	5	6	7	8	9	Total	%
Forward	-	-	-	10	1	1	-	3	-	15	31.25
Backward	-	-	1	9	4	1	2	-	-	17	35.41
SC/ST	-	-	2	6	4	4	-	-	-	16	33.33
Total	-	-	**3**	**25**	**9**	**6**	**2**	**3**	-	48	**100.00**
%		-	6.25	52.08	18.75	12.5	4.17	6.25		**100.00**	

1. Literate 2. Primary 3. Upper Primary 4. High School & +2

5. Graduate 6. Post graduate 7. Technical 8. Professional Degree.

9. Skilled worker

Monthly Family Income

Personal Income (Rs.) Family Income (Rs)

	0-2500	2500-7500	7500-10000	> 10000	Total	%
Nil	13	2	5	2	**22**	**45.83**
0-1000	4	4	2		10	**20.83**
1000-2000	2				**2**	**4.17**
2000-5000	2	1	5	2	**10**	**20.83**
> 5000			2	2	**4**	**8.33**
Total	**21**	**7**	**14**	**6**	**48**	**100**

Monthly Personal Income : Mean Rs. 866.67 SD 186.25

Monthly Family Income : Mean Rs. 3944.36 SD 473.86

Occupation

Occupation	Caste				
	Forward	Backward	SC/ST	Total	%
Agriculture	**3**	**5**	**4**	12	25.00
Poultry & A.H	4	8	11	**23**	**47.92**
Fisheries			1	**1**	**2.08**
Manual Labour				**0**	**0.00**
Skilled Profession	3	2		**5**	**10.42**
Office Work	1	1		**2**	**4.17**
Teaching	1	1		**2**	**4.17**
Bank	1			**1**	**2.08**
Trade and Business	2			**2**	**4.17**
Total	**15**	**17**	**16**	**48**	**100**

Control Group - Non - Members of the Library

N = 48

AGE DISTRIBUTION

Age (in Years)	Frequency	Percentage (%)
10 – 20	12	25.00
21 – 30	22	45.83
31 – 40	3	6.25
Above 40	11	22.92
TOTAL	48	100.00

Mean Age = 27.97 Years S.D = 12.25

Marital Status

Age	Married	Unmarried	Separated	Widow	Divorced	Total	%
10 – 20		12				**12**	25.00
21-30	4	17	1			**22**	45.83
31-40	1	1			1	**3**	6.25
Above 40	6			4	1	**11**	22.92
Total	**11**	**30**	**1**	**4**	**2**	**48**	**100.00**
%	22.92	62.50	2.08	8.33	4.17	100	

Level of Education

Caste	Level of Education 1	2	3	4	5	6	7	8	9	Total	%
Forward	-	-	2	10	4		-	-	-	**16**	33.33
Backward	-	-	-	10	2	3	1	-	-	**16**	33.33
SC/ST	-	-	2	2	5	3	2	2	-	**16**	33.33
Total	-	-	4	22	11	6	3	2	-	48	100.00
%		-	8.33	45.83	22.91	12.50	6.25	4.16			**100.00**

1. Literate
2. Primary
3. Upper Primary
4. High School & +2
5. Graduate
6. Post graduate
7. Technical
8. Professional Degree.
9. Skilled worker

Monthly Family Income

Personal Income (Rs.)	Family Income (Rs) 0-2500	2500-7500	7500-10000	> 10000	Total	%	
Nil	18	2	6	2	**28**	**58.33**	
0-1000	4	1	2		**7**	**14.58**	
1000-2000		3	1			**4**	**8.33**
2000-5000		3		4	1	**8**	**16.66**
> 5000				1	**1**	**2.08**	
Total	28	4	12	4	48	100	
%	**58 33**	**8.33**	**25.00**	**8.33**			

Monthly Personal Income : Mean Rs. 539.12 S D 332.55

Monthly Family Income : Mean Rs. 3812.15 S D 497.06

Occupation

Occupation	Caste Forward	Backward	SC/ST	Total	%	
Agriculture	**5**	**1**		6	12.50	
Poultry & A.H	2	6	4	**12**	**25.00**	
Fisheries		1	1	**2**	**4.16**	
Manual Labour				4	**4**	**8.33**
Skilled Profession		1	2		**3**	**6.25**
Office Work	4	4	4	**12**	**25.00**	
Teaching	1	2	1	**4**	**8.33**	
Bank			**0**	**0.00**		
Trade and Business		3		2	**5**	**10.42**
Total	16	16	16	48	100	
%	33.33	33.33	33.33	**100**		

The distribution of the Experimental and the Control group is uniform , considering the indicators of age, caste, marital status, education and income. Age, caste, and educational profile of the two groups are significantly matched. While 18.75% of the experimental group is above the age of 40 years, 22.92% of the control group also fall under this category.The mean age of the two groups is 27.98 years (S.D 12.50) and 27.97 (S.D 12.25) years respectively . The caste distribution pattern among the two groups is almost identical, and represents the larger population of Pinarayi panchayat in Kannur district. 58.33% of the experimental group have not been educated beyond High school +2, compared with 54.16% for the control group.

Some difference can be noted in the marital status and family income between experimental and control groups. But this difference is not statistically significant to consider normalization of benchmark data. Among the experimental group 35.42% of respondents are married , while only 22.92% from control group are married. The National Sample Survey (1994) which found the percentage of women in Kerala under the age group less than 20 years was 8.21%. Corresponding to this figure the number of married women above the age of 20 years in 73.22%. In our study the percentage of women below the age of 20 years is very high and hence the low percentage of married women in both the samples can be attributed to age. The incidence of separation after marriage in control group (2%) is not related to age or education of women. There are no previous studies to compare the success of the institution of marriage. The mean monthly family income of the experimental group is Rs. 3944 (S.D 473.86) and that of the control group is Rs. 3812 (S.D 497.06). The same pattern is also reflected in the difference in personal incomes between the groups. This difference can be explained by the fact that only 45.83% of the experimental group declared their personal incomes as nil, while 58.33 % of control group members indicated no incomes. Thus the differences in the parameters of marital status and income does not affect the validity of benchmark data and can be attributed to random causes.

Quantitative Evaluation of Experimental and Control Groups

Criteria Mean S.D Std. Error Range Dispersion Coefficient

Age (Years) 27.97 12.25 1.7 18 - 60 **0.95**

27.98 12.50 1.6 17 - 65

Monthly Personal Income (Rs.) 866.67 186.25 38.2 400 – 8000 **0.67**

539.12 332.55 33.4 400 - 6500

Other Income (Rs.) 469.73 371.22 60.2 100 - 3500 **0.52**

585.10 308.10 69.1 100 - 4500

Total Monthly Family Income (Rs.) 3944.36473.86 42.7 800 – 14000 **0.83**

3812.15497.06 48.5 500 - 12000

Quantitative assessment of the two groups reveals close similarities in the economic status. The dispersion coefficients for age and total family income establishes the uniform patterns among the two groups. The average family income is higher among women with better educational status. This may also be due to the fact that the average family size among better educated women is smaller.

EFFECTIVENESS OF THE LIBRARY AND RELATED SERVICES

The Library being a social product , has in it's functioning certain social objectives in enriching the community . The three main objectives of a Library can be listed as :

1. To assemble, preserve, and administer books and related educational materials in organised collections, in order to promote through guidance and stimulation an enlightened citizenship and enriched personal lives.

2. To serve the community as a general center of reliable information.
3. To provide opportunity for individuals in the community to educate themselves continuously and engage in social interaction through participation in collaborative activities.

It is important to note that the role of a public library has not been a single one or uniform , irrespective of it's location and membership. The effectiveness of a library and related services is determined by the needs of the local community and it's adaptation to changing times.

Asset Ownership among family

Type of Asset	Members	%	Non-Member	%
Land & Building only	20	41.67	21	43.75
Agricultural Land only	1	2.08	1	2.08
Bank Deposits only	0	0.00	0	0
Buildings & Bank Deposits	8	16.67	8	16.67
Agricultural Lands & Bank Deposits	10	20.83	12	25.00
All types of assets	9	18.75	6	12.50
Total	48	100	48	100

Awareness to Join Library

Source of Information about Library	Frequency	%
Not aware before joining	3	6 25
From Teachers and Elders	7	14.58
Proximity to Library	6	12.50
Friends and Relatives	28	58.33
Participation in programs of Library	4	8.33
Total	48	100

The decision to join a library and to use it's services requires personal initiative. Ownership of assets empowers families and consequently individuals belonging to those families to take decisions. In this study it is seen that all the families of experimental group and control had some asset base. 18.75% of the members reported that their families had collective asset holdings compared to 12.50% of non-members. The co-relation between the family income and ownership of asset is very strong (0.92) . Additional earning members in the family, other sources of income and awareness about income generating opportunities are the key factors in economic status of individuals. The economic status results in better social and cultural interaction among community members. The awareness about the library is directly related to the scope and level of social interaction. School attendance, family gatherings, public functions and casual visits are the important activities that promote awareness. Only 6.25 % of the experimental group were not aware about the library, prior to becoming members. Contrary to general assumptions, awareness about library created by teachers and elders is only 14.58%. This study reveals that there is no effective linkage between school education and public libraries .

Awareness about the Library among Non - members

Level of Education	*Yes*	*No*	*% Awareness*
Literate	-		0.00
Primary	-		0.00
Upper Primary	4	2	8.33
High School & +2	21	1	43.75
Graduate	9	1	18.75
Post Graduate	5		10.42
Technical	3		6.25
Professional	2		4.17
Total	44	4	91.67

There is a significantly high level of awareness (91.67%) about the library among the non-members. Comparison of the experimental and control group establishes that the activities of the library and the conduct of the members are well known among the general population of the Pinarayi panchayat of Kannur district. The reading behaviour of an individual is governed by motivation and pre-disposition. Since the members of both groups had school education and were socially active, the external motivation to join the Library would have made the same impact. Then the difference between experimental and control groups can only be attributed to pre-disposition. This refers to the academic and intellectual environment in the family, the importance to reading imparted during early years at school and availability of good reading material to pursue the habit. Even though the Library as an institution has a multi-dimensional role, reading is the primary need for which local people join as members.

Reason for Not Joining the Library

Reason for Not Joining Library Educational Level

	Upper Primary	High School	+2	Graduate	PG and Others	**Total**
Distance	1	15	5	7	**28**	
No Spare Time	2	3	5	2	**12**	
Not Useful	1	1		2	**4**	
Others in Family are members				3	1	**4**
Total	**4**	**22**	**11**	**11**	**48**	

Reason for Not Joining Library Mean Family Income

	1500	**2500**	**3500**	**4500**	**> 5000**	**Total**
Distance	15	2	1	2	8	**28**

No Spare Time 6 6 **12**

Not Useful 2 1 1 **4**

Others in Family are members 2 1
1 **4**

Total 25 3 1 3 16 48

The main reason for not joining the Library as member can be attributed to the lack of available reading time. 58.33% of the control group expressed the distance from the library as the most important factor in limiting their use of it's services. 25.00% informed that they did not have spare time for reading. Considering the impact of accessibility and leisure time, it can be inferred that domestic responsibilities of women prevent them from joining libraries. The distribution of non-members is independent of educational level (P > 0.25) and family income (P > 0.25).

Measures of Library Use Pattern by Members

Library Use Criteria	Mean	S.D	Std. Error	Range	Dispersion Coefficient
Duration of Membership (Years)	6.30	3.42	0.49	0.5 - 15	0.72
Distance from Library (Km)	0.99	0.54	0.07	0.5 – 3.0	0.88
No. of Visits in a Month	21.18	5.18	0.74	12 - 30	0.63
No. of Hours in a Month	43.67	6.36	3.69	12 – 105	0.99

The Library use data shows interesting findings. Being the important social institution in the panchayat, the library is an integral part in the lives of the experimental group. The mean duration of membership is 6.3 years and the mean hours of use is 43.67 . This shows that members find the library useful and visits to the library is routine. There is significant co-relation between duration of membership and the hours spent. New members use the library more frequently and for more number of hours , than old members (Pearsons coefficent -0.91). Since there is an immediate purpose in joining the library, new members depend on the library and it's services, more than old members. Among the members there is no influence of distance on the library use pattern (P > 0.50) .

Motivation to Join the Library

Motivating Factors	Age 10-20	20-30	30-40	> 40	Total	%
Self	14	13	8	3	**38**	**79.17**
Friends & Relatives	1		2	3	**6**	**12.50**
Teachers & Elders					**0**	**0.00**
Librarian or Office bearer			1	3	**4**	**8.33**
Total	15	13	11	9	48	

Aim of Joining the Library

Purpose	Age 10-20	20-30	30-40	> 40	Total	%
Reference & Study	12	10	1	0	**23**	**47.92**
Leisure Reading	2	3	8	2	**15**	**31.25**
Social Interaction			1	4	**5**	**10.41**
Information Centre	1				**1**	**2.08**
Cultural Activities			1	3	**4**	**8.33**
Total	15	13	11	9	48	100

Co-relation Age and Self Motivation

Model	R^2	d.f	Std. Error	P
Regression	0.299	2	0.75	< 0.05

Co-relation Age and Aim

Model	R^2	d.f	Std. Error	P
Regression	0.126	2	0.80	< 0.05

Age is the key factor in determining the motivation and purpose for which members join the library. The inference that younger women are self motivated ($P < 0.05$) and their purpose is for study and self development ($P < 0.05$) is significant. Among older women the librarian and office bearers have to canvass for membership. Contrary to generally held beliefs women above the age of 30 , join libraries to participate in cultural activities. In the experimental group respondents above 30 stated that their aim in joining libraries was to improve social interaction with others in the community and participate in cultural activities.

In this study the relation ship between educational level, occupation , family income and the motivation to join the library was also analysed.

Motivation to Join the Library

Motivating Factors Educational Level

Upper Primary High School +2 Graduate PG and Others **Total**

Self 2 18 8 10 **38**

Friends & Relatives 4 1 1 **6**

Teachers & Elders **0**

Librarian or Office bearer 2 2 **4**

Total **4** **22** **11** **11** **48**

Aim of Joining Library

Purpose	Educational Level					
	Upper Primary	High School	+2	Graduate	PG and Others	**Total**
Reference & Study	2	12	6	3		**23**
Leisure Reading		6	2	7		**15**
Social Interaction		2	2	1		**5**
Information Centre			1			**1**
Cultural Activities	2	2				**4**
Total	**4**	**22**	**11**	**11**		**48**

Co-relation Education and Self Motivation

Model	Ç^2	d.f	Std. Error	P
Chi-Squared	0.251	2	0.38	<0.25

Co-relation Education and Aim

Model	Ç^2	d.f	Std. Error	P
Chi-Squared	**0.311**	**2**	**0.62**	**<0.50**

The better educational status also contributes towards self motivation ($P < 0.25$) and use of library for reference and study ($P < 0.50$). The findings are not as significant as the co-relation with age.

LIBRARY AND EDUCATIONAL DEVELOPMENT OF WOMEN

Transformation for gender equality begins with assertion of women's rights and equal access to economic resources. Educational value adds the women to be more productive and empowered. Education confers on women the awareness about their current status and opportunities to achieve better socio-economic conditions. The privileges of education, hitherto administered as a means of establishing the men as the earning members of the family, is now equally enjoyed by the women also. Literacy and Education of women has a two-fold influence on the family :

I. Increase the Family income and control over expenditure

II. Contribution to children's education , especially encouragement to the girl child to pursue education, thus ensuring that the next generation will attain a higher socio-economic status.

While the former process denotes a removal of family barriers and economic subordination, the latter emphasizes the social acceptance of legitimate women's aspirations. This study has tried to analyse the role of Library that promote better literacy & educational levels among women and the awareness about opportunities for employment and income generation.

The purpose for using the library and other services may be varied. Academic and non-academic pursuits would require different information resources. In this study the educational level of women was higher compared to the state average. Hence their needs are not confined to general awareness and public announcements. The actual use of the library by the members and the perceived benefits of using the library among control group was elicited and compared. The hypothesis regarding the reading habit of rural women can be tested from this collected data.

Role of Library in Literacy and Education Experimental Vs Control Group

Role	Frequency of Responses							
	No		Little		Average		High	
	Exp.	Con.	Exp.	Con.	Exp.	Con.	Exp.	Con.
For Studies and Reference	0	1	1	9	9	8	38	30
General Awareness	0	0	1	1	6	3	41	44
Business Information	7	19	8	11	10			

11 23 7

Employment Information 2 29 5 8

27 7 14 4

Discussion Group 0 14 1 22 11

4 36 8

Government Notifications 19 25 6 11

8 15 15 0

Library has improved the reading habit of rural women

Test of Hypothesis

Model	t^2	d.f	Std. Error	P
T - test	0.196	2	0.16	<0.10

Model	Ç^2	d.f	Std. Error	P
Chi-Squared	0.039	2	0.02	<0.05

The t-test confirms that the experimental and control sample comes from the same population. Therefore any difference in the reading habit can be co-related with the role of the library. Analysis of the two groups reveals strong co-relation between the level of awareness of rural women and their use of library ($P < 0.05$).

The role of the public library is not very important with regard to reference source and providing study material for formal education. 79.17% of the experimental group used the library for the purpose of their course study. 62.50% of the control group also used other libraries. There was no significant difference in the extent of assistance rendered by the library and related services. It is assumed that books and study materials for curriculum are purchased by individuals and therefore the role of library in formal education is minor. Nevertheless the library can always function as second reference.

Public library is truly effective as a repository of business and employment information and government announcements. This study reveals that the public library is the most preferred information centre in the community. The experimental group respondents used the public library extensively for business information (47.92%) , employment information (29.17%) and discussions(75.0%) . In sharp contrast to this the control group had very little access to business (14.53%), employment (8.33%) information and discussions(16.67%) with others in community. Public libraries are the only source for government notifications in the rural community. While 39.55% of experimental group had no information about government notifications on a regular basis, 52.08% of control group were not at all aware of any source of government information. 31.25 % of experimental group regularly obtained government notifications and public announcements from the library. Public library makes information more accessible to rural women and thus contributes towards improving their literacy skills and educational status.

Average number of Books read per month

Yrs. Of Membership	*2 Books*	*3 Books*	*4 Books*	*Total*
1 – 5	7	8	9	**24**
5 – 10	4	8	2	**14**
> 10	1	8	1	**10**
Total	12	24	12	48

Type of Books preferred

Yrs. Of Membership	*Fiction*	*Non-fiction*	*Both*	*Total*
1 – 5	1	9	14	**24**
5 – 10	3	1	10	**14**
> 10	3	2	5	**10**
Total	7	12	29	48

Benefits from Library membership

Benefits	***Age in Years***				
	10 – 20	***21 – 30***	***31 – 40***	***> 40***	***Total***
Literacy					
Personality	1	1	4	2	**8**
Academics	13	8			**21**
Awareness	1	4	7	6	**18**
Economic				1	**1**
No Benefit					**0**
Total	**15**	**13**	**11**	**9**	**48**

The data from members suggest that Library has a significant role to play in the educational levels and general awareness of rural women. 50% of the members read atleast 3 books during the past month. The number of books read is co-related to the duration of membership i.e as the years increased the reading habit increased (0.92). This may also be explained by the fact that , as older members do not attend school or college , they would have more of spare time to use the library. 56.25% of the members had non-academic benefits like improved personality, general and social awareness and direct economic gains.

Mode of Information Dissemination (N = 48)

Type of Activity	*Nil*	*Low*	*Average*	*High*
Reading Books & Periodicals			4	44
Reference			11	37
Government Publications	1	2	4	41
Discussions		1	11	36
Seminars			1	47
Teach Family members		2	18	28
Teach friends, neighbours		4	12	32

The indirect impact of the Library is clearly brought out in the above table. Besides being a repository of published body of knowledge, the library is an institution of social intercourse and peoples interaction. 33.33% of members engaged in discussions and 97.92% participated in seminars organised by the library management. Members also actively involved in knowledge dissemination among their family and neighbourhood. Library members rendered more assistance to friends and neighbors (66.67%) compared to immediate family members (58.33%). Since the educational and economic status of member's families is higher than others in the locality, near relatives would require less educational assistance compared with others.

LIBRARY AND SOCIO – CULTURAL DEVELOPMENT OF WOMEN

Education and employment are the major platforms supporting the participation of women in democratic processes. Education prepares the individual to understand the democratic process, makes them aware of the roles & responsibilities of individuals in nation building and communicate with the society to be identified as empowered women. Employment confers economic independence and the power to make decisions. Once , women participate in the socio-cultural and political activities then there is increased awareness about health, family welfare , economic opportunities and children's education . The role of the government in development and welfare activities of rural women is monitored by empowered women within the community.

The outcome of historical subordination of women in Kerala , leads to their lower status, which is perceived as natural, immutable and even correct for the modern times. Kerala's matrilineal heritage has been unearthed by many social actors including researchers, activists and feminist scholars as a vital link in the re-emergence of women as agents of development. In the present context, the contribution of women in improving the health, education , family welfare and agricultural productivity conditions in Kerala cannot be downplayed. For women the lack of power has meant lack of access to, and control of resources. dimensions in education.

This study has tried to co-relate the access to information and role of Library services in the participation of rural women in socio – cultural and political process. Women's aspirations are raised , when their access to media like newspapers & television are facilitated. This results in participating in the democratic process and influencing the decision making. Women's access to public sphere cannot be total without competing with men for the same socio – cultural and political space.

In this study socio – cultural and political participation is quantified by the attitudes, opportunities and utilisation of leisure time in community activities. Awareness about culture , history and arts is the result of access to books and media like newspapers & TV. Participation in political activity is recognised by primary membership in any political, trade union or socio-cultural organisation. Gender equality is measured in the elevation of primary functionaries to the position of elected / nominated representatives

Role of Library in Socio – cultural Development Experimental Vs Control Group

Role Frequency of Responses

No Little Average High

Exp. Con. Exp. Con. Exp. Con. Exp.

Con.

Access to Audio and Visual media 5 12 10

2 18 28 15 6

Read Books on Culture & history 10 9 18

37 14 2 6 0

Newspaper and periodicals 7 22 8 12

10 6 23 8

Social and cultural activities 12 46 4 2
1 0 31 0

Awareness of Culture & history 1 3 2
39 9 5 36 1

Other Leisure activities 4 30 27 12
16 1 1 5

Improved social status 0 23 2 22 16
2 30 1

Library has improved the Social status of rural women

Test of Hypothesis

Model	t^2	d.f	Std. Error	P
T - test	0.196	2	0.16	<0.10

Model	Ç^2	d.f	Std. Error	P
Chi-Squared	0.210	2	1.02	<0.10

In this study the role of library in the social and cultural development of rural women is compared for experimental and control groups. The data compiled for the relevant indicators , show that the awareness and status of Library members is higher than non – members. 64.58% of the experimental group were very active in social and cultural activities, 75.0% were aware of history and culture and 62.5% responded that their social status improved after joining the library. The figures for non – members is less than 5% for the respective indicators cited. The test of population and hypothesis also shows the statistical validity of the inference (P < 0.10)

Attitude towards Social Problems
Experimental Vs Control Group

Social Attitude	Frequency of Responses					
	Opinion Change		Approve		Disapprove	
	Exp.	Con.	Exp.	Con.	Exp.	Con.

Communal Harmony	2	NA	43	41	3	7
Dowry System	5	NA	29	41	14	7
Widow remarriage	0	NA	8	10	40	38
Superstition	1	NA	10	22	37	26
Atrocities against women	3	NA	3	4	42	44

Attitude towards Women's Problems

Experimental Vs Control Group

The analysis of data shows that membership of the library is a significant driver in changing the attitudes about society and focus groups. Social attitudes are moulded by interaction with peer groups, self determination and influence of media. In the sample population 10.42% of the experimental group and 25.0% of the control group were members or sympathizers of political parties. Library members prefer to have individual opinions rather than be influenced by local opinion makers and political leaders. The change in attitude brought about by library membership is confined to women's issues . The belief systems of rural women changed after using the resources and information in the library. Significant proportion of library members changed their opinion in matters regarding disapproval of dowry system (10.42%), awareness about atrocities against women (6.25%), approval for family planning (12.5%), need for women's empowerment (12.5%) and environmental protection (33.33%).

ECONOMIC IMPACT OF LIBRARY ON RURAL WOMEN

A desegregated view of women as constituting different categories , is essential to understand women's relationship to economic development and the labour market. In case of upper castes and class the caste rules deny women access to independent income or employment and they often end up undertaking domestic & household responsibilities. The data collected by Central Social

Welfare Board and NGO's indicate that illiterate and women with low levels of education work in extremely adverse and formidable conditions. In this study the educational level of the population was higher compared to the state average. Library is not an institution of production or economic activity. Thus the library can at best function as a facilitator in economic development of rural women. Library can provide information regarding government assistance, income generation schemes, market potential and institutions for techno-commercial viability study and consulting.

Role of Library in Economic Development of Rural Women
Experimental Vs Control Group

Role	Frequency of Responses							
	No		Little		Average		High	
	Exp.	Con.	Exp.	Con.	Exp.	Con.	Exp.	Con.
Increased Family Income	27	47	14	1	7	0	0	0
Reduced Expense for Education	38	44	8	4	2	0	0	0
Employment related information	2	29	5	6	27	6	12	7
Self employment	41	28	0	19	0	1	7	0
Market & Price	0	0	0	8	3	11	45	29
Business contacts	8	16	30	32	6	0	4	0
Banks & Savings	28	30	14	16	6	2	0	0
Agricultural loan	2	9	8	15	20	18	18	6

Library creates economic benefits for rural women

Test of Hypothesis

Model	t^2	d.f	Std. Error	P
T - test	0.196	2	0.16	<0.10

Direct Economic Benefit

Model	Ç2	d.f	Std. Error	P
Chi-Squared	**0.011**	**2**	**2.02**	**>0.25**

Indirect Economic Benefit (Information)

Model	Ç2	d.f	Std. Error	P
Chi-Squared	**0.467**	**2**	**0.44**	**<0.10**

In this study the role of Library as agent of change in the economic status of women, should be interpreted against the economic resources of the institution and occupation profile of the samples. Unlike banks and co-operatives libraries do not have monetary and non-monetary resources. Direct intervention in economic activity is not envisioned in the objectives of the library. Members of the library may represent financial institutions . Thus the role of the library is limited to economic information dissemination and facilitate interaction between economic decision makers and beneficiaries. the experimental group 47.92% were housewives with additional income from agriculture and animal husbandry. Among the control group only 25.0% had similar occupation. 20.83% of experimental group were salaried class while 39.58% of control group were of this category. The economic impact of the library will be significant among the students and unemployed sections of the society.

Analysis of the data shows that there is no difference in the direct economic benefits among members and non-members of the library. 56.25 % of the members and 97.9 % of non-members did not receive any benefits. This data is not statistically significant (P > 0.25). Indirect benefits like market information, information about agricultural loans and employment related information can be attributed to the services provided by the library (P < 0.10).

FINDINGS

1. The reading habits of rural women have improved after joining the Library.
2. Libraries have contributed to the education, awareness and empowerment of rural women.
3. Library as an institution which promotes participation in social and cultural activities.
4. Rural vanitha Library adequately meets the educational and information needs of the local population.
5. Library helps rural women to utilize their leisure time for entertainment and social interaction.
6. In rural areas the library is the only source of information about history, culture and arts.
7. The level of participation in the programs organised by the library is high.
8. Library does not have direct economic impact on the rural women.
9. Library improves the educational and socio- cultural status of rural women.

REFERENCES

1. S.C. Behar, National System of Education in India, *The Encyclopaedia of Higher Education,* Vol. 1, National Systems of Higher Education, Pergmon Press, Oxford, 1992, pp 304-321
2. S.S. Jagnayak, *Role of Libraries in Socio-economic, Cultural and Educational Development among Rural People,* Classical Publishing Company, New Delhi, 1997, pp 1-3.
3. W.F. Ogburn, Library and the New Social Order, *Wilson Library Bulletin,* Vol. B, No. 8, H.W. Wilson Co., New York, 1934, p 443

4. Patrick R. Penland, Community and the Library, *Encyclopaedia of Library and Information Science* Vol. 5, Marcel Dekker Inc., New York, 1968, p. 483

5. E. N. O. Adimorah, An Analysis of Progress Made by Public Libraries as Social Institution In Nigeria, *UNECO Journal of Information Science, Librarianship and Archives Administration,* Vol. V, No. 3, UNESCO, Paris, 1983, p 162.

6. D. R. Kalia, *A Report on Role of Cultural Institutions in Adult Education,* Education Commission, Govt. of India, New Delhi, 1965, p. 15

7. Patrick R. Penland, op. cit. 1968, p. 477

8. Cyril O. Houle, *Libraries in Adult and Fundamental Education: The Report of the Malmo Seminar,* Paris, 1951.

9. Quoted by Ruth W. Gregory, Search for Information About Community Needs, *Library Trends*. Vol. 17, No. 1, 1968, p. 18.

10. Ann P. Drennan and Ann Shelby, Library and Information Needs of the Geographically Remote, *'In Library and Information Service Needs of the Nation* (Eds. Carlos A. Caudara and Marcia J. Bates), Washington, 1974, p. 17.

11. Mary Jo. Lynch, Educational, Cultural and Recreational Services of the Public Library for Adults, *Library Quarterly.* 48(4) p. 484.

12. J.A. Hennessy, Choices for Library Services: Comments on the Socio-economic Dimension, *Journal of Librarianship.* 11(2) , 1979, p. 128.

13. F.A. sharr, Functions and Organisation of a Rural Library System, UNESCO Bulletin for Libraries. 2(1), 1972, p.6.

14. Gardner Hanks and James C. Schmidt, An Alternative Model of a Profession for Librarians, College and Research Libraries, 36(3) 1975. p 181

15. Sarada K., *Rural Library Services in India,* ESS ESS Publication, New Delhi, 1986, p. 163

16. UNESCO, *Transfer and Utilisation of Information for Development in the 1980s – Main Problems and Strategies for their Solution* , Paris, 1981, p.2

17. India, Advisory Committee for Libraries (1959), *Report of Advisory Committee for Libraries,* New Delhi, 1959, p. 95.

18. John Lowe, *The Education of Adults : A world Perspective,* Paris, 1975, p. 22.

19. Cyril O. Haule, op.cit p. 24

20. John Lowe, op. cit , 1975, p22

21. UNESCO Public Library Manifesto, *UNESCO Bulletin for Libraries.*26(3), 1972, p 129-131

22. G. L. Tehran, *Modern Public Library Movement and Services In India.* Library Literature House, Chandigrah, 1982, p.105

23. J. H. Shera, *Sociological Foundations of Librarianship*, Asia Publishing House, Bombay, 1970 p 44-52

24. K. C. Harrison, *Library And the Community*, Andre Deustch Ltd., London, 1962, p. 15

25. A. G. Gopinatha Menon, *'Adoption Behaviour of Small Farmers in Relation to their Attitude towards Agricultural Innovation,* Unpublished Ph. D. Thesis, Department Of Sociology, University Of Kerala, Thiruvananthapuram, 1982, p. 16

26. Ansuya T. Shethi, *Nonformal Education And Community Development – A System Alalysis,* Unpublished Ph. D. Thesis, Department Of Education, South Gujarath University, Surat, 1981, p.4

27. Shiv R. Mehta, *Rural Development – Policies And Programmes – A Sociological Perspective*, Sage Publications, New Delhi, 1984, p. 5

28. S.R. Mittal, *Organising A Village Library,* Publication Unit,

National Council Of Educatuional Research And Training, New Delhi, 1964, p.1.

29. Robert J. Stalcup, *Sociology And Education*, Charles E. Merril Publishing Company, Ohio, 1968, p 29

30. Sachdev And Gupta, *A Simple Study of Sociology*, Ajanta Prakashan, New Delhi, 1980, p 248-250

31. Padma Ramachandran, Libraries as Catalysts of Change, *Trivandrum Public Library Jubilee Souvenir*, Government of Kerala, Trivandrum , 1974 , p 105

32. P. N. Kaula, A Study of Public Library Development and Services for Rural Upliftment, *Herald Of Library Science*. 39, (3-4) , 2000, p. 185

33. Ibid, p 187

34. Ibid, p 189

35. Ibid, p 190

36. S.S. Jagnayak, op.cit. 1997, p 10

37. Nittala V. Ratnam and B. Bhaskara Rao, *The Measurement of Social Development in Rural Areas* , Newman Group of Publishers, New Delhi, 1982, p. 8.

38. S.K. Mangal, *Educational Psychology,* Prakash Brothers , Ludhiana, 1981, p. 117.

39. R. Owens, The State Government and Libraries , *XXVth All India Library Conference – Seminar Papers,* Indian Library Association, New Delhi, 1980, p.28.

40. P. Raymond Williams, *Culture,* William Colins Sons and Co. Ltd. , Glasgon, 1981, p. 13.

41. C.N. Shankar Rao, *Sociology,* S. Chand and Company Ltd. New Delhi, 2000. p. 190

42. Ibid, p.192

43. M.C. Jingan, *The Economic Development and Planning,* Vikas Publishing House Pvt. Ltd., New Delhi, 1976, p 4-6.

44. Charles M. Moharhardt, a Building Programme for a Public Library, *Public Library of Asia* , Delhi Seminar, UNESCO, Paris, 1956, p. 83.

45. P.N. Kaulas, op. cit. 2000, p. 190.

46. C.N. Shankar Rao, op. cit, 2000, p. 400.

47. K. Sharada, op. cit. 1986, p. 128.

48. J. J. Thabah, Information Needs and Information Seeking Behaviour of Housewives, *Library Hearld*, 39(142), 2001, p. 65.

49. Ibid p. 70

50. P.N. Kaula, op. cit. p 190.

51. Elizabeth Bumiller, *May you be the Mother of a Hundred Sons, A Journey among the Women in India,* Raindom House, New York, 1990.

52. Sarala R. Murgai, 'Motivation to Manage : A Comparative Study between male and Female Library and Information Science. Students in the United States of America and India, *50 years of Indian Librarianship,* G. Devarajan (ed). ESS ESS Publications, New Delhi, 1999, p. 286

53. V.K. Thomas , *Public Libraries in India – Development and Finance*, Vikas Publishing House Pvt. Ltd., New Delhi, 1997, pp. 37-55.

54. G.D. Bhargava and B.S. Nigam, 'Madhya Pradesh Needs Library Legislation' in *Library Movement and Library Development in India,* 30th All India Library Conference Papers, Ed. C.P. Vasisth, Indian Library Association, Delhi 1994, pp. 52-60.

55. Raman Nair, *Public Library Development*, S.S. Publications, New Delhi , 1993, pp. 21-22.

56. R.S.P. Singh , Public Library Development in Bihar, *Indian Journal of Library Studies* , 2(2), 1991, pp. 193-204.

57. V.K. Thomas , op. cit, pp. 45-58

58. Ibid, p. 55 –65

59. S.S. Jagnayak, Public Library Development in India – An Historical Perspective since 1947, *50 years of Indian Librarianship* , Ed. G. Devarajan, ESS ESS Publications, New Delhi, 1999, pp. 71-92

60. V. K. N. Menon, The Trivandrum Public Library, *Trivandrum Public Library Platinum Jubilee Souvenir,* 1974, p.15

61. Koya Pakkar, Some Major Libraries in Kerala, *Trivandrum Public Library Platinum Jubilee Souvenir,* 1974, p.118.

62. K. Sivadasan Pillai (Ed). *Kerala Granthasala Sangham (1945-80),* Trivandrum, 1981, p. 2

63. K.A Issac , Library Movement in Kerala, *Timeless Fellowship,* 1973, p. 46.

64. T.K. Vellupillai, *Trvancore State Manual*, Vol. 2, Government Press, Trivandrum, 1958, p. 43.

65. Vettoor Raman Nair, Kerala Granthasala Sangham Pravarthanacharithavum Khadanayum (Kerala Granthasala Sangham; History and Constitution), *Kerala Granthasala Directory,* Trivandrum , 1964, p. 53.

66. Krishna Kurup, Malabar Granthasala Prasthanam (Library Movement in Malabar), Granthalokam 9(4), *Kerala Granthasala Sangham,* Trivandrum, 1957, p. 197.

67. Krishna Kumar (Ed), *XXVI All Indian Library Conference,* Indian Library Association , New Delhi, 1980.

68. T. Vasudea Menon , Library Movement in Kerala, *Library Movement in India*, Delhi Library Association, Delhi, 1958, p. 98.

69. S.S. Jagnayak, op. cit. 1997, pp 24-31.

70. S.S. Jagnayak, *Literacy and Educational Status of women in Kerala,* (Unpublished Report), Kerala Women's

Commission , Government. Of Kerala, Trivandrum, 2001, pp. 12-13.

71. Hepzi Joy, Women's Education and Social Change in Kerala, *International Congress on Kerala Studies* , Vol 2, 1994, p. 102.

72. T. Vasudeva Menon, op. cit, p. 98.

73. P. Udayabhanu, Sanganthinte Sargatmaka Paripadikal (Sangam's Developmental Activities), *Keralathile Granthasala Prasthanam (Library Movement In Kerala)*, Trivandrum, 1992, p 269-270

74. Kerala Granthasala Sangham, Granthasala Niyamavali, p. 2

75. Bernard Reuben Berelson, *Library's Public,* Columbia Universiy, New York , 1949.

76. Jesse Hauk Shera, *Foundations of the Public Library : Origins of the Public Library in New England, 1629-1815*, University of Chicago Press, Chicago, 1949,

77. Sydney H. Ditizon, Arsenals of a Democratic culture, *A Social History of the American Public Library movement in new England and the Middle States from 1850-1900*, American Library Association, Chicago, 1947.

78. A. Stuart, Reading Habits in Three London Boroughs, *Journal of Documentation* ,Vol. 8, No. 4, 1952, pp 34-39.

79. Brian Groombridge, *The Londner and His Library*, London 1965

80. Bryan Luckham, *The Library In Society : A Study of the Public Library in an Urban Setting,* London, 1971

81. Barry Totterdell and Jean Bird, *The Effective Library Report of the Hillingdon Project on Public Library Effectiveness* (Ed) Margaret Redfern, London, 1976.

82. Joseph L Wheeler, *The Library and the Community*, Chicago, 1924

83. Leon Carnovosky And Lowell Martin (Eds), *The Library in the Community* Chicago, 1944.

84. Bernard Berelson, *The Library's Public : A Report of The Public Library Inquiry*, New York, 1949.

85. Ching-Chih Chen, Citizen's Information Needs : A Regional Investigation. Robert D. Stuart (Ed) *Information Needs of the 80's* , Jain Press, London, 1982.

86. Kain W. Schade Van Westrun, What Public Libraries have to Offer : Collection Building in the Field of Women's Information Bibliothek En Samenleving, 18[10], 1990.

87. E.A. Chatman, Channels To A Larger Social World : Older Women Staying in Contact with the Great Society, *Library and Information Science Research*.3(3), 1991.

88. Frank M. Gardner, *Delhi Public Library: An Evaluation Report* , UNESCO, Paris, 1957.

89. M.N. Srinivas, *India's Villages,* Bombay, 1960.

90. A.H. Somjee *Democracy And Political Change In Village India*, Delhi, 1971

91. S.C. Dube, *Indian Village* , London, 1955.

92. Biplab Das Gupta (Ed) , Village Studies In The Third World, Delhi, 1978.

93. M. Kumar and B.S. Biradar, Use of Mass Media and Public Library by the Rural Community : A Study, *Annals of Library Science and Documentation,* 44(3),1998.

94. K. Sarda, Library Facilities for women in Andhra Pradesh Public Library System, *Indian Librarian,* 31(1), 1976.

95. L. Moore, The Provision of Women's Reading Rooms in Public Libraries, *Library History*, 9 (5&6), 1993.

96. Shrinath Shahi, *Library And the Community* , Today and Tomorrow's Printers and Publishers, New Delhi, 1973.

97. .K. Sarada , op cit. p1.

98. S. S. Jagnayak op cit. 1997.
99. Gerald W. Johnson, Role of Public Library, *Public Library Service*, American Association, Chicago, 1956, p 31.

9

INFORMATION NEEDS AND USE PATTERN OF PURE SCIENTISTS

P.Geetha

Information could be considered as an indispensable resource, which human beings receive throughout the day. Now a day, we are living in an age of 'information explosion'. Information is the communication of knowledge about an event, given condition, or the spread of knowledge derived from observation, study, experience or instruction. According to Shannon and Weaver [1], 'Information is any stimulus that reduces uncertainty'. Ching-Chih Chen and Peter Hernon defines information as 'all knowledge, ideas, facts, data and imaginative works of mind which are communicated formally and/or informally in any format' [2]. Information may be stored in different ways. For getting knowledge, the users may depend on printed or other forms of information. In order to make the information sources easily available, facilities should be provided in such a way that, these sources could be made accessible to the right user at the right time.

Information has become an essential ingredient for research and development, and it is the raw material from which knowledge is derived. During the second quarter of the 20th century, tremendous growth of research activities in science and technology was observed. India also has a unique position in the field of scientific and technical research. It is from research that new information is generated. Research in the field of science and technology result in the generation of information, which is beneficial to the whole society. Also, for carrying out research, information is necessary.

The primary aim of research is to extend the boundaries of knowledge. Research is the search for knowledge through objective and systematic methods for finding a solution to a problem. Research is a self-perpetuating activity, where each new invention suggests a new problem. If the desired result is not found, one should re-search again. Busha [3] defines research as "... any systematic quest for knowledge that is characterised by disciplined inquiry".

According to Best [4], research is " a more systematic activity directed towards discovery and development of an organised body of knowledge. It is based on critical analysis of hypothetical propositions for the purpose of establishing cause-effect relationships, which must be tested against objective reality". Wise[5] and others quotes research as "It is characteristically and inevitably a systematic inquiry for verified knowledge".

Research is of different types. According to functional characteristics, research can be categorised into the following groups[6].

1. Pure or Basic or Fundamental or Theoretical Research.
2. Applied or Industrial or Field Research.
3. Action Research.
4. Evaluation Research.

The first two categories i.e. Pure and Applied research are the major components of scientific research. The latter two are mainly carried out in the fields of Social Science and Humanities. In Universities and similar institutions, pure research is carried out, which is aimed at the expansion of knowledge. It develops theories by discovering broad generalisations or principles for further understanding of a phenomenon.

The scientific discipline is categorised into Pure Science and Applied Science disciplines. The researchers in scientific disciplines use scientific information. According to Busha [7], " science is an organised body of knowledge and a method of modifying and extending what is known by careful research". Scientific information has certain properties. It is universal, especially in the case of disciplines like Physics, Chemistry and Biological Sciences. It becomes obsolete in fast developing disciplines, and the exponential growth in scientific publications causes difficulty in their accessibility and availability. So in order to carry out research, right information should be provided to the researchers at the right time.

Researchers need information to keep them updated, with the latest trends in their subject fields. For this, an effective information service, which is inexpensive compared to the expensive scientific research is of great help. By providing effective information services by agencies and libraries, and by improving the efficiency of these services to researchers, duplication in research could be minimised and R&D could be made more effective.

Research can be successfully carried out only when the necessary information is provided to the scholars as and when they are needed. For information connected with their work, the researchers may conduct comprehensive literature survey and use sources like primary, secondary, tertiary, audio-visual sources, computer based sources etc. It is very difficult to satisfy the information needs of research scholars in scientific disciplines, due to many factors like exponential growth of literature, its complexity, scattering of literature, language barriers, multi-disciplinary nature etc. So it is necessary to study the information needs and information gathering behaviour of research scholars.

Information gathering activity of individuals include aspects like types of information sought, ways of accessing information, searching and acquiring information, use of their own libraries as well as others etc. Behaviour studies are usually conducted to find out the interaction of the user community with the communication system. So in order to provide the information to research scholars, according to the needs, their information needs, use pattern and information seeking behaviour should be ascertained. This will help to take measures to improve the information services by libraries and other agencies and help to provide need-based information to researchers belonging to various disciplines. For this reason, user studies are of great significance.

Universities act as the premier centers of research activities. Usually pure research is carried out here and the universities are playing an important role in promoting research in the field of Pure Sciences. Progress in research is impossible without the support of information. So, before embarking on research for doctorate, the researchers invariably conduct comprehensive literature search. Hence an investigative study about the information gathering behaviour of research scholars in Pure Science will help to get an understanding of the information needs and use pattern of researchers in their subject fields.

RELEVANCE OF THE STUDY

Research scholars often need specialised information for carrying out their works. In developing countries, most of the researchers are not aware of the role of information in research activities. Due to lack of competitive situations and research environments, researchers in developing countries do not properly use information. In India, even the existing resources of the scientific and technical library remains underutilized. So studying the information needs and information gathering behaviour of research scholars is relevant.

A doctoral thesis deal with the field of study, not previously treated, and so it is a source of original information. For its preparation, the research scholars seek various types of information from various sources. With the help of user studies, the specific needs of the research scholars regarding the use of information, as well as their satisfaction with the available facilities can be analyzed, based on which improvements in facilitating information could be made. These studies also help in providing effective and efficient information services and also to improve the public relations of a library with its users.

By assessing the user needs and use pattern, library services could be provided in such a way as to meet the demands of the users. The present study also aims to assess the information needs, use pattern and behaviour of research scholars in Pure Science disciplines of the University of Kerala. It is also tried to study the difference in the need, use pattern and information seeking behaviour of research scholars in different Pure Science fields. This information will help to provide better services and to improve existing services in both the department libraries and the University library. The study also help to understand the types of resources and services most needed by research scholars in the different Pure Science disciplines, which in turn is needed for the provision of the required information.

TITLE OF THE STUDY AND DEFINITION OF KEY TERMS

The title of the study is "Information Needs and Information Gathering Behaviour of Research Scholars in the Pure Science Departments of the University of Kerala".

The definitions of key terms are given below. Some of them are self-explanatory.

Information needs - According to Maurice B. Line [8], information need is "what an individual ought to have for his work, his research, his edification, his recreation etc.". The Librarians' Thesaurus [9] defines information need as "that need which library services or materials are intended to satisfy".

Information gathering behaviour - This include aspects like the motives and purposes of information gathering, the nature and type of information sought, the mode and means to access, search, identify and acquire information, and the use of their own as well as other libraries. T.D. Wilson [10] defines 'information behaviour' as "those activities a person may engage in when identifying his or her own needs for information, searching for such information in any way, and using or transferring that information".

Research scholar - A research scholar in this context includes students, working towards an advanced degree of M.Phil and Ph.D.

Pure science - Pure Science is a theoretical discipline that is not governed by practical theories. These are disciplines with wide-ranging objectives and studies laws behind phenomena.

OBJECTIVES OF THE STUDY

The main objective of the study is to examine the information needs and information gathering behaviour of research scholars in the pure science departments of the University of Kerala. The other objectives of the study include:

1. to find out the information needs of research scholars in Pure Science fields, in relation to their qualification, sex, category and discipline.
2. to examine the type of information sources required by the research scholars in Pure Science and to identify their approach to information contained in different information sources;
3. to identify the communication channels through which information is acquired by Pure Science research scholars, and to examine the frequency of use of various sources of information;
4. to ascertain the opinion of the researchers in Pure Science regarding the adequacy of information sources and services in libraries;
5. to find out the problems faced by research scholars in Pure Science, in using the libraries and their response towards

the existing systems, and under utilization if any, of the existing facilities;

6. to make a comparative study of the use pattern of research scholars in various Pure Science disciplines;
7. to assess whether the research scholars in Pure Science are satisfied with the facilities of the Kerala University Library System;
8. to examine the search strategy for an exhaustive information search on a specific topic;
9. to identify the nature of search done for current information;
10. to examine whether the resources and services of libraries are properly used by the research scholars and to understand their awareness of various services offered by external agencies.
11. To identify the most favourite journals in Pure Science discipline;
12. To examine the awareness of electronic or computer based sources in libraries and approach followed in CD/Online search method; and
13. To identify the most used libraries by Pure Science researchers.

METHODOLOGY

The methodology adopted for the study includes survey using questionnaire, supplemented by interview wherever clarification was required. In order to get an idea about similar studies carried out in this area, an exhaustive literature search was carried out. For this, many primary periodicals, secondary periodicals like LISA and its CD-version called LISA Plus, bibliographies etc. were consulted. Details about the studies made in the area of information needs, use pattern and information seeking behaviour of scientists and researchers in pure sciences were reviewed.

Since the study is about the information needs and use pattern of research scholars in the field of Pure Science, it is necessary to have background information about the different Pure Science disciplines, their history and development, institutional infrastructure available in the field of Pure Science research etc. For this, a comprehensive literature search was carried out. Much reference sources like Encyclopedias, Handbooks, Yearbooks, Directories etc., and on-line sources were consulted to collect the background information.

After collecting the background information, the samples of research scholars were surveyed. A pre-structured questionnaire was prepared anticipating the information needs, information gathering behaviour and the use pattern of research scholars in the various Pure Science disciplines. The questionnaires were distributed to the respondents by personal visit. Around 170 questionnaires were distributed, and 159 were returned duly filled. Wherever clarification was required, brief interview was also carried out.

The questionnaire consisted of questions under the heads, personal data, use of various sources, use of various services, as well as information seeking behaviour and use pattern. The data collected were then subjected to a detailed analysis. Wherever found suitable, the dependence of different variables were tested statistically.

HYPOTHESES

1. There are significant variations in the information needs and information gathering behaviour among research scholars in various Pure Science disciplines.
2. The resources and services available in the Kerala University Library System is only partially adequate to meet the information needs of the Pure Science research scholars.

SIGNIFICANCE OF THE STUDY

For a long time, librarians and information scientists had

neglected one of the most important components of the library i.e. the user.

Unless appropriate research is carried out, the library community will not be able to transform itself. The utilization process of scientific literature is one of the less understood phases of scientific communication. So research aimed at understanding the methodology and information gathering behaviour of research scholars in Pure Science is significant. Direct questioning of research scholars in Pure Science will help to discover the characteristics, information requirements, behaviour, attitudes, opinions, priorities, problems and evaluation of the users. An adequate knowledge about the researchers and their demands is necessary to make the library and information services for them more effective.

LIMITATIONS OF THE STUDY

The study is limited to full-time research scholars in the Pure Science faculties Viz. Aquatic Biology and Fisheries, Biochemistry, Botany, Chemistry, Geology, Mathematics, Physics, Statistics and Zoology.

ORGANISATION OF THE STUDY

The study is organised under six chapters, as follows:

Chapter 1 : Introduction

In this chapter a brief description of the whole study is provided.

Chapter 2 : Review of Literature

This chapter provides a brief review of related literature and similar studies conducted in the field of Pure Science.

Chapter 3: Pure Science: Genesis, Scope and Development

In this chapter a brief historical background and development of various Pure Science subjects are discussed.

Chapter 4: Institutional Infrastructure in Pure Science Research

This chapter provides a short description of the institutional infrastructure available in scientific disciplines, their development in India as well as in Kerala. It also provides a short account of the history and development of the different Pure Science departments of the University of Kerala.

Chapter 5 : Analysis of Data

The statistical analysis and interpretation of the data collected is provided in this chapter.

Chapter 6: Findings and Conclusion

The findings and conclusions derived from the analysis of data collected are given in this chapter

FINDINGS AND CONCLUSION

The study is aimed at investigating into the information needs and information gathering behaviour of research scholars in the Pure Science departments of the University of Kerala, which forms the main objective of the study. In order to carry out the study, the certain specific objectives were also formulated, as mentioned earlier.

A survey was conducted among the research scholars of the nine Pure Science departments of the University of Kerala, with the help of questionnaires. Interview was also carried out wherever clarification was required. A total of 159 scholars took part in the survey, from a total of about 207 researchers present. The major findings of the study are summarized in the subsequent sections.

CATEGORY-WISE DISTRIBUTION OF PURE SCIENCE RESEARCHERS

Analysis of the category-wise distribution of pure science researchers revealed that, out of the total 159 respondents, Ph.D. scholars dominate in number. Among the respondents, the number of Ph.D. scholars numbered 112 (70.44%), compared to 47 (29.56%) M.Phil scholars.

GENDER-WISE DISTRIBUTION OF RESPONDENTS

Gender-wise distribution of pure science researchers shows that, female scholars dominate in number compared to males. Out of the total 159 respondents, 94 (59.12%) are females and 65 (40.88%) are males. It is further observed that male researchers dominate only in the Geology (100%) and Statistics (66.66%) disciplines.

QUALIFICATION-WISE DISTRIBUTION OF RESPONDENTS

The qualification of pure science researchers when examined, it is found that 66.04% of them possess only a basic M.Sc degree. Only 33.96% researchers possess an additional M.Phil degree.

DISCIPLINE-WISE DISTRIBUTION OF RESPONDENTS

The discipline-wise distribution of respondents when examined, it is found that, maximum numbers of researchers are from the Biochemistry and Chemistry disciplines – 17.61% each. Researchers of Botany (16.35%) discipline follow this. The least number of researchers are in the Geology (1.89%) and Statistics (3.77%) disciplines. From this it can be seen that, Biochemistry, Chemistry and Botany are the Pune Science disciplines where most of the research is being carried out.

AREAS OF RESEARCH

The field in which the pure science scholars carry out research was analysed. It is found that, most of the scholars in Aquatic Biology discipline are carrying out research in the field of Fisheries Biology. In this the main studies include Pollution studies. Biotechnology, including Tissue Culture studies formed the main area of research in Botany discipline.

Majorities of the Biochemistry researchers are carrying out

research in the area Immunology, Microbiology etc. Many of them are conducting research in areas related to medical field. Inorganic and Organic chemistry are the main areas of research in Chemistry. Geology researchers are mainly carrying out research in Structural Geology, Weathering and Environmental Geology.

Graph theory is the main area of research in Mathematics discipline. Majority of the Physics scholars is interested in Space Physics. Most of the studies in Statistics discipline are conducted in the area of Order Statistics. Endocrinology is found to be the most studied area in Zoology discipline.

STAGES OF RESEARCH WORK

The data relating to the various stages of research work in which the researchers are engaged, is examined and found that majority i.e. 64.78% are engaged in the laboratory or experimentation stage. This is because laboratory works form an important part in many of the pure science disciplines. 44.03% researchers are in the literature survey stage and 15.09% are in the thesis writing stage.

YEAR OF JOINING IN RESEARCH WORK BY PURE SCIENCE RESEARCHERS

Majority of the researchers i.e. 80 (50.31%), are found to join for research during the year 2001. Out of these, 47 are M.Phil scholars. As far as Ph.D. scholars are concerned, 33 researchers each joined for research during the years 2000 and 2001.

PARTICIPATION OF RESEARCHERS IN CONFERENCE AND SEMINARS

82.39% of the pure science research scholars are found to attend conferences, seminars etc. which shows the importance of these sources in the information communication process of the researchers. Out of the total research scholars attending conference and seminars, 72.52% are Ph.D. scholars and 27.48% are M.Phil scholars.

It is further observed that, 57.25% of the researchers who attends conference and seminars are female scholars and 42.75% are males. But when examined within each of the gender, it is found that, among the total female scholars only 79.79% attend conferences and seminars. But 86.15% of the total male researchers are found to attend these. Thus, though the female researchers attending conference, seminars etc. are more in number, in relative participation male scholars dominate in attending conferences and seminars.

DISCIPLINE-WISE ANALYSIS OF RESEARCHERS ATTENDING CONFERENCE

Seminars etc. shows that, maximum number of researchers attending conference and seminars is in the Biochemistry discipline – 19.85%. The researchers in Botany discipline (16.79%) follow this. The least number of researchers attending conference and seminars is in the Geology discipline (2.29%).

PUBLICATION PATTERN OF PURE SCIENCE RESEARCHERS

The publication pattern of pure science researchers shows that, out of the total 159 pure science scholars studied, only 22.01% have published papers in learned periodicals. All the M.Phil scholars and 71.43% of Ph.D. scholars have not published any papers. It is observed that, altogether 89 papers were published by a total of 35 Ph.D. scholars. Majority i.e. 42.86% research scholars have published one paper each. Those publishing more than 2 papers are less in number.

Out of the 89 papers published by pure science researchers, 10 (28.57%) researchers together contribute majority i.e. 20 (22.47%) papers. It is also found that two researchers together published 14 papers, and a single scholar has contributed 10 (11.23%) of the total papers published.

SUBJECT-WISE ANALYSIS OF PUBLICATION PATTERN OF RESEARCHERS

Discipline-wise analysis of papers published by researchers shows that, maximum number of papers i.e. 24 (26.97) out of the total 89 papers published, are from the Botany discipline. 6 research scholars published these papers. The least number of papers is published from Statistics discipline (1.12%). The maximum number of papers published by a single person i.e. 10 paper, is also from Botany discipline. The maximum number of researchers publishing papers are in the Chemistry and Biochemistry disciplines i.e. 7 persons each.

PUBLICATION PATTERN OF RESEARCHERS VS YEAR OF JOINING RESEARCH

When the publication pattern of researchers was analysed in relation to the year of joining research, it is observed that, researchers joined during the year 1999 published the maximum number of papers is 30 papers. This is followed by those joined during the year 1998. It is found that during the year 2001, 20 papers were published and these are by a total of only 4 researchers.

It is further observed that, during the 1990s, 41 researchers joined for research and out of these 25 scholars have published papers. They published all together 58 papers. But during the year 2000 and after, 117 researchers joined for research, of which only 9 researchers have published their works. These 9 researchers together contributed 28 papers, which is more than three fold their total number. This shows that, as the year of experience increases, more scholars equip themselves to publish papers. But the number of papers published is found independent of the year of experience.

PUBLICATION PATTERN OF RESEARCHERS VS QUALIFICATION

The qualification of the 35 research scholars who had published papers in learned periodicals when examined it is found that, 54.29% of them had only M.Sc as their basic qualification. Only 45.71% possess an additional M.Phil degree. This shows that, higher qualification has not much influence on the publication pattern of researchers.

PUBLICATION PATTERN OF RESEARCHERS Vs GENDER

Gender-wise analysis of pure science researchers who had published papers in learned periodicals shows that, 62.86% of them are male scholars. Only 37.14% of these scholars are females. This shows that male researchers dominate in publishing papers in learned periodicals. They are found contributing 65.17% of the total papers published.

FINDINGS FROM ANALYSIS OF DATA BASED ON QUALIFICATION OF THE PURE SCIENCE RESEARCHERS

Adequacy of Information Sources for Researchers Vs Qualification of Researchers

Majority of the research scholars with M.Sc as their basic qualification, and also those with an additional M.Phil, finds sources like Textbooks, Periodicals, Indexing and Abstracting sources, Computer-based sources, Reference sources etc. in Kerala University Library System as only partially adequate to meet their research needs. This finding substantiates the validity of the second hypothesis of the study.

Only the Dissertation and Theses collection in the Kerala University Library System is found adequate to majority of researchers of both the categories. Most of the M.Sc as well as M.Phil holders find the collection of Patents, Standards, Reports and Non-book materials as inadequate to meet their needs. This shows that the need for various sources of information is similar for both M.Sc as well as M.Phil qualified researchers. It can be inferred that the collection of various information sources in the Kerala University Library System should be improved and updated.

FREQUENCY IN THE USE OF DIFFERENT INFORMATION SOURCES VS QUALIFICATION OF RESEARCHERS

The most frequently used information source by both M.Sc as well as M.Phil holders is found to be Journals. 77.14% M.Sc holders and 72.22% M.Phil holders are found frequently using Journals. Other sources like Textbooks, Thesis and Reference sources are also found to be frequently used by both the categories of researchers. Majority occasionally uses Conference Papers and Catalogues.

As far as the frequency of use of Computer-based sources are concerned, these are frequently used by majority i.e. 40.74% of M.Phil holders and occasionally used by most of the M.Sc holders (31.48%). Reports are occasionally used by most of the M.Sc holders, while M.Phil holders rarely use these. When 45.71% M.Sc holders frequently use sources like Index, Abstracts and Reviews, 44.44% M.Phil holders only occasionally use them.

Variations in the frequency of use is observed between M.Sc and M.Phil holders, in the case of certain sources like Computer-based sources, Reports, Indexing and Abstracting sources and Reviewing sources. Non-book materials are found using rarely by both M.Sc and M.Phil holders, and sources like Patents and Standards are found never used by more than 40% researchers of both the categories. In the case of many of the sources, the frequency of use is found more or less similar by both the categories. A study of the use pattern of pure science researchers of University of Kerala made by Sheena Kumari also reveals that, qualification of the researchers have no significant role in their use pattern.

MOST PREFERRED INFORMATION SOURCES BY PURE SCIENCE RESEARCHERS VS QUALIFICATION OF RESEARCHERS

The researchers with M.Sc degree and those with additional M.Phil are found to prefer Current Periodicals most. M.Sc holders give next preferences to Textbooks, Back volumes, Thesis and Reference sources respectively. After Current Periodicals, the next four preferred sources by M.Phil holders are found to be in the order Back volumes, Reference sources, Textbooks and Thesis respectively. Thus it is observed that, information sources namely, Periodicals, Back volumes, Thesis, Textbooks and Reference sources come under the first five preference of the pure science researchers with M.Sc as well as those with M.Phil degree. But the orders of preference to certain sources are found to vary.

CHANNELS OF ACQUIRING INFORMATION IN VARIOUS INFORMATION SOURCES SOURCES VS QUALIFICATION OF RESEARCHERS

Information is arranged in different ways in various information sources. While seeking information in certain important sources like Textbooks, Journals, Reference sources, Abstracts etc., the approach followed by the researchers with M.Sc degree and those with additional M.Phil was observed. Variations are observed between M.Sc holders and M.Phil holders, in their approach of seeking information in many of the information sources.

Only in the case of Reference sources, both the categories preferred similar approach i.e. consulting subject index first, followed by the use of alphabetical listings.

For seeking information contained in Textbooks, majority of M.Sc holders prefers to consult the index first, while M.Phil holders prefer content pages. In the case of Journals, both the categories prefer to read contents page first. M.Sc holders give next preference to indexing periodicals, while M.Phil holders give it to browsing the whole book. While consulting Abstracts, M.Sc holders prefer to use subject index, while M.Phil holders prefer keyword index.

DEMAND FOR SOURCES NOT AVAILABLE IN THE UNIVERSITY/ DEPARTMENT LIBRARIES VS QUALIFICATION OF RESEARCHERS

53.33% M.Sc holders and 62.96% M.Phil holders are found demanding sources, which are not available in the University or Department libraries, that are needed for their research works. Among the 56 M.Sc holders who ask for such sources, majority i.e. 32 of them got the required sources mainly from other special libraries. But among the 34 M.Phil holders, who demanded such sources, majorities i.e. 22 of them are found not getting the required sources.

USE OF SCIENTIFIC JOURNALS BY PURE SCIENCE RESEARCHERS VS QUALIFICATION

74.29% M.Sc holders and 72.22% M.Phil holders are found using 1-5 journals regularly. Only 4.76% M.Sc holders and 5.55% M.Phil holders are found using more than 10 journals regularly. 13.33% M.Sc holders and 5.56% M.Phil holders are found not reading any scientific journals regularly. Altogether 94.44% researchers with additional M.Phil degree are found using scientific journals regularly. But in the case of M.Sc holders, the number is comparatively less i.e. 86.67%.

The use of foreign language periodicals other than English by M.Sc and M.Phil qualified researchers was examined. Out of the total 105 researchers with M.Sc degree and 54 with additional M.Phil, only 5 researchers from each category are found using foreign language periodicals.

USE OF VARIOUS LIBRARY SERVICES VS QUALIFICATION OF RESEARCHERS

The use of various library services by pure science researchers shows that, majority of researchers is aware of the various library services. Certain library services like Inter Library Loan, Translation service, Addition Lists etc. are unaware to majority of researchers of both the categories.

55.24% M.Sc holders are found using Photocopying service the most. Next most used library services by M.Sc holders include Literature search (45.71%) and Computer-based Information Service (39.05%). The most used service by M.Phil holders is found to be Literature Search Service (55.56%), which is followed by the use of Computer-based Information Service (53.70%), Indexing and Abstracting Service (48.15%) and Photocopying Service (44.44%) respectively.

ADEQUACY OF SERVICES OFFERED BY KERALA UNIVERSITY LIBRARY SYSTEM FOR RESEARCHERS VS QUALIFICATION OF RESEARCHERS

In order to ascertain the adequacy of services offered by Kerala University Library System to pure science researchers, a question was asked to them. 64.76% M.Sc holders and 79.63% M.Phil holders opined that the services offered by Kerala University Library System is only partially adequate to meet their needs, which substantiate the validity of second hypothesis of the study. From this finding, it can be inferred that, the services of Kerala University Library System in the field of pure science should be improved.

AWARENESS OF SERVICES RENDERED BY EXTERNAL AGENCIES VS QUALIFICATION OF RESEARCHERS

When the awareness of services provided by external agencies to researchers is examined, it is found that, majority i.e. 66.67% M.Sc holders are unaware of the services rendered by such agencies to research scholars. As far as M.Phil scholars are concerned, majorities i.e. 53.70% are aware of such services. More research experience of M.Phil holders may be the reason for this. It is further observed that, many of the M.Phil scholars, though aware of the services provided by external agencies, have not utilised these facilities.

The study reveals that 60% M.Sc holders and 51.72% M.Phil holders are aware of the services provided by INSDOC. But only around 17% researchers of both these categories have utilised these services. A small percent i.e. less than 9% of researchers of both the categories are found utilising the services provided by agencies like NCSI, Patent Information Center etc.

USE OF INTERNET BASED SERVICES VS QUALIFICATION OF RESEARCHERS

Among the various Internet-based services, e-mail is found to be the most used service by pure science researchers. It is utilised by 76.38% of the M.Sc holders and 83.33% of the M.Phil holders. 70.48% M.Sc holders and 79.63% M.Phil holders give next preference to On-line database search. Researchers with M.Phil qualification are found to be using the Internet based services more frequently.

TIME SPEND FOR READING IN LIBRARIES AT DIFFERENT STAGES OF RESEARCH WORK VS QUALIFICATION OF RESEARCHERS

It is found that, during the literature survey stage, 50.48% M.Sc holders and 57.41% M.Phil holders use to spend 1-5 hours/ week in libraries for reading. At the laboratory stage while majority of the M.Sc holders spend 1-5 hours/week in libraries, most of the M.Phil holders spend 5-10 hours/week in libraries for reading. During the writing stage also, 53.06% M.Sc holders and 60% M.Phil holders use to read only 1-5 hours/week in libraries.

Thus, it is observed that, during the literature survey and writing stages, most of the researchers of both the categories use to spend 1-5 hours/week in libraries for reading purpose. But during the laboratory stage of work, majority of M.Sc holders are found spending 1-5 hours/week while M.Phil holders spend 5-10 hours/ week in libraries for reading purpose.

TIME SPEND FOR READING IN DIFFERENT PLACES VS QUALIFICATION OF RESEARCHERS

Most of the M.Sc holders (60.95%) and M.Phil holders (70.37%) use to spend 1-5 hours for reading, per week, in University library. The Department and Campus library is the next most used library by M.Sc holders where, 45.71% scholars use to spend 1-5 hours per week for reading purpose. But in the case of M.Phil holders, after University library, majority i.e. 50% researchers use to spend 1-5 hours/week in other special libraries, for reading. In all the libraries and also at home, most of the researchers of both the categories are found spending an average of 1-5 hours/week for reading purpose.

6-10 hours of reading per week is mainly carried out in the Department libraries by 33.33% each researchers of both the categories. Both M.Sc and M.Phil holders mostly do more than 10 hours of reading per week at home.

The Department libraries are found to be the most favourite reading place by both the categories of scholars. 100% M.Phil holders and 96.19% M.Sc holders are found utilising the Department libraries for reading purpose.

DIFFICULTY IN CONDUCTING LITERATURE SEARCH VS QUALIFICATION OF RESEARCHERS

Majority of the researchers i.e. 56.19% M.Sc holders and 55.56% M.Phil holders opined that they did not felt any difficulty in conducting literature search in connection with their works. This may be due to the fact that, many of them are not aware of the various library services and are satisfied with the existing services.

USE OF LIBRARIES OUTSIDE KERALA VS QUALIFICATION OF RESEARCHERS

Only 20% of the M.Sc holders and 33.33% of the M.Phil holders are found utilising the facilities of libraries outside Kerala.

Majority of the scholars of both the categories are not using the facilities of libraries outside Kerala. Compared to M.Sc holders, the percentage of M.Phil holders using these libraries are more.

METHOD USED TO FIND SPECIFIC INFORMATION VS QUALIFICATION OF RESEARCHERS

The most followed method by M.Sc holders and M.Phil holders, to find out specific information on a topic is found to be similar. Consulting Reference sources is the most used method by both the categories of researchers. 68.57% M.Sc holders and 77.77% M.Phil holders follows this method. Next most used method by both the categories of scholars is found to be searching the Internet and asking teachers/colleagues respectively.

MOST PREFERRED METHOD OF INFORMATION SEARCH VS QUALIFICATION OF RESEARCHERS

Maximum number of M.Sc holders and M.Phil holders are found to prefer manual information search methods. Majority of scholars gives next preference to On-line search method, followed by a combination of these two methods.

KNOWLEDGE OF THE USE OF ELECTRONIC/ COMPUTER-BASED SOURCES VS QUALIFICATION OF THE RESEARCHERS

70.48% M.Sc qualified and 77.78% M.Phil qualified researchers are found to know the use of electronic or computer-based sources available in the library. Thus, compared to M.Sc holders, the percentage of M.Phil holders who know the use of these sources is more. Most of the M.Sc holders learned to use these sources from their colleagues, while M.Phil holders learned their use from colleagues as well as through previous experience.

TYPES OF DATABASE USED AND APPROACH FOLLOWED BY RESEARCHERS IN ON-LINE SEARCH VS QUALIFICATION

The different types of database preferred by researchers with M.Sc degree and those with an additional M.Phil degree were examined. It is observed that majority of the scholars of both the categories preferred both National and International database equally, while conducting online searches. Bibliographic database is found frequently used by majority of the researchers of both the categories.

It is also observed that, while conducting CD/Online searching, most of the researchers of both the categories prefer keyword search.

While conducting online search, 41.90% M.Sc holders are found to formulate the search strategy by themselves. But in the case of M.Phil holders, 51.85% scholars formulate the search with the help of others like, scientists, teachers, librarian etc. This may help them to retrieve more precise information.

APPROACH FOLLOWED BY RESEARCHERS TO FIND CURRENT INFORMATION VS QUALIFICATION

In order to find out current information published in their respective discipline, the first three methods preferred by both M.Sc and M.Phil holders are found similar. The methods include scanning periodicals, using current contents, and consulting indexing and abstracting sources respectively. Discussion and searching the shelves are the next two preferred methods by M.Sc holders, while M.Phil holders prefer consulting catalogues and OPACs, followed by searching the shelves. Addition lists, Book trade catalogues etc. are given least preference by both the categories.

SEEKING ADVICE OF SCIENTISTS IN OTHER INSTITUTES BY RESEARCHERS VS QUALIFICATION OF RESEARCHERS

Majority of the researchers of both the categories is found

seeking the advice of scientists working in other institutions, in connection with their research works. When compared to M.Sc holders, the percentage of M.Phil holders seeking such advises are very high i.e. while 57.14% M.Sc holders sought the advice of scientists, it is 81.48% in the case of M.Phil holders.

Z-Test of significance was applied to test statistically whether there is any significant difference between both the categories in this regard. The value is calculated as 2.18, which shows significance at 5% level. From this it is concluded that there is significant difference in the use pattern of both the categories in this regard.

FINDINGS FROM ANALYSIS OF DATA BASED ON GENDER OF THE PURE SCIENCE RESEARCHERS

Adequacy of Information Sources for Researchers Vs Gender of Researchers

When the adequacy of various information sources for male and female scholars was examined, it is found that, the only source in the Kerala University Library System that was adequate for the research needs of the scholars is the Dissertation and Theses collection. For 43.08% males and 52.13% females, this source is adequate for their research purpose. 40.43% female scholars also found the collection of Textbooks as adequate, whereas for 46.15% males, it is only partially adequate.

Majority of the male and female scholars found the collection of Reference sources, Indexing and Abstracting sources, as well as Computer-based information sources in the Kerala University Library System as only partially adequate to meet their needs. While the Periodical collection is only partially adequate for 50% females, it is inadequate for 46.15% male scholars.

Majority of male and female scholars does not know about the sources namely, Patents and Standards. 47.87% female scholars are unaware of the Non-book materials whereas for 44.62% male scholars it is inadequate.

FREQUENCY IN THE USE OF DIFFERENT INFORMATION SOURCES VS GENDER OF RESEARCHERS

Majority i.e. 72.31% male scholars and 72.34% female scholars are found utilising Textbooks frequently. 80% males and 72.34% females uses Journal sources frequently. Dissertation and Theses as well as Reference sources are the other sources frequently used by maximum number of researchers of both the categories.

Information sources like Reports and Conference papers are occasionally used by majority of scholars in both the categories. Some other sources like Indexing and Abstracting sources, Catalogues and Computer-based sources are used frequently by majority of females, whereas these are occasionally used by most of the male scholars. Non-book materials are found rarely used by most of the male scholars, while these sources are never used by majority of females.

MOST PREFERRED INFORMATION SOURCES BY PURE SCIENCE RESEARCHERS VS GENDER

Current Periodicals are found to be the most preferred source of information by both the categories of research scholars. The 2nd preference is given to Textbooks by male researchers and to Theses and Dissertation by female researchers. Textbooks and Reference sources are given the 3rd and 4th preferences respectively by both the categories of researchers. The order of preference given to many of the information sources by the male and female scholars are found similar. Only in the case of certain sources like Back Volumes, Computer-based sources, Dissertation and Thesis etc. the choice varied.

CHANNELS OF ACQUIRING INFORMATION IN VARIOUS INFORMATION SOURCES VS GENDER OF RESEARCHERS

The route chosen by male and female researchers for seeking information in most of the information sources are found similar.

In the case of Textbooks and Journals, both the categories prefer reading the content page first. In the case of Reference sources, they prefer consulting subject index most. Only in seeking information in Abstracting sources, their preference varies. Here most of the male researchers prefer consulting keyword index, while females prefer subject index.

DEMAND FOR SOURCES NOT AVAILABLE IN THE UNIVERSITY/ DEPARTMENT LIBRARIES VS GENDER OF RESEARCHERS

When the demand of research scholars for sources that are not available in the University or Department library are examined, it is revealed that 52.31% male scholars and 59.57% female scholars demanded for such sources. The availability of such sources was examined, and found that 35.29% male scholars and 41.07% female scholars got these sources, which is mainly from other special libraries. When compared to male scholars, larger percentage of female researchers are found demanding for such sources and more number of them are getting the required sources, than male researchers.

USE OF SCIENTIFIC JOURNALS BY PURE SCIENCE RESEARCHERS VS GENDER

Majority i.e. 72.31% male scholars and 74.47% female scholars use to read on an average of 1-5 journals regularly. Only around 10% researchers of both the categories are found using 6-10 journals on a regular basis. Compared to female researchers, the percentage of male scholars reading more than 10 journals are high. They constitute 9.32%, compared to 2.12% female scholars.

As far as the use of foreign language periodicals are concerned, only 10 out of the total 159 scholars use these. Out of these 10 researchers, majorities i.e. 6 of them are females and 4 of them are males. So the female researchers are found using foreign language periodicals more, compared to males.

USE OF VARIOUS LIBRARY SERVICES VS GENDER OF RESEARCHERS

Literature Search service and Reprographic service are found to be the most used service by majority of male and female scholars. 56.92% male researchers and 47.87% female researchers are found using Reprographic service. Literature Search service is utilised by 47.69% males and 50% females. Newspaper Clipping service and Bibliographic services is aware to most of the researchers belonging to both the categories, but the use of these services is less.

Majorities of female researchers (46.81%) are unaware of Referral service, while 38.46% males have utilised this service. Similarly, services like Interlibrary Loan, Translation service and Addition Lists are unaware to most of the male and female researchers.

As far as the utilisation of various library services are concerned, the percentage of male scholars using the various services are more compared to females.

ADEQUACY OF SERVICES OFFERED BY KERALA UNIVERSITY LIBRARY SYSTEM VS GENDER OF RESEARCHERS

76.92% female scholars and 64.89% male scholars opined that the services of the Kerala University Library System is only partially adequate to meet their research needs. The percentage of male scholars who are satisfied with the services of Kerala University Library System is less compared to females – 23.08% and 35.11% respectively.

AWARENESS OF SERVICES RENDERED BY EXTERNAL AGENCIES VS GENDER OF RESEARCHERS

The awareness of services rendered by external agencies to researchers was examined and found that, while majority i.e. 56.92% male researchers are aware of such services, only 28.72% females are aware of them. So the awareness of services rendered by external agencies to researchers, is high in the case of male scholars, compared to females.

On in-depth analysis, it is found that among those who are aware of the services rendered by external agencies, 24.32% male scholars have utilised the services of INSDOC. In the case of females, it is only 7.41%. The number of male researchers utilising the services provided by external agencies like NCSI, Patent Information Center etc. are also higher compared to female scholars.

In order to test statistically whether there is any significant difference between male and female scholars in their awareness of services provided by external agencies, Z-Test was applied. The significance level was found to be at 5%, which proves that there is significant difference in the awareness of male and female researchers in this regard.

USE OF INTERNET BASED SERVICES VS GENDER OF RESEARCHERS

It is found that, the percentage of male scholars using the Internet based services is very much higher compared to females. E-mail service is the most used Internet based service by both male (81.54%) and female (72.34%) scholars. Online search is the next most frequently used Internet based service by both the categories of scholars. When compared to male researchers, the percentage of female researchers using the various Internet based services is very less.

TIME SPEND FOR READING IN LIBRARIES AT DIFFERENT STAGES OF RESEARCH WORK VS GENDER OF RESEARCHERS

The time spend by male and female scholars, at different stage of research work is examined and found that, during the Literature survey stage, 100% researchers of both the categories used libraries for reading purpose. 53.19% females and 52.31%

males use to spend 1-5 hours/week in libraries for reading at this stage of work and 35.38% males and 31.92% females use to spend 5-10 hours per week.

At the laboratory or experimentation stage, majority of male scholars (29.23%) is found reading more than 10 hours/week in libraries. But in the case of female scholars, majority i.e. 42.55% uses to read only 1-5 hours/week, in libraries. At the laboratory stage, more number of females are found spending time for reading in libraries, than male scholars – 85.11% and 73.84% respectively.

During the writing stages of research work, the number of researchers using libraries for reading purpose is very less. They constitute 50% females and 41.54% males. This is because, most of the researchers have not yet reached the writing stages. Among those who have reached this stage of work, majority of male and female researchers is found spending 1-5 hours/week in libraries.

TIME SPEND FOR READING IN DIFFERENT PLACES VS GENDER OF RESEARCHERS

The average time spend by male and female scholars per week, for reading at various libraries and at home was examined. It is observed that, majority of researchers i.e. 67.7% each male and female scholars use to spend 1-5 hours/week for reading, in the University library.

In the Department library and Campus library, 40% male and 50% female scholars are found spending 1-5 hours/week for reading. Here 33.84% male and 32.98% females use to spend 6-10 hours/week and 23.08% and 14.89% male and female scholars respectively spend more than 10 hours/week, for reading. Department libraries are found to be the reading place that is used by maximum number of male and female researchers.

In Other libraries connected with research institutions, 41.54% male researchers and 39.36% female scholars use to spend 1-5 hours/week for reading. In these libraries, the number of male researchers spending more than 5 hours of reading per week is very less. Next to University library, majority of male scholars is found using other libraries for 1-5 hours of reading per week and then only prefers Department libraries. But in the case of females, after University library, majority do their reading in Department libraries.

As far as the time spend by researchers for reading at home is concerned, majority of male scholars (27.69%) use to read more than 10 hours/week at home. But majority of the females (38.30%) prefer 1-5 hours of reading at home, per week.

Department library is found to be the most used library by both the categories of researchers. Here 96.92% male scholars and 97.87% female scholars use to spend 1-10 hours or more time in a week for reading purpose. 1-5 hours of reading is done by majority of researchers of both the categories in the University library.

Next to Department library, the most favourite reading place by majority i.e. 80% of male scholars is the University library. But in the case of females, next to Department library, majority i.e. 76.60% prefers reading at home. It is also observed that researchers of both the categories do more than 10 hours of reading per week, mostly at home.

DIFFICULTY IN CONDUCTING LITERATURE SEARCH VS GENDER OF RESEARCHERS

58.46% male researchers and 54.26% female scholars opined that they felt no difficulty in conducting literature search as part of their research works. 41.54% male scholars and 45.74% females felt difficulty in conducting literature search. Thus the number of female scholars feeling difficulty in conducting literature search is more compared to males.

USE OF LIBRARIES OUTSIDE KERALA VS GENDER OF RESEARCHERS

It is observed that, majority of the scholars using libraries outside Kerala are males. They constitute 46.15%. Compared to male researchers, the percentage of female scholars using libraries outside Kerala is negligible i.e. 9.57%. In order to test this statistically, Z-Test was applied. The value is found significant at 5% level. This shows that there is significant difference in the use pattern of libraries outside Kerala by male and female research scholars in Pure Science.

METHOD USED TO FIND SPECIFIC INFORMATION VS GENDER OF RESEARCHERS

In order to seek specific information on a topic, the method most used by both male and female scholars is consulting Reference sources. 73.04% females and 69.23% males use this method. Searching the Internet is the next most preferred method. It is seen that more number of females, compared to males consults Reference sources. But in the case of Internet searching, it is vice versa. The other methods sought by both categories of researchers are found to be similar.

MOST PREFERRED METHOD OF INFORMATION SEARCH VS GENDER OF RESEARCHERS

Majorities of researchers of both the categories are found preferring manual information search method to other modern sophisticated methods. On-line search is given the 2nd preference by both the categories.

KNOWLEDGE OF THE USE OF ELECTRONIC/ COMPUTER-BASED SOURCES VS GENDER OF THE RESEARCHERS

81.54% male researchers and 67.02% female researchers have knowledge of the use of electronic or computer-based sources available in the libraries. This show that, the percentage of male scholars having knowledge of electronic sources are high compared to females. Majority of scholars of both the categories has learned to use these sources from their colleagues.

TYPES OF DATABASE USED AND APPROACH FOLLOWED BY RESEARCHERS IN ON-LINE SEARCH VS GENDER OF RESEARCHERS

Majority of research scholars belonging to male and female sex are found using both National and International database equally, while carrying out on-line search. Female scholars are found to prefer both bibliographic and full text databases equally. Male scholars prefer to use bibliographic database mostly.

When conducting literature search online, most of find the male scholars do this themselves while most of the females do this with the help of others like library staff. Keyword search is found to be the most preferred approach by majority of researchers of both the categories.

APPROACH FOLLOWED BY RESEARCHERS TO FIND CURRENT INFORMATION ON THE SUBJECT VS GENDER OF RESEARCHERS

The method most preferred by majority of scholars, to find out current information published in their respective field is, scanning Current Periodicals. The 2nd preference is given to the method of consulting Abstracting and Indexing sources by male researchers and to Current Contents by female researchers. Current Periodicals, Indexing and Abstracting sources, Current Contents, Catalogues/ OPACs and Searching the shelves are the five most preferred methods used by male and female scholars to find current information in their fields. Only in the order of preference, certain variations are observed.

SEEKING ADVICE OF SCIENTISTS IN OTHER INSTITUTES BY RESEARCHERS VS GENDER OF RESEARCHERS

A large number of male and female scholars are found seeking the advice of scientists working in other institutions, in connection with their research. But the percentage of male scholars seeking such advises are very high compared to females i.e. when 73.85% male scholars sought such advises, it is only 59.57% in the case of females.

FINDINGS FROM ANALYSIS OF DATA BASED ON THE CATEGORY OF THE PURE SCIENCE RESEARCHERS

ADEQUACY OF INFORMATION SOURCES FOR RESEARCHERS VS CATEGORY OF RESEARCHERS

Majority i.e. 49.11% of the Ph.D. scholars and 46.81% M.Phil scholars finds the collection of Dissertation and Theses in the Kerala University Library System as adequate to meet their research needs. 46.81% of M.Phil scholars finds the Textbook collection also as adequate, while for most of the Ph.D. scholars it is only partially adequate.

The collection of sources like Periodicals, Reference sources, Indexing and Abstracting sources and Computer-based sources in the Kerala University Library System is found as only partially adequate for both M.Phil and Ph.D. scholars.

Many of the Ph.D. (48.21%) and M.Phil (38.30%) scholars do not know about the collection of Patents and Standards. Majority of the researchers is unaware to collection of Non-book materials.

FREQUENCY IN THE USE OF DIFFERENT INFORMATION SOURCES VS CATEGORY OF RESEARCHERS

The most frequently used information source by pure science researchers is found to be Journals, Textbooks, Thesis and Reference sources. 81.25% of the Ph D. scholars uses journals frequently.

This is followed by the use of Textbooks (74.11%), Theses (50%) and Reference sources (50%). In the case of M.Phil scholars, Textbooks are frequently used by majority i.e. 68.09%, followed by Journals (61.70%), Theses (51.06%) and Reference sources (48.94%).

Sources like Reports, Conference papers, Catalogues etc. are occasionally used by majority of scholars of both the categories. Indexing and Abstracting sources are found frequently used by majority of the Ph.D. scholars (48.21%), while majority (42.55%) of M.Phil scholars only occasionally uses these. The use of Computer-based sources when examined, it is found that, while 35.71% Ph.D. scholars used these sources frequently, most of the M.Phil (36.17%) scholars have never used these sources.

Non-book materials are occasionally used by 32.14% Ph.D. scholars and are rarely used by 48.94% M.Phil scholars. Sources like Patents and Standards are never used by majority of both categories of researchers.

MOST PREFERRED INFORMATION SOURCES BY PURE SCIENCE RESEARCHERS VS CATEGORY OF RESEARCHERS

Among the various sources of information, Current periodicals are found to be the most preferred source of information in the case of both Ph.D. and M.Phil scholars. M.Phil scholars give the next four preferences to Textbooks, Reference sources, Theses and Back volumes respectively. In the case of Ph.D. scholars, after Current periodicals the next four preferred sources are in the order Back volumes, Textbooks, Theses and Computer-based sources.

CHANNELS OF ACQUIRING INFORMATION IN VARIOUS INFORMATION SOURCES VS CATEGORY OF RESEARCHERS

In consulting Textbooks, the channel followed by researchers doing Ph.D. and M.Phil are found to vary. In the case of other sources, they showed a similar pattern for seeking information.

While seeking information contained in Textbooks, the Ph.D. scholars preferred consulting the contents page first, while M.Phil scholars preferred consulting the index.

In the case of Journals, both M.Phil and Ph.D. scholars prefer to read contents page first, to seek the required information. Subject index is consulted by most of the M.Phil and Ph.D. scholars, while seeking information in Reference sources.

DEMAND FOR SOURCES NOT AVAILABLE IN THE UNIVERSITY/ DEPARTMENT LIBRARIES VS CATEGORY OF RESEARCHERS

It is found that, while majority i.e. 53.19% of M.Phil scholars does not ask for sources that are not available in the University or Department library, 60.71% Ph.D. scholars ask for such sources. This shows that, Ph.D. scholars are more in demand for various information sources not available in the University or Department libraries. As far as the availability of the required sources are considered, it is observed that, while 54.55% of the M.Phil scholars got the required sources, only 36.76% Ph.D. scholars got them. The scholars are found getting the required sources from other libraries. It can be inferred that a large number of Ph.D. scholars are not getting the required information sources, compared to M.Phil scholars.

USE OF SCIENTIFIC JOURNALS BY PURE SCIENCE RESEARCHERS VS CATEGORY OF RESEARCHERS

97.32% of the Ph.D. scholars and 70.21% of the M.Phil scholars are found to read scientific journals regularly. Compared to 2.26% Ph.D. scholars, who do not read any scientific journals regularly, the percentage of M.Phil scholars not reading scientific journals is high i.e. 29.79%.

Majority of Ph.D. and M.Phil scholars is found to read 1-5

journals regularly. The number of Ph.D. scholars reading scientific journals regularly is high compared to M.Phil scholars – 77.68% and 63.83% respectively. It is further observed that, while 19.64% Ph.D. scholars used to read more than 5 journals regularly, it is only 6.25% in the case of M.Phil scholars.

USE OF VARIOUS LIBRARY SERVICES VS CATEGORY OF RESEARCHERS

A large number of M.Phil and Ph.D. scholars are unaware of sources like Inter library loan, Addition lists, Translation service etc. The percentage of M.Phil scholars unaware of the various library are more compared to Ph.D. scholars, in most of the cases. It is observed that, while 37.50% Ph.D. scholars have utilised Referral service, most of the M.Phil scholars (44.68%) are unaware of this.

Reprographic service and Literature Search services are found to be the most used services by both the categories of researchers. Indexing and Abstracting service, as well as Computer-based Information service is utilised by a large number of Ph.D. scholars. But the M.Phil scholars are less using these services.

Other services like Newspaper clippings, Bibliographic service etc. is aware to majority of researchers of both the categories. But the utilisation of these services is found to be very less. Only a single Ph.D. scholar is found using the Inter library loan facility.

ADEQUACY OF SERVICES OFFERED BY KERALA UNIVERSITY LIBRARY SYSTEM VS CATEGORY OF RESEARCHERS

The adequacy of services offered by Kerala University Library System to pure science researchers is examined. It is found that, for 57.45% M.Phil scholars and 75% Ph.D. scholars, the services are insufficient or only partially adequate to meet their research needs.

AWARENESS OF SERVICES RENDERED BY EXTERNAL AGENCIES VS CATEGORY OF RESEARCHERS

Majority of the M.Phil scholars (76.60%) and Ph.D. scholars (52.68%) are not aware of the services provided by external agencies to researchers. But it is seen that the percentage of Ph.D. scholars who are aware of these services are more compared to M.Phil scholars.

Out of the total 53 Ph.D. scholars who are aware of the services provided by external agencies, 20.75% have utilised the services of INSDOC, 9.43% each have utilised the services of NCSI and Patent Information Center respectively, and about 5% had utilised the services of other agencies. In the case of M.Phil scholars, many of them are aware of the services provided by external agencies to researchers, but none of them have utilised these services.

USE OF INTERNET BASED SERVICES VS CATEGORY OF RESEARCHERS

Among the various Internet based services, e-mail service is found to be the service used by majority of Ph.D. (82.14%) and M.Phil (61.70%) scholars. This is followed by on-line search, which is used by 80.36% Ph.D. scholars and 57.45% M.Phil scholars. When the use of various Internet based services are considered, the number of Ph.D. scholars utilising the various Internet based services are very high compared to M.Phil scholars.

TIME SPEND FOR READING IN LIBRARIES AT DIFFERENT STAGES OF RESEARCH WORK VS CATEGORY OF RESEARCHERS

During the literature search stage, majority i.e. 53.19% M.Phil scholars and 52.68% Ph.D. scholars are found spending 1-5 hours/week in libraries for reading. At the laboratory stage also, majority i.e. 31.25% Ph.D. scholars and 36.17% M.Phil scholars use to spend 1-5 hours/week for reading, in libraries. Only in the writing stage of research work, majority of researchers of both the categories are found spending either less than one hour or do not spend any time in libraries for reading purpose. Maximum number of researchers of both the categories are found using libraries for reading purpose, during the literature survey stage.

TIME SPEND FOR READING IN DIFFERENT PLACES VS CATEGORY OF RESEARCHERS

Maximum number of M.Phil and Ph.D. scholars are found to spend an average time of 1-5 hours/week for reading in University library, Department library, other libraries and at home. University library is the place where majority of Ph.D. scholars (61.61%) and M.Phil scholars (70.21%) are spending 1-5 hours of reading per week. Department library is found to be the library used by majority i.e. 100% M.Phil and 96.43% Ph.D. scholars. The next favourite reading place for both the categories of researchers is home. It is further observed that, 1-5 hours of reading per week is done more by M.Phil scholars, whereas over 10 hours of reading per week is done more by Ph.D. scholars.

DIFFICULTY IN CONDUCTING LITERATURE SEARCH VS CATEGORY OF RESEARCHERS

63.83% M.Phil scholars and 52.68% Ph.D. scholars felt no difficulty in conducting literature search in connection with their works. Among those who had difficulty in conducting literature search, the percentage of Ph.D. scholars are more compared to M.Phil scholars.

USE OF LIBRARIES OUTSIDE KERALA VS CATEGORY OF RESEARCHERS

None of the M.Phil scholars are found utilising the facilities of libraries outside Kerala. Among the Ph.D. scholars, 34.82% are found using the facilities of these libraries.

METHOD USED TO FIND SPECIFIC INFORMATION VS CATEGORY OF RESEARCHERS

In order to acquire information regarding a specific topic, majority of M.Phil and Ph.D. scholars prefer to use the methods of consulting reference sources. Searching the Internet is found to be the next most preferred method by Ph.D. scholars, whereas the M.Phil scholars prefer Internet searching and consulting teachers and colleagues, equally.

MOST PREFERRED METHOD OF INFORMATION SEARCH VS CATEGORY OF RESEARCHERS

The information search method most preferred by researchers when examined, it is found that, maximum number of researchers doing M.Phil and Ph.D. prefers manual information search methods. While Ph.D. scholars give 2nd preference to on-line search, M.Phil scholars prefers a combination of both these methods.

KNOWLEDGE OF THE USE OF ELECTRONIC/ COMPUTER-BASED SOURCES VS CATEGORY OF THE RESEARCHERS

80.36% of the Ph.D. scholars and 55.32% M.Phil scholars are found to possess knowledge of electronic or computer-based sources available in the library. This shows that the percentage of Ph.D. scholars having knowledge about these sources is very high compared to M.Phil scholars. Many of the researchers of both the categories learned to use these sources from their colleagues, and many of them learned by self.

In order to test statistically whether there is any significant difference in the knowledge of these sources by M.Phil and Ph.D. scholars, Z-Test was carried out. The value was found to be 2.588, which is significant at 1% level. This proves statistically, there is highly significant difference in the knowledge of electronic/ computer-based sources, between both the categories of researchers.

TYPES OF DATABASE USED AND APPROACH FOLLOWED BY RESEARCHERS IN ON-LINE SEARCH VS CATEGORY OF RESEARCHERS

Maximum number of researchers doing M.Phil and Ph.D. are found to prefer both National and International database equally, while carrying out online information search. Bibliographic database are used most by researchers belonging to both these categories, while conducting online searches.

Most of the M.Phil and Ph.D. scholars are found to prefer keyword searching followed by title and subject approach, while conducting online search. Majority of Ph.D. researchers opined that they formulate the search strategy by themselves. Most of the M.Phil scholars are found to formulate the search strategy with the help of colleagues, while carrying out on-line search.

APPROACH FOLLOWED BY RESEARCHERS TO FIND CURRENT INFORMATION VS CATEGORY OF RESEARCHERS

The first 5 methods preferred by M.Phil scholars and Ph.D. scholars for seeking current information in their subject field are found to be similar. The methods used by them are in the order, Scanning Periodicals, Current contents, Index and Abstracts, Searching shelves and consulting Catalogues/OPACs. Methods of consulting Addition lists, Book Trade Catalogues etc. are given least preference.

SEEKING ADVICE OF SCIENTISTS IN OTHER INSTITUTES BY RESEARCHERS VS CATEGORY OF RESEARCHERS

Most of the M.Phil scholars (57.45%) do not seek the advice of scientists working in other institutions. But as far as the Ph.D. scholars are considered, 75% of them consult with scientists working in other institutions, in connection with their work. This may be due to the need of in-depth studies in Ph.D. works. When tested statistically using Z-Test, the value obtained is found significant at 5% level. This shows that, there is considerable difference in the information seeking behaviour of M.Phil and Ph.D. scholars, in this regard.

FINDINGS FROM THE ANALYSIS OF DATA BASED ON DISCIPLINE OF THE PURE SCIENCE RESEARCHERS

ADEQUACY OF INFORMATION SOURCES VS DISCIPLINE OF RESEARCHERS

The Periodical collection in the Kerala University Library System is only partially adequate to majority of research scholars in the disciplines namely Aquatic Biology (76.47%), Biochemistry (50%), Botany (50%) and Physics (57.14%). For majority of scholars in Chemistry (50%) and Mathematics (54.55%), Periodical collection is found to be inadequate. Only in the Statistics (50%) and Zoology (36.84%) disciplines majority of scholars responded that these sources are adequate for their needs.

The Textbook collection of Kerala University Library System is adequate to majority of researchers in Biochemistry (67.86%), Statistics (66.67%) and Zoology (42.11%). For 38.10% Physics researchers Textbooks are inadequate. In all other fields, the maximum number of researchers responded that the Textbook collection as only partially adequate.

When the adequacy of Reference sources in Kerala University Library System for pure science researchers was examined, it is found that only for majority of Geology scholars, it is felt adequate. For majority of Physics (52.38%) and Chemistry (35.71%) researchers, Reference sources are inadequate. For majority of researchers in all other disciplines, Reference sources are only partially adequate to meet their needs.

The Indexing and Abstracting sources in the Kerala University

Library System is found to be only partially adequate to majority of researchers in all the pure science disciplines. In Mathematics discipline, 36.36% researchers did not know about these sources.

Dissertation and Theses collection in Kerala University Library System is the only source found to be adequate to majority of researchers in most of the pure science disciplines. Only in Geology (66.66%), Mathematics (54.55%) and Physics (52.38%) disciplines, most of the researchers felt these sources as partially adequate. In Statistics discipline, while for 33.33% researchers these sources were adequate, for another 33.33% it is felt inadequate to meet their needs.

The Computer-based information sources are found as only partially adequate to majority of researchers in all disciplines except Mathematics and Physics. Majority of researchers in these two disciplines felt these sources as inadequate to meet their needs.

The collection of Patents and Standards are unaware to majority of scholars in most of the disciplines. For 66.67% Geology scholars these sources are partially adequate, while for 83.33% Statistics scholars and 47.62% Physics scholars these sources are inadequate.

In the case of Non-book materials, only in Geology discipline majority of researchers opined that these collections as adequate. They constitute 66.66%. In disciplines viz. Biochemistry (39.29%) and Botany (38.46%), these sources are only partially adequate to majority of researchers. A large number of researchers in Aquatic Biology (70.59%), Chemistry (46.43%) and Zoology (42.11%) are unaware of the non-book material collection. Majority of Mathematics, Physics and Statistics researchers responded these sources as inadequate for their research needs.

The above findings prove the hypothesis that the resources in Kerala University Library System are only partially adequate to meet the needs of pure science researchers. From the findings it can be inferred that the collection of various information sources in the Kerala University Library System in pure science field should be improved. Proper awareness about the different information sources should also be provided.

FREQUENCY IN THE USE OF DIFFERENT INFORMATION SOURCES VS DISCIPLINE OF RESEARCHERS

More than 66% of researchers in all the disciplines except Aquatic Biology (52.94%) are found using Textbooks frequently. Journals are frequently used by more than 80% researchers in Botany, Aquatic Biology, Zoology and Geology disciplines; more than 50% researchers in Statistics and more than 60% scholars in the rest of the disciplines. Journals and Textbooks are found to be the most frequently used information sources by pure science researchers. This finding is similar to the findings of a study conducted by Dumanova[12], on the information needs of physicists. In another study conducted by Mubeen[13], on the use pattern of chemistry researchers also, a similar finding is observed.

Theses and Dissertation are occasionally used by majority of scholars in the fields of Chemistry, Mathematics, Physics and Geology, while in the rest of the disciplines the scholars use these sources frequently. In Physics discipline, a considerable percent of 33.33% scholars are found using these sources rarely.

Reference sources are found used occasionally by majority of scholars in all the disciplines except Chemistry and Mathematics, where majority uses these sources occasionally.

When the frequency of use of Indexing and Abstracting sources are examined, it is found that most of the Chemistry, Zoology and Aquatic Biology researchers use these sources frequently. In other disciplines except Mathematics, majority occasionally uses these sources. This may be due to the absence of sufficient indexing and abstracting sources in this field. Majority i.e. 45.45% Mathematics scholars are found using these sources rarely.

Conference papers are occasionally used by majority of researchers in disciplines except Physics and Statistics, where majority only rarely uses these sources. Catalogues are frequently used by majority of researchers only in the Zoology and Biochemistry disciplines. Reports are rarely used by most of the scholars in the disciplines, Aquatic Biology and Statistics, and never used by majority of scholars in Mathematics discipline (66.67%). In other disciplines, these sources are used occasionally by most of the researchers.

Computer-based sources are found frequently used by maximum number of researchers in Biochemistry and Geology disciplines. Majority of Mathematics (36.36%) and Statistics (66.67%) scholars has never used these sources. In all other disciplines, majority occasionally uses these sources.

Non-book materials are found frequently used by majority of Zoology scholars (31.58%). Many of the scholars in Biochemistry and Geology disciplines use these sources only occasionally. 83.33% researchers in Statistics and 52.38% in Physics discipline rarely use these sources. In all other disciplines, majority of scholars is found not using these sources, for their research works.

Patents and Standards are never used by majority of researchers in most of the disciplines. In Chemistry, 42.11% are found using these sources occasionally, while in Biochemistry 46.43% use these sources rarely. A study conducted by Amba[14] on the extent of use of Patent documents by pure scientists also shows that the use of these sources by pure scientists are less compared to that of applied scientists.

The above findings show that there are variations in the use of different sources by pure science scholars belonging to different disciplines, which substantiates the validity of the first hypothesis of the study.

MOST PREFERRED INFORMATION SOURCES BY PURE SCIENCE RESEARCHERS VS DISCIPLINE OF RESEARCHERS

Based on the preference given by pure science scholars to

various information sources, a rank list was prepared. The research scholars in all the disciplines except Statistics gave first preference to Current Periodicals. Statistics researchers gave first preference to Textbooks and 2nd preference to Periodicals. This may be due to the lack of sufficient Periodicals in this discipline in the library.

Most of the scholars in Botany and Chemistry gave 2nd preference to Back volumes, whereas most of the Aquatic Biology and Geology researchers prefers Theses and Dissertation secondly. Textbooks are given the 2nd choice by majority of researchers in Mathematics, Physics and Geology. Only in Biochemistry discipline, most of the scholars prefer reference sources secondly. Thus certain variations are observed in the order of preferences to various sources of information by pure science researchers.

In order to test statistically, the extent of correlation between the ranks given by scholars in various pure science disciplines, Spearman's Rho method of rank correlation was applied. Except between Statistics and Physics researchers, the ranks given by researchers in all other disciplines when compared, the significance level was found to be at 1%. This shows that except between Statistics and Physics scholars, high correlation exists between the preferences given by researchers in all other disciplines. The ranks given by Statistics and Physics researchers to various information sources when compared show more variations.

The study reveals that researchers in most of the pure science disciplines prefer to obtain the required information from published literature. This finding has some correlation with the study made by Wood[15] about the information seeking behaviour of pure scientists. He found that the pure scientists used formal communication channels more and they obtained more information directly from published literature.

NEED FOR ORIENTATION IN THE USE OF INFORMATION SOURCES BY PURE SCIENCE RESEARCH SCHOLARS

Only in Statistics discipline majority i.e. 66.67% opined that orientation in the use of various information sources are not helpful. In all other disciplines, majority of researchers feels the need for orientation in using different information sources. This necessity is felt more by researchers in Aquatic Biology discipline – 94.12%.

Orientation in the use of library resources and services helps much in carrying out effective research. In a similar study, Alire[16], points out the importance of the knowledge of library and its resources for the academic success of the research scholars, and stresses the need for bibliographic instruction.

DEMAND FOR SOURCES NOT AVAILABLE IN THE UNIVERSITY/ DEPARTMENT LIBRARIES VS DISCIPLINE OF RESEARCHERS

On examination it is found that, out of the total 159 researchers, 56.60% often ask for sources not available in the University or Department libraries. More than 60% researchers in Biochemistry, Statistics, Zoology and Geology disciplines and 50%-58% researchers in Chemistry, Botany, Physics and Aquatic Biology demand for such sources often. Only in Mathematics discipline, majority i.e. 81.82% did not ask for such sources.

Among the research scholars who demands for sources not available in the University or Department libraries, only in Biochemistry, Physics and Mathematics disciplines 50% or more scholars got the required sources, usually from other libraries. In Aquatic Biology discipline, only 10% scholars got the required sources.

USE OF SCIENTIFIC JOURNALS BY PURE SCIENCE RESEARCHERS VS DISCIPLINE OF RESEARCHERS

In all the nine pure science discipline, majority of researchers is found reading an average of 1-5 scientific journals regularly. In Chemistry, Biochemistry, Aquatic Biology and Geology disciplines more than 75% researchers are found using 1-5 journals regularly. 33.33% Statistics scholars use to read 6-10 journals on a regular basis. More than 10 scientific journals are used by Zoology scholars – 15.79%. It is in Mathematics discipline, majority of researchers i.e. 45.45% is found not reading any scientific journals regularly. In Aquatic Biology, Mathematics and Geology disciplines, none of the scholars are found using more than 5 journals regularly.

USE OF FOREIGN LANGUAGE PERIODICALS VS DISCIPLINE OF RESEARCHERS

Out of the total 159 pure science scholars, only 10 (6.29%) researchers are found using foreign language periodicals other than English. Among these 10 researchers, 5 of them belong to Chemistry discipline, 3 in Botany and 2 in Zoology discipline.

Russian, French and Chinese journals are used most by Botany researchers. Zoology scholars are found using French and German journals mostly, whereas Chemistry scholars mostly use German journals.

MOST PREFERRED JOURNALS BY PURE SCIENCE RESEARCHERS

The journals most preferred by researchers in each pure science discipline were examined. NAGA is the most preferred journal in Aquatic Biology discipline. In Biochemistry discipline it is the Indian Journal of Experimental Biology. Current Science is the journal ranked first by Botany scholars and Journal of American Chemical Society by Chemistry scholars. Journal of the Geological Society of India is the most read journal by Geology scholars and

Journal of Graph Theory by Mathematics scholars. The most favourite journal of Physics researchers is found to be Annales Geophysicae and that of Statistics and Zoology scholars are Sankhya and Nature respectively. Among these 9 top ranked journals, only 4 of them are found to be Indian and the rest are foreign journals.

As far as the uses of different journals are considered, researchers in Chemistry and Physics disciplines respectively uses a maximum of 35 and 27 journals. The use of journals is found less in Mathematics, Statistics and Geology disciplines – only 5 or 6 journals. This may be due to the lack of sufficient journals in these fields. Thus it can be inferred that, the availability of journals in the Physical, Chemical and Biological fields are more compared to Mathematics and Geology disciplines.

USE OF VARIOUS LIBRARY SERVICES VS DISCIPLINE OF RESEARCHERS

Among the various library services, Reprographic service is found to be the service utilised by more than 50% researchers in all the disciplines. Literature Search is another most used service. It is in Mathematics discipline majority i.e. 81.82% is found utilising this service. 50%-60% researchers in Botany, Biochemistry, Aquatic Biology and Statistics utilised this service. In other disciplines, the use of this service is comparatively less.

39.29% researchers in Biochemistry discipline and 42% to 66% researchers in other disciplines except Mathematics, Zoology and Geology use indexing and Abstracting service. In Mathematics (27.27%) and Zoology (26.32%) disciplines, the researchers using this service are less. In Geology, none of the researchers have utilised these services. The reason may be due to the lack of such services in these disciplines.

Between 50%- 58% researchers in the fields of Botany, Biochemistry, Zoology and Aquatic Biology are found utilising Computer-based information services. 50% researchers in Statistics and more than 60% researchers in the rest of the disciplines are aware of these services, but use is comparatively less. Only very few researchers in Mathematics (18.18%) and Statistics (16.67%) disciplines are found using Computer-based services.

16% -38% researchers in disciplines except Mathematics use Bibliographic service, where none of the scholars are found using this service.

Newspaper Clipping service is utilised by majority of researchers in Geology and Statistics disciplines – 66.67% each. In all other disciplines, only less than 30% scholars are found using this service and in Physics discipline it is only 4.76%.

Referral service is used by most of the Statistics scholars i.e. 83.33%. In all other disciplines except Mathematics also, a considerable percentage of researchers are found using this service. As far as the Interlibrary Loan service is concerned, none other than a single person in Biochemistry discipline has utilised this service.

The Addition List service is unaware to majority of scholars in all the disciplines. Between 8% - 33% researchers in disciplines except Statistics have used this service. Translation service is also found utilising by only a few researchers in Biochemistry, Botany, Chemistry, Aquatic Biology and Statistics.

ADEQUACY OF SERVICES OFFERED BY KERALA UNIVERSITY LIBRARY SYSTEM FOR RESEARCHERS VS DISCIPLINE OF RESEARCHERS

Only in Statistics discipline 50% researchers opined the services of Kerala University Library System as sufficient. In all other fields, for a large number of scholars, the services are only partially adequate to meet their needs. This finding also substantiate the validity of the 2nd hypothesis of the study. Majority of researchers in all the disciplines is found expecting more and more Current Periodicals and foreign journals in their respective fields.

A study of the information needs of pure science researchers of the University of Kerala, carried out by Devarajan[17] also observes that the collection and services provided by the Kerala University Library System for pure science scholars is only partially adequate to meet their needs.

AWARENESS OF SERVICES RENDERED BY EXTERNAL AGENCIES VS DISCIPLINE OF RESEARCHERS

Majority of the researchers in Geology (66.67%) and Botany (53.85%) disciplines are found aware of the services provided by external agencies. In all other fields, majorities of scholars are unaware of such agencies.

Out of the total 159 scholars, only 64 (40.25%) are found aware of services provided by external agencies. Among them, 36 scholars are aware of INSDOC services, but only 11 of them have utilised the services of INSDOC. They include 3 researchers each from Botany and Physics, 2 researchers each from Biochemistry and Zoology and one in Aquatic Biology. Few scholars in Mathematics, Biochemistry, Zoology and Botany have used the services of NCSI, and another few researchers in the fields Botany, Physics and Biochemistry discipline have utilised the services of Patent Information Center. Botany and Biochemistry scholars are found using the services of various external agencies more.

USE OF INTERNET BASED SERVICES VS DISCIPLINE OF RESEARCHERS

Out of the 159 researchers, majority i.e. 121 (76.10%) are found using e-mail service most. This is followed by online search (73.58%). Majority of researchers in Chemistry (82.14%), Mathematics (45.45%) and Statistics (50%) use e-mail service most. But majority of the researchers in Biochemistry (89.28%), Aquatic Biology (94.11%) and Zoology (78.95%) are found using online search. 80.77% researchers in Botany are found utilising these two services equally, while most of the Geology scholars prefer to use e-mail, e-journals and online search equally.

TIME SPEND FOR READING IN LIBRARIES AT DIFFERENT STAGES OF WORK VS DISCIPLINE OF RESEARCHERS

During the literature search stage, majority i.e. 50% of the researchers in Chemistry are found spending 5-10 hours/week in libraries for reading purpose. In Aquatic Biology, while 47.06% use to spend 1-5 hours, another 47.06% spend 5-10 hours in a week. In all other disciplines, most of the scholars use to spend 1-5 hours/week in libraries for reading, during the literature search stage.

During the laboratory or experimentation stage of work, majority i.e. 42.11% researchers each in Zoology discipline are found spending 1-5 hours and 5-10 hours per week respectively, in libraries for reading. Majority of scholars in Biochemistry (35.71%), Aquatic Biology (47.06%) and Physics (42.86%) use to spend 1-5 hours/week for reading purpose. 38.46% researchers in Botany and 66.67% in Geology spend 5-10 hours/week in libraries at this stage. Majority i.e. 35.71% Chemistry researchers spend more than 10 hours/week in libraries for reading purpose.

During the writing stage of work, majority of scholars in all the disciplines spends 1-5 hours/week in libraries. Many of the researchers in Aquatic Biology, Statistics and Zoology are also found to spend more than 10 hours/week in libraries for reading, during the writing stage of research work.

TIME SPEND FOR READING IN DIFFERENT PLACES VS DISCIPLINE OF RESEARCHERS

It is found that more than 71% of research scholars in all the discipline except Mathematics (36.36%) and Physics (47.62%) are using the University library for 1-5 hours of reading per week.

Department library is found to be the library used by majority of researchers in all the disciplines. Most of the scholars in disciplines except Statistics, Physics, Zoology and Geology spend an average of 1-5 hours/week here. In Physics, Zoology and Geology disciplines more than 52% researchers use to spend 6-10 hours/week here for reading. Majority i.e. 66.66% scholars in Statistics use to spend more than 10 hours/week in Department libraries. This finding has some relation with the findings of a study made by Martin[18], on the information use of pure scientists. It showed that most of the scientists prefer information to be available conveniently in places of their own.

The use of other libraries by researchers, when examined, it is found that majority of scholars in disciplines except Mathematics and Geology use to spend 1-5 hours/week for reading, in these libraries. 33.33% Geology scholars spend more than 10 hours/week in other libraries. In Mathematics discipline none are found using other libraries.

27.27% researchers each in Mathematics discipline use to spend 1-5 hours and 6-10 hours/week at home for reading purpose. 31.58% Zoology scholars also spend 6-10 hours/week at home for reading. Most of the scholars in Biochemistry, Statistics and Geology use to spend more than 10 hours/week at home for reading. In all other disciplines, majority uses to spend 1-5 hours/week here for reading purpose.

As far as the use of various libraries are concerned, 70% to 100% researchers in all disciplines except Mathematics (where it is 45.45%) are found using University library. All the researchers in most of the disciplines use Department library. A considerable number of scholars in all the disciplines except Mathematics use other libraries. 65-100% scholars in all the disciplines are found spending time for reading at home.

DIFFICULTY IN CONDUCTING LITERATURE SEARCH VS DISCIPLINE OF RESEARCHERS

Majority of researchers in the disciplines viz. Biochemistry (53.57%), Physics (52.38%) and Geology (66.67%) found difficulty in conducting a comprehensive literature search in connection with their works. In other disciplines, majority of scholars does not feel any difficulty in conducting literature search.

Non availability of books, journals, back volumes etc. are the difficulty encountered by most of the researchers in Aquatic Biology, Botany and Statistics. Inadequate collection of journal especially foreign journals is the major difficulty faced by researchers in Biochemistry, Chemistry, Geology, Mathematics and Zoology disciplines. Physics scholars are often faced with the difficulty of locating the required sources.

LIBRARIES DEPENDED BY PURE SCIENCE RESEARCHERS FOR LITERATURE SEARCH

The pure science scholars are found to depend on a number of libraries for literature search. Majority of research scholars i.e. 100% in Statistics, Zoology and Geology, more than 90% researchers in Botany, Mathematics and Physics, and over 78% researchers in Biochemistry and Aquatic Biology have depended on Department libraries for carrying out literature search. Only in Chemistry discipline majority i.e. 78% scholars depends on University library for literature search. The 2nd position goes to University library in most of the disciplines. In Chemistry 2nd most depended library is Department library (83.33%), and in Statistics it is Campus library (66.67%).

Next to Department libraries and University library, majority of researchers in Mathematics (18.18%), Zoology (63.16%) and Geology (66.67%) are found to depend on Campus library for literature search. In other disciplines most of them depends on other libraries.

Among the other libraries consulted by pure science scholars, CMFRI library at Vizhinjam and Kochi are consulted most by researchers in Aquatic Biology. 38.46% Botany scholars use to consult TBGRI library at Palode. Most of the Biochemistry scholars (39.29%) consult SCTIMST library at Trivandrum. 57.14% of Chemistry and 66.66% of Physics scholars consults VSSC library, Trivandrum. GSI library at Trivandrum, IISc library at Bangalore, and library of IIT, Mumbai, are used by 33.33% each of Geology scholars. 18.18% Mathematics scholars use IMS library at Chennai whereas CUSAT library at Kochi, CDS library at Trivandrum and VSSC library at Trivandrum are consulted by 16,67% Statistics scholars. Among the other libraries, British Library, Trivandrum is consulted mostly by Zoology (36.84%) scholars.

USE OF LIBRARIES OUTSIDE KERALA VS DISCIPLINE OF RESEARCHERS

It is found that the library facility of I.I.Sc, Bangalore is used by many of the researchers in all the disciplines except Statistics. Only in Statistics discipline none of the researchers are found utilising the facilities of libraries situated outside Kerala. Researchers using the libraries outside Kerala are found more in Chemistry discipline.

DEPENDENCE ON LIBRARIES BY PURE SCIENCE RESEARCHERS AT DIFFERENT STAGES OF WORK

It is found that, in all the disciplines except Statistics, researchers felt the dependence on libraries more during the literature search stage. Most of the Statistics scholars felt the dependence on libraries more during the time of topic selection and at the writing stages of work.

TYPES OF INFORMATION SOUGHT AT DIFFERENT STAGES OF RESEARCH WORK VS DISCIPLINE OF RESEARCHERS

During the literature search stage, majority of scholars in all the disciplines preferred current information. Retrospective and Bibliographic information are given the next preferences. In Mathematics and Statistics discipline, experimentation stage is absent. In other fields except Chemistry, majority of scholars prefers methodological information most during the experimentation stage. Most of the Geology scholars are found using statistical information also, along with methodological information, at this stage. At the experimentation stage also, most of the Chemistry scholars prefers Current information first.

During the literature survey and experimentation stage, the types of information sought by researchers in most of the disciplines are found more or less the same. But during the writing stage of work, the types of information sought by researchers in various pure science disciplines are found to vary.

A similar study on the information needs of researchers of Burdwan University, made by Barua and Tripadi[19] also reveals that the information requirements of researchers varied and it further observes that majority of researchers wanted current and bibliographic information, for their research works.

USE OF STYLE MANUALS BY PURE SCIENCE RESEARCHERS

On analysis of data, it is observed that majority of researchers are only in the literature survey or experimentation stage of work. About 31.47% scholars are in the initial writing stages and only 24 (15.09%) have started writing the thesis completely. When these 24 researchers were asked about the use of style manuals, only 7 of them responded as using these. Of these researchers, two each belongs to Botany and Biochemistry disciplines and one each in Chemistry, Physics and Aquatic Biology disciplines. Majority i.e. 4 researchers are found using other theses submitted earlier, as guidelines for writing thesis. The researchers in Biochemistry prepared thesis according to the pattern suggested by their supervising teachers. Only one research scholar in the Botany discipline, used an authoritative style manual titled "How to write a thesis". This shows that proper awareness about the use of these sources is required for researchers.

METHOD USED TO FIND SPECIFIC INFORMATION VS DISCIPLINE OF RESEARCHERS

Out of the total 159 researchers, maximum number of scholars in Botany (80.77%), Chemistry (60.71%), Physics (76.19%) and Zoology (84.21%) use to consult Reference sources for seeking specific information on a topic. The methods of consulting reference sources as well as the method of consulting teachers and colleagues are equally preferred by majority of researchers in Aquatic Biology and Statistics disciplines. All the Geology researchers and 78.57% Biochemistry researchers prefer the method of searching the Internet, whereas 90.91% Mathematics scholars follow the method of consulting with teachers and colleagues, to find specific information on a topic.

MOST PREFERRED METHOD OF INFORMATION SEARCH VS DISCIPLINE OF RESEARCHERS

The information search method preferred most by pure science researchers when examined, it is found that, majority of scholars in all the disciplines other than Geology and Biochemistry prefers manual search method to other modern methods. Equal number of Geology scholars are found to use manual, online and a combination of both these respectively. Only in Biochemistry discipline, majority of scholars is found preferring online search to manual search method.

KNOWLEDGE OF THE USE OF ELECTRONIC/ COMPUTER-BASED SOURCES VS DISCIPLINE OF RESEARCHERS

Out of the total 159 scholars, 72.96% are found to possess knowledge about the use of electronic or computer based sources available in the library. 100% Geology scholars and more than 80% Botany, Biochemistry and Zoology scholars had knowledge of these sources. Only in Mathematics discipline, majority i.e. 63.64% is found unaware of the use of electronic or computer-based sources. In all other fields 50% or more number of scholars know the use of these sources.

TYPES OF DATABASE USED AND APPROACH FOLLOWED BY RESEARCHERS IN ON-LINE SEARCH VS DISCIPLINE OF RESEARCHERS

Majority of research scholars in all the disciplines except Mathematics and Geology are found preferring both National and International database equally, while carrying out online search. Majority of researchers in Mathematics and Geology prefer to use International database. On further examination, it is found that, Zoology scholars use full text database more. Biochemistry and Physics scholars prefer to use both full text and bibliographic database equally. Most of the scholars in the rest of the disciplines are found using bibliographic database more.

While conducting CD/Online search, most of the pure science scholars used subject approach, which is followed by Keyword search. Researchers in disciplines except Botany, Physics and Zoology are found to formulate the search strategy by themselves, while carrying out CD/online search. In Botany, Physics and Zoology disciplines, most of the scholars are found formulating the search strategy with the help of library staff.

In all the disciplines except Zoology, the number of researchers using CD/online database are found more compared to the total scholars who have knowledge of the use of computer-based sources. This shows that many of the researchers are carrying out CD/Online search indirectly, with the help of others.

APPROACH FOLLOWED BY RESEARCHERS TO FIND CURRENT INFORMATION VS DISCIPLINE OF RESEARCHERS

In order to find out current information published in their subject fields, majority of scholars in all the disciplines except Aquatic Biology and Statistics prefer the method of scanning current periodicals. In the Aquatic Biology and Statistics disciplines, majorities of scholars are found to give 1st preference to Indexing and Abstracting sources, and then to Current Periodicals. The 2nd choice is given to Indexing and Abstracting sources by Physics researchers, while in the rest of the disciplines majority prefers Current Contents as their second preference. It is found that, Scanning Periodicals, Current Contents, Indexing and Abstracting sources, Searching the shelves in libraries, using Catalogues/OPAC, asking Library Staff and Discussion with teachers and colleagues are the methods that come within the first 5 preferences of researchers in most of the disciplines. But the order of preference is found to vary.

Spearman's Rho test of rank correlation when applied, it is found that a high correlation exists between the ranks given by researchers in various disciplines. The value is found significant at 1% level. Between Mathematics and Aquatic Biology researchers, Mathematics and Physics researchers and Geology and Statistics researchers, when compared the correlation between the ranks is found less. When the ranks given by Mathematics and Biochemistry, as well as Mathematics and Statistics scholars are compared, no correlation between ranks is observed.

SEEKING ADVICE OF SCIENTISTS IN OTHER INSTITUTES BY RESEARCHERS VS DISCIPLINE

It is observed that, in all other disciplines except Statistics and Mathematics, maximum number of scholars uses to seek the advice of scientists and persons working in other institutions. 100% scholars in Geology, over 80% scholars in Aquatic Biology and

Zoology, 71.43% in Physics, 64.29% in Chemistry and 57.69% researchers in Botany are found to seek the advice of scientists working in other institutions. Majority i.e. 90.91% Mathematics scholars and 83.33% Statistics scholars are found as not seeking such advises.

RELATED SUBJECT DOCUMENTS CONSULTED BY PURE SCIENCE SCHOLARS

Many of the researchers in various pure science fields are found to consult documents in the fields other than their core subjects. 100% researchers in Geology, 70.59% scholars in Aquatic Biology, 66.67% researchers in Statistics, around 57% researchers in Physics and Zoology, 46.15% researchers in Botany and 25% researchers in Biochemistry are found to consult related subject documents. The number of researchers consulting other subject documents is very less in the case of Mathematics scholars – 1.09%.

Many of the researchers in Botany are found to consult documents in the area of Biochemistry and Statistics. Biochemistry scholars usually consult Chemistry documents. Most of the Chemistry scholars are found consulting Physics documents. Many Aquatic Biology scholars use Zoology documents. The other subject documents consulted by Physics scholars are in the fields of Computer science and Electronics, Chemistry and Mathematics. Many of the Geology scholars use to consult documents in the field of Biochemistry. Mathematics scholars are found consulting Statistics documents alone and vice versa. It is observed that researchers in most of the disciplines commonly use statistics documents. This shows that,- Statistics is applicable in every discipline.

In addition to the above mentioned subjects a number of other subject documents are also consulted by many of the pure science scholars. The reason for this may be the interdisciplinary nature of the research works. In a similar study on the information needs of scientists, Mote[20] observed that the more interdisciplinary is the subject studied, the more scattered is its literature. So large amount of literature has to be consulted to keep abreast of the developments.

CONCLUSION

The findings of the study reveal the various characteristics of the information needs and information gathering behaviour of pure science researchers. It has helped to get an idea of the information requirements, behaviour, priorities, opinions and problems of the pure science scholars. Such studies help to provide a guideline, based on which improvements could be made in the information system.

The study started with the hypotheses that (1) there is significant variations in the information needs and information gathering behaviour among research scholars in various pure science disciplines and (2) the resources and services available in the Kerala University Library System is only partially adequate to meet the information needs of the research scholars. The findings enumerated in this chapter substantiate the validity of these hypotheses.

From the analysis, it can be concluded that current periodicals are the most preferred and used information source by pure science research scholars. But these sources are only partially adequate to majority of the scholars. Since latest developments in any subject field are covered in these sources, their significance is high.

The types of information sought by the pure science researchers are also found to vary according to the stage of work and discipline of the researchers. Documentary sources of information are given importance by majority of pure science scholars in most of the disciplines. But in some disciplines like Mathematics and Statistics, informal communication is given much importance.

A large number of pure science researchers are found to depend on other libraries connected with research institutions, in order to satisfy their information requirements. On the whole, the resources and services rendered by Kerala University Library System to pure science scholars are found as only partially adequate to meet their needs. Variation in the information need, use pattern and information seeking behaviour are also observed among researchers, in relation to variables such as sex, qualification, category and discipline.

The present study is not a complete one, since it deals with the information needs, information gathering behaviour and use pattern of researchers in the pure science discipline only. Future researchers can explore other similar areas also. They can attempt comparative studies on the information needs, information gathering behaviour and use pattern of research scholars in the areas of Pure Science and Applied Science disciplines. Studies on the Information needs and use pattern of research scholars in different Universities in Kerala, as well as in India and their comparative studies can also be attempted. Investigation into the difference in the information needs and use pattern of researchers in science and non-science disciplines is another area where further research can be carried out. From such detailed analysis, a complete picture of the information needs, use pattern, information gathering behaviour etc. of research scholars can be ascertained.

Research in science and technology is very essential for the development of the society. In order to carry out effective research in this field, scientific information should be organised effectively and made available to the users according to their needs. Pure science research is a base for applied research. So a study of the information requirement and use pattern of research scholars in this field will provide a basis for reorganising libraries and information centers in this field. It will also help to provide sufficient resources and services to researchers in this field based on their requirements.

REFERENCES

1. **Shannon, C. and Weaver, W.** The mathematical theory of communication. Urbana: University of Illinois press, 1949.

2. **Chen, C. and Hernon, P.** Information seeking: assessing and anticipating user needs. New York: Neal-Schuman, 1982.

3. **Busha, C.H.** Research methodology in librarianship. *In*. Encyclopedia of Library and Information Science, 25, 1978. P.254 - 293.

4. **Best, J.W.** Research in education. Ed. 2. New Jersey: Prentice Hall, 1970.

5. **Wise, J.E. et.al.** Methods of research in education. Boston: D.C.Heath & Co., 1967.

6. **Sengupta, I.N.** Research in librarianship and glossary of technical terms relating to the strategies of research. *IASLIC Bulletin* 31 (3), 1986. P.113.

7. **Busha, C.H.** Op. Cit.

8. **Line, Maurice B.** Draft definitions: information and library needs, want, demand and uses. *ASLIB Proceedings* 26, 1974. P.87.

9. **Soper, M.E.** The librarian's thesaurus: a concise guide to library and information terms. Chicago: American Library Association. P.2.

10. **Wilson, T.D.** On user studies and information needs. *Journal of Documentation* 37 (1), 1981. P.3-15.

11. **Sheena Kumari, P.K.** Information needs and use pattern in purescience: a study with special reference to Ph.D. scholars in the University of Kerala. Kerala University: MLISc dissertation, 1994.

12. **Dumanova, Aleksandra.** A study of the information needs of physicists. *Biblioteker* 33 (5), 1986. P.18-21.

13. **Mubeen, M.A.** Citation analysis of doctoral dissertation in chemistry. *Annals of Library Science and Documentation* 43 (2), 1996. P.48-58..

14. **Amba, S.** A study on the extend of use of patent documents. *IASLIC Bulletin* 23 (2), 1978.

15. **Wood, D.N.** User studies, a review of literature, 1966-1970. *ASLIB Proceedings* 23 (1), 1971. P.11-23.

16. **Alire, Camila Ann.** A nation wide survey of education doctoral students attitude regarding the importance of the library and the need for bibliographic instruction. *Dissertation Abstract International* 45 (3), 1984. P.673A.

17. **Devarajan, G.** Users approach to information in libraries. New Delhi: Ess Ess, 1989. P.33-43.

18. **Martin, M.W. and Ackoff, Russel L.** Dissemination and recorded scientific information. *Management science* 9, 1963. P.322-36.

19. **Barua, P, and Tripadi, Tridip.** An analysis of information seeking behaviour of research scholars vis-à-vis existing information sources and services of Burdwan University Library: a case study. *IASLIC Bulletin* 33 (2), 1988. P.93-98.

20. **Mote, L.J.B.** Reasons for the variations in the information needs of scientists. *Journal of Documentation* 18 (4), 1962.

Index